Securing the Cloud
Cloud Computer Security
Techniques and Tactics

Securing the Cloud
Cloud Computer Security
Techniques and Tactics

Vic (J.R.) Winkler

Technical Editor
Bill Meine

**Vincennes University
Shake Learning Resources Center
Vincennes, In 47591-9986**

AMSTERDAM • BOSTON • HEIDELBERG • LONDON
NEW YORK • OXFORD • PARIS • SAN DIEGO
SAN FRANCISCO • SINGAPORE • SYDNEY • TOKYO
Syngress is an imprint of Elsevier

ELSEVIER

Acquiring Editor: Angelina Ward
Development Editor: Matt Cater
Project Manager: Jessica Vaughan
Designer: Alisa Andreola

Syngress is an imprint of Elsevier
225 Wyman Street, Waltham, MA 02451, USA

Notices

Knowledge and best practice in this field are constantly changing. As new research and experience broaden our understanding, changes in research methods or professional practices, may become necessary.
Practitioners and researchers must always rely on their own experience and knowledge in evaluating and using any information or methods described herein. In using such information or methods they should be mindful of their own safety and the safety of others, including parties for whom they have a professional responsibility.

To the fullest extent of the law, neither the Publisher nor the authors, contributors, or editors, assume any liability for any injury and/or damage to persons or property as a matter of products liability, negligence or otherwise, or from any use or operation of any methods, products, instructions, or ideas contained in the material herein.

Library of Congress Cataloging-in-Publication Data
Application submitted

British Library Cataloguing-in-Publication Data
A catalogue record for this book is available from the British Library.

ISBN: 978-1-59749-592-9

For information on all Syngress publications
visit our website at *www.syngress.com*

Typeset by: diacriTech, Chennai, India

Printed in the United States of America
10 11 12 13 14   10 9 8 7 6 5 4 3 2 1

Working together to grow
libraries in developing countries

www.elsevier.com | www.bookaid.org | www.sabre.org

ELSEVIER   BOOK AID International   Sabre Foundation

This book is dedicated to my parents Gernot and Renate, wife Rebecca, daughter Carra, and to Rebecca's father William Payne. Rebecca: Thank you for putting up with me (and not only because of this book) during this time. I owe you a great deal. Carra: You are embarking on your own story; watch your punctuation. Blue skies and may the wind always be at your back.

My father-in-law William Payne passed away this past year. Bill embodied Southern charm and he left a legacy not only with his daughter but also as the Chief Engineer of the C130.

Contents

Acknowledgments

I would like to thank Rachel Roumeliotis for contacting me out of the blue, first to act as Technical Editor for this book and later to assume the role of Author. I never imagined this to be both so hard and consuming. Oddly, I am thankful!

We all come from somewhere—I'd like to thank two companies that no longer exist: Planning Research Corporation and Sun Microsystems. I can't begin to express the joy I felt at the many opportunities I discovered in both places. May the spirit of these companies persist. At PRC, Wayne Shelton and others presented me with one opportunity after another. At Sun Microsystems, I found myself in the heart of the Silicon Valley revolution.

To many Sun Microsystems colleagues over the past few years: You taught me more than you'll ever know. To the incomparable Bill Meine, Thom Schoeffling, Joe Carvalho, Dan Butzer, Layne Jester, David Rodgers, Brian Foley, Dan Hushon, Jim Parkinson, Rinaldo DiGiorgio, and several dozen others whom I joined in designing and then building rather safe and rather cool platforms for grid and cloud computing: We achieved an incredible feat, several times over. At Sun, I learned the difference between marketing, innovation, engineering, and magic.

But life goes on, and I have found new opportunities at Booz Allen Hamilton, so I would like to thank Bob Harbick, who convinced me to join his team of talented engineers. I am grateful for this experience as well.

...Did I thank Jimmy Page, Jimi Hendrix, and Tommy Bolin? O.K., here we go: Thank you Mordaunt-Short, Parasound, PS Audio, Apple Computer, "the Google," late night TV, bad monster movies, uncertain walks in pitch dark with my dog Uli, great cigars, dangerously excellent spirits and wine, the attention my dog Bella lavishes on me, the truth of fiction, sea and air, mountains and snow, fireworks, a beautiful girl whose name I still remember after nearly 40 years, old friends, young friends, the existence of the power grid, the fact that NY is intact, and that star over there.

I will again thank Bill Meine, who agreed to be the Technical Editor for this book. After many conversations with Bill, it is not surprising that many of his words and ideas should be in this book. Lastly, Matt Cater: Thank you for being a great shepherd for this project.

About the Author

Vic (J.R.) Winkler is a Senior Associate at Booz Allen Hamilton, providing technical consultation to U.S. Government clients. He is a published InfoSec and cyber security researcher as well as an expert in intrusion/anomaly detection. At Sun Microsystems, Vic served as the Chief Technologist for Security for the Sun Public Cloud. He was also Chairman of the Board for the Sun Security Technology Ambassador program (presales security engineers). In 2010, he became a member of the Advisory Board for StratuScape (a Silicon Valley startup). Vic's background includes positions as an R&D principal investigator at Planning Research Corporation (PRC), where he was the lead designer and Program Manager for a trusted B1 UNIX OS. At PRC, he also conceived of and built one of the first network/host Intrusion Detection Systems (IDS). Vic has over 30 years' experience in InfoSec/cyber security, cloud computing, systems and applications engineering, and IT operations and management. He has numerous technical conference publications, and as a visiting cyber security expert, Vic was the author of the Information Security policy for the Government of Malaysia. Vic resides in Reston, Virginia, with his family: Rebecca, Carra, Uli, Bella, and Toby.

About the Technical Editor

Bill Meine recently moved to the other side of the cloud delivery system by joining Software-as-a-Service startup Evergreen Energy, where he is the product owner for the agile software development effort. Part of his time is spent on the security concerns for delivering cloud service applications to customers in the power generation business. Previously, Bill was the chief architect for the infrastructure, security, and operations on Sun Microsystems' public cloud, where he led the design of a large cloud infrastructure and operational processes that offered a leap in security at commodity prices. He instituted a lean manufacturing model with agile techniques for all aspects of the construction, development, and delivery of the cloud infrastructure. In his 25+ years at Sun, he was an architect for their *dollar an hour* public grid offering, enterprise IT architect, *fly-and-fix smoke jumper*, and staff engineer. Somewhere in his dark past, he wrote software for mine planning, controlling a laser-fusion experiment, and locating earthquakes. Bill lives in Denver, Colorado, with his family: Melinda and Kalen.

Introduction

BOOK AUDIENCE

This book will prove to be a practical resource for anyone who is considering using, building, or securing a cloud implementation. Security professionals may refer to this book as a source of detailed information for evaluating and verifying cloud security policy and requirements. Cloud infrastructure engineers, cloud services engineers, and integrators will find value in learning about relevant security approaches and cloud security architecture. It will also provide value to those who are interested in understanding cloud security. Executive-level management will gain an understanding of the security advantages and developing trends that are likely to mature as cloud computing progresses.

TERMINOLOGY

In this book, we use the term *cloud* in a broad way to refer to *cloud computing* and *cloud services*. By *cloud computing* we mean: The Information Technology (IT) model for computing, which is composed of all the IT components (hardware, software, networking, and services) that are necessary to enable development and delivery of *cloud services* via the Internet or a private network.

By *cloud services*, we mean those services that are expressed, delivered, and consumed over the Internet or a private network. Cloud services range from Infrastructure-as-a-Service (IaaS), Platform-as-a-Service (PaaS), and Software-as-a-Service (SaaS) and include everything else that uses these more basic services to create new services. These services may be deployed privately, publically, or in some combination.

Cloud computing is far broader a field than *public cloud* services. There are different advantages and even risks in adopting either a private, community, public, or hybrid cloud deployment. Likewise, there are different value propositions and risks with the three main cloud services.

RISK, PERCEPTION OF RISK AND CLOUD COMPUTING

A good way to view cloud computing is as a landscape that already offers great value and services, but one that is not yet at the *Goldilocks* stage, where every customer's computing needs are met by a *just right* solution. As a new paradigm for computing, cloud introduces challenges even as it offers advantages. Not all cloud deployment models (public, hybrid, private, and community) are appropriate for each service, each service customer, or all tenants. Likewise, it is not cost effective for all cloud providers to implement high assurance security or offer the same level of security. However, cloud computing is compelling, it is a rapidly growing trend in IT, and it is forcing significant advances in supporting technologies.

In this book, we address some of the common security issues or questions that prospective cloud adopters face:

- **Network Availability** Network reliability is a key lynchpin for cloud computing and cloud services. Since a public cloud is by definition accessed over the Internet, the cloud provider must address the potential for catastrophic loss of Internet backbone connectivity. The same concern should be a primary consideration for cloud service consumers who entrust critical infrastructure to the cloud. Similar concerns exist for private clouds.

- **Privacy and Data** Data may not remain in the same system, the same data center, or within the same cloud provider's systems. Conceivably, data may even be stored in another country, incurring considerable concern.

- **Control over Data** A given user or organization's data may be comingled in storage or processing with data belonging to others. At minimum, data should be encrypted at the granularity of files belonging to given users or organizations.

- **Cloud Provider Viability** Since cloud providers are relatively new to the business, there are questions about provider viability and commitment. This concern is exacerbated when a provider requires that tenants use nonstandards-based application program interfaces (APIs), thus effecting lock-in (impeding a tenant in migrating to an alternative provider).

- **Security Incidents** Tenants and users need to know what information the provider will share when an incident is discovered. This concern is related to questions about transparency that providers may offer into security processes, procedures, and internal policies.

- **Disaster Recovery and Business Continuity** Tenants and users must understand how they can continue their own operations and services if the underlying production environment is subject to a disaster.

- **Systems Vulnerabilities and Risk of Common Attacks** All software, hardware, and networking equipment is subject to exposure of new vulnerabilities. Some components may pose greater risks based on a history of vulnerabilities and exploits. Tenants may not tolerate specific vulnerabilities or risk areas for a range of reasons. A specific cloud may be subject to new attack types, or it may be immune to common attack types based on various reasons.

- **Regulatory or Legislative Compliance** It is difficult to utilize public clouds when your data is subject to legal restrictions or regulatory compliance. Building a cloud that can be certified may be challenging due to the current stage of cloud knowledge and best practices.

CLOUD COMPUTING AS A TECTONIC SHIFT

Cloud computing and cloud-based services (or *cloud*) are exciting for many reasons. Cloud is a significant step in the evolution of computing paradigms and a revolution in delivering IT services. At the same time, cloud threatens destabilization for the IT status quo. We appear to be at the early stages of a tectonic shift that will force changes in: Information security approaches, application development models, capital and operational expense decisions, and the IT operations workforce size and skill set. In many ways, cloud is breaking down our models of what we accept as being possible and even reasonable to do with computers. Being able to *lease* a dozen servers and have them be delivered in a fully provisioned manner within mere moments is astonishing, but doing so for a miniscule fraction of the traditional cost is revolutionary.

Cloud computing has raised concerns about the erosion of control as information and software move off of *organic* resources and into someone else's IT management sphere. Despite concerns from many security professionals, cloud computing isn't innately more or less secure. But the cloud model does force a movement toward a more robust and capable foundation of security services. The mere act of transitioning from legacy systems gives us hope that we can regain control over gaps and issues that stem from poorly integrated or *after-thought security*. With cloud, greater investment for in-common security services has great potential for return on investment (ROI) given cloud scale.

Even as it evolves and matures, cloud computing is being adopted at a fast pace. Despite the hype, cloud brings multiple fundamental shifts in how computing infrastructure is acquired and managed. Despite often shameless marketing by vendors and cloud providers, the opportunities with cloud computing may prove challenging to IT, business, and government. Already today, significant security concerns about cloud computing are coloring many early cloud adoption decisions. But we see cloud as a driver for better security, and we see security as an enabler and foundation for better cloud computing.

STRUCTURE OF THE BOOK

We begin by examining cloud computing in light of the continuing evolution of IT. Later, we will build a set of guidelines and simple tools that we can use to plan or evaluate security in different cloud deployment models and for different service models—SaaS, PaaS, and IaaS. Together, we refer to these as the SPI service model. Developing guidelines entails a review and understanding of security principles, security risks, and security architecture. What we aim to do is to describe the security issues associated with cloud computing and how to apply security to cloud computing.

We recognize that security requirements and solutions will vary greatly, and thus our underlying goal for the book is that the reader becomes better prepared to evaluate the conditions under which we should adopt Cloud Computing services and technologies.

Chapters in This Book

This book is organized in a top-down manner that begins with an introduction to cloud computing and security, progresses to an examination of cloud security architectures and issues, then presents a series of key strategies and best practices for cloud security, discusses the major security considerations for building or selecting a cloud provider, and concludes with an examination of what it means to securely operate a cloud.

Chapter 1: Introduction to Cloud Computing and Security

Chapter 1 "Introduction to Cloud Computing and Security" presents an overview to cloud computing along with its IT foundations, the historical underpinnings, and the cost benefits. Also covered are the essential qualities of clouds and a brief security and architecture background to support the remaining chapters. The bottom line with cloud computing is the combination of cost advantages it brings along with the pervasive changes it is unleashing.

Chapter 2: Cloud Computing Architecture

Chapter 2 "Cloud Computing Architecture" examines cloud computing, the NIST Cloud Computing Model, and identifies the essential characteristics of clouds. Also covered is the SPI cloud service model (SaaS, PaaS, and IaaS) along with the four cloud delivery models (public, private, hybrid, and community). The chapter also covers the relative degree of security control a tenant or consumer has with the different models.

Chapter 3: Security Concerns, Risk Issues, and Legal Aspects

Chapter 3 "Security Concerns, Risk Issues, and Legal Aspects" takes a closer look at the security concerns and issues with clouds along with surveying the legal and regulatory considerations of different types of clouds.

Chapter 4: Securing the Cloud: Architecture

Chapter 4 "Securing the Cloud: Architecture" identifies a number of security requirements for cloud computing. Proceeding from those requirements we identify common security patterns and architectural elements that make for better security. We then look at a few representative cloud security architectures and discuss several important aspects of those. This chapter also details several key strategies that if considered during design can present considerable operational benefits.

Chapter 5: Securing the Cloud: Data Security

Chapter 5 "Securing the Cloud: Data Security" examines data security in cloud computing along with data protection methods and approaches. Cloud security countermeasures must comprise a resilient mosaic that protects data at rest and data in motion. Security concerns around storing data in the cloud are not inherently unique compared to data that is stored within the premises of an organization; nonetheless there are important considerations for security when adopting the cloud model.

Chapter 6: Securing the Cloud: Key Strategies and Best Practices

Chapter 6 "Securing the Cloud: Key Strategies and Best Practices" presents an overall cloud security strategy for effectively managing risk. Also covered is a treatment of cloud security controls and a discussion of the limits of security controls in cloud computing. The chapter also includes a detailed treatment of best practices for cloud security and a discussion of security monitoring for cloud computing.

Chapter 7: Security Criteria: Building an Internal Cloud

Chapter 7 "Security Criteria: Building an Internal Cloud" discusses the various motivations for embarking on a private cloud strategy along with an overview of what adopting a private cloud strategy entails in terms of benefits to both the enterprise and to security. The remainder of the chapter details the security criteria for a private cloud.

Chapter 8: Security Criteria: Selecting an External Cloud Provider

Chapter 8 "Security Criteria: Selecting an External Cloud Provider" ties together the material from the previous chapters in providing guidance for selecting a cloud service provider (CSP). In doing so, it addresses the gaps between vendor claims and the various aspects of information assurance, including those elements that are critical in selecting a CSP. That discussion includes an overview of vendor *transparency* and the prudent limits of disclosure. The chapter includes a discussion on the nature of risks in cloud computing along with the probability, impact affected assets, and factors that may be involved. The chapter concludes with a lengthy discussion of security criteria to enable selection of a CSP.

Chapter 9: Evaluating Cloud Security: An Information Security Framework

Chapter 9 "Evaluating Cloud Security: An Information Security Framework" builds on previous chapters and presents a framework for evaluating cloud security. This framework augments the security criteria identified in Chapter 8 and serves to provide a set of tools to evaluate the security of a private, community, or public cloud.

Chapter 10: Operating a Cloud

Chapter 10 "Operating a Cloud" discusses the relationship between underlying architecture and numerous security-relevant decisions that are made during all phases of a system and their impact on security operations, associated costs, and agility in operation. The chapter covers the numerous activities that are part of security operations, including patching, security monitoring, and incident response.

CONCLUSION

Depending on how you adopt the cloud model or how you deliver cloud-based services, cloud computing will bring fundamental change. Adopting cloud computing as a model for IT allows organizations to transition away from more traditional device-centric models and toward information and services based ones. Cloud offers many benefits that go beyond leaner and more agile IT infrastructure. The cloud model allows greater scalability and the change from a capital-heavy model of IT spending toward an operating model that is subscription-based brings new opportunities for a broader set of users and tenants to place larger bets with lower risk. But there are clear trade-offs that involve control over data and applications, compliance with laws and regulations and even with security. The bottom line with cloud security is that when a cloud is implemented with appropriate security, then there is no reason why cloud security can't be equal to or exceed traditional IT implementations.

Introduction to Cloud Computing and Security

INFORMATION IN THIS CHAPTER

* Understanding Cloud Computing
* The IT Foundation for Cloud
* The Bottom Line
* An Historical View: Roots of Cloud Computing
* A Brief Primer on Security: From 50,000 ft
* A Brief Primer on Architecture
* Security Architecture: A Brief Discussion
* Cloud Is Driving Broad Changes

Cloud computing is an evolutionary outgrowth of prior computing approaches, which builds upon existing and new technologies. Even as *cloud* presents new opportunities around *shared resources*, the relative newness of the model makes it difficult to separate reasonable claims from hype. In part, excessive marketing claims have led to completely unrealistic perspectives of cloud security. Claims that cloud computing is inherently insecure are as absurd as are claims that cloud computing brings no new security concerns. Prospective cloud users can sense that there is value here, but their understanding of the issues is often incomplete.

UNDERSTANDING CLOUD COMPUTING

Just as the Internet revolutionized and democratized access to information, cloud computing is doing the same for Information Technology (IT). Cloud computing represents a paradigm shift for delivering resources and services; this results in important benefits for both cloud providers and cloud consumers. From how we build IT systems and how we use them to how we organize and structure IT resources, cloud is refactoring the IT landscape. Instead of uncrating computers and racking them in your server closet, the cloud allows for virtually *downloading* hardware and associated infrastructure. By abstracting IT infrastructure and services to be relatively transparent, the act of *building* a virtual data center is now possible in minutes, with minimal technical background and at a fraction of the cost of buying a single server.

How is this possible?

> **NOTE**
>
> Living up to its name, the term *cloud* conveys a nebulous quality. The term has historical roots in describing telephone networks as well as the Internet and has recently been applied to a seemingly endless range of products, services, technologies, and infrastructure. This makes for a difficult situation if we are to have a shared understanding of cloud computing.
>
> This book uses the term *cloud* very broadly to include both *cloud computing* and *cloud services*. We will refine and build on this broad description in the course of this book, but initially we define these two terms:
>
> - **Cloud Computing** An IT model or computing environment composed of IT components (hardware, software, networking, and services) as well as the processes around the deployment of these elements that together enable us to develop and deliver *cloud services* via the Internet or a private network.
> - **Cloud Services** Services that are expressed by a cloud and delivered over the Internet or a private network. Services range from infrastructure-as-a-service (IaaS), to platform-as-a-service (PaaS), and software-as-a-service (SaaS), and include other services that are layered on these basic service models (more on these in Chapter 2).

Cloud Scale, Patterns, and Operational Efficiency

First, a detour: Upon entering a data center that hosts a cloud infrastructure, you will notice the immense size of the space and the overwhelming noise that comes from countless identically racked computers that are all neatly cabled and look the same. Massive scale, a disciplined appearance, and repeated patterns are three qualities of successful cloud implementations. These qualities are obviously not unique to the cloud, but they do contribute to the advantages of the cloud model. And it isn't simply the scale or the disciplined uniformity of a cloud infrastructure build: By developing appropriate repeated patterns and implementing them at a massive scale, you will gain cost advantages at all phases of the cloud life cycle: From procurement, build-out to operations, costs can be minimized through multiplied simplification. These same advantages benefit security as well.[1]

> **NOTE**
>
> The following quotes about the noise of thousands of fans and disk drives in the *Sun Public Cloud* come from a friend and former manager Dan Butzer as he was interviewed on NPR: "This is the sound of lots of data being crunched and lots of data being stored" and "This amount of power has a certain sound to it, and it kind of sounds like a buzz. All around you, the other end of these machines, there may be tens of thousands or millions of people doing what they need to do. They have no idea that these things are here. This is the Internet. We're sitting in the Internet."[2]

Our short detour through the server room can serve as an introduction to the cloud model, but before we exit the facility, let's take a look at a different collection of racked servers. This non-cloud server cage is being visited by a tired-looking engineer whom you can see standing alone in the din, rubbing the back of his head while clearly perplexed by a complete rat's nest of Ethernet and other cabling. You can almost hear him thinking: "Where is the other end of this cable ...?" By following regular patterns in infrastructure to the point of cabling, inefficiencies as these can largely be designed out, along with the errors in operation that are correlated with a less-disciplined implementation.

A Synergistic Trick

As we saw in our server room tour, at the IT infrastructure level, cloud computing involves assembling or *pooling* computing resources in huge aggregate quantities. Additional hardware can be added to the infrastructure as demand for resources approaches oversubscribed levels. Using virtualization, servers appear to multiply inside hardware per *The Sorcerer's Apprentice*. But traditional IT had the same tools, so what is different with cloud?

The cloud model performs a synergistic trick with its constituent technology components. The cloud model benefits from a convergence between technologies, from their synergies, and from complimentary approaches for managing IT resources. This results in a critical mass of compelling value that we can operate and deliver at an acceptable cost. There are few facets of the cloud model that are entirely new. What makes cloud computing so compelling can be summed up in the saying from Aristotle: "The whole is more than the sum of the parts."[3]

Elasticity, *Shape Shifting*, and Security

The need for elasticity in cloud computing has spawned new solutions for managing infrastructure. Providing elasticity in cloud computing goes beyond simply flexing resource allocation as a customer requires more servers or more storage. Cloud elasticity entails continual reconfiguration in network and related controls from the cloud Internet ingress through core switches and down to individual virtual machines (VMs) and storage. This amounts to infrastructure *shape shifting*.

There are profound security implications to performing such dynamic changes to security controls; each one must be orchestrated correctly and performed to successful completion. Internet Protocol (IP) addresses and VMs can come and go, only to reappear elsewhere in the infrastructure, traceability becomes ephemeral, and thus elasticity greatly complicates security monitoring.

This elastic and shape-shifting quality demands a sophisticated management infrastructure that continually reflects both the desired state and the actual state of infrastructure configuration controls along with all resource allocation. One approach to achieve this is to use a database as a continually current and authoritative information source that operates in conjunction with *all* cloud infrastructure management and control functions—security included. Specific solutions for managing infrastructure are sometimes called *configuration management databases* (CMDBs), a term that stems from the configuration management process in the Information Technology Infrastructure Library (ITIL).[A] Notably, to support the automation in a cloud, the CMDB must span a far wider set of information than ITIL acknowledges.

THE IT FOUNDATION FOR CLOUD

In this section, we take a high level look at the underlying technology pieces from which cloud computing infrastructure is built. These can be broadly categorized as follows:

- **Infrastructure** Cloud computing infrastructure is an assemblage of computer servers, storage, and network components that are organized to allow for incremental growth well beyond typical infrastructure scale levels. These components should be selected for their capability to support requirements for scalability, efficiency, robustness, and security. Commodity or typical enterprise servers may not offer appropriate network support, reliability, or other qualities to efficiently and securely deliver against service level agreements (SLAs). Also, cloud servers may prove less expensive to operate, and they may be more reliable without internal disks in each server.
- **IP-based Networks** In cloud infrastructure, the network serves as the means to connect users to the cloud as well as to interconnect the internal cloud. An enterprise model of networking does meet the needs for efficient and secure cloud provisioning and operation. At cloud scale, network needs drive toward specifying carrier-grade networking along with optimized networking strategies. Multiple switches in datapaths become single points of failure (SPOF) and compound cost in various ways.

  Although optimization may point to a single unified network, security requires that the network be partitioned or virtualized to effect separation between different classes of traffic. Although networking can become flatter, you should expect to see multiple parallel networks in order to support security. Some of these segregate platform management from public data and service traffic, and others may be necessary to enable patterns for scale. These additional networks entail additional cost, but for the price, you also get physical separation and superior security.
- **Virtualization** With deep roots in computing, virtualization is used to partition a single physical server into multiple VMs—or a single physical resource (such as storage or networking) into multiple virtual ones. Virtualization allows for

---

[A]ITIL is a registered trade mark of the Office of Government Commerce, UK.

server consolidation with great utilization flexibility. For cloud computing, virtualization has great value in rapid commissioning and decommissioning of servers. Cloud virtualization software also presents a dynamic perspective and unified view of resource utilization and efficiencies for cloud IT operations. Virtualization is the primary enabling technology for achieving cost-effective server utilization while supporting separation between multiple tenants on physical hardware. Virtualization is not the only way to achieve these benefits, but its advantages make it the approach of choice.

- **Software** Enables all aspects of cloud infrastructure management, provisioning, service development, accounting, and security. It is critical that cloud infrastructure is able to dynamically enforce policies for separation, isolation, monitoring, and service composition. The regular patterns of cloud infrastructure enable software to automate the tasks providing elasticity and *shape shifting* in order to present services that are composed of servers, VMs, storage, services, and other IT components. With software, we can automate provisioning and deprovisioning.

- **Service Interfaces** The service interface between the provider and the consumer is a key differentiator for cloud. It represents a contract that enforces the value proposition with SLAs and price terms. It is largely this interface that makes clouds stand out as new. It makes for competitive value, and it enables competition between providers. With the addition of self-service interfaces, we gain further optimizations. Cloud customers can engage cloud resources in an automated manner without having IT act as an impediment. Storage and other resources are expressed through graphical interfaces that the user can manipulate to define and subsequently instantiate virtual IT infrastructure. A Web browser, a credit card, and it's off to build your own virtual data center.

Figure 1.1 represents the relationship between individual components and their aggregation into a set of pooled and virtualized resources that can be allocated to specific uses or users—in essence, *cloud computing* that supports *cloud services*.

Cloud Computing as Foundation for Cloud Services

Taking the underlying IT components together, we can represent their relation as implementing cloud computing and cloud services. Depicted in Figure 1.2, at the bottom of the cloud stack, we have IT components that comprise cloud computing, above that we have one or more layers of cloud services. Networking is the lynchpin that enables the composition of hardware, storage, and software to allow orchestration of resources along with service development, service deployment, service interaction with other services, and finally service consumption. Although Figure 1.2 is a very generalized depiction of service delivery and cloud computing, and it does not depict SaaS as layered on PaaS or PaaS layered on IaaS, these services can very well be layered in implementation.

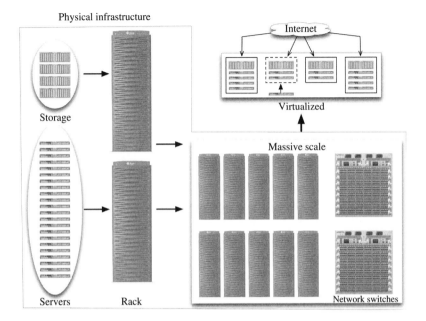

FIGURE 1.1

Physical infrastructure is virtualized.

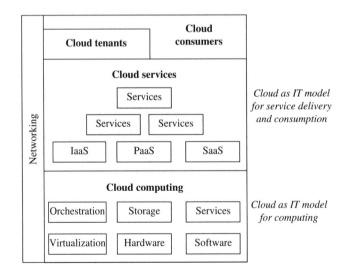

FIGURE 1.2

Cloud computing enables cloud services.

> **NOTE**
>
> In the cloud model, *tenants* are users who typically *lease* a dynamically provisioned piece of the cloud infrastructure in the form of either IaaS or PaaS in order to express value-added services to their users. *End users* typically interact with or consume specific application services that are expressed from a cloud.

Cloud Computing Qualities

In light of what we now understand of the foundations of cloud computing and cloud services, what qualities does the cloud model exhibit?

- **Pooling Resources at Massive Scale** Cloud demands scalability at every level. When we assemble computing hardware, we graduate to a higher grade of networking requirements than typical infrastructure demands. Cloud generates cost benefits at scale, cloud presents computational and storage value at scale, and with scale, we get new opportunities. This aspect of aggregating servers and network capacity to scale holds true for both public and private clouds.

- **Repeated Patterns** At a basic level, infrastructure patterns rule how countless duplicated IT components are configured. From system components to power and network cabling and from hardware nomenclature to configuration management, patterns are optimized to eek small margins in building and provisioning and managing and operating cloud infrastructure. *Lights out management*, *remote operations*, and *fail in place* objectives such as these drive the refinement of patterns.

- **Greater Automation** Scale is impossible to manage manually, and so provisioning must be automated and should operate against a common and current model of resource allocation and status. This must be done at every level from the network to servers and VMs. Automation also contributes to cloud provider profitability and more competitive services for consumers.

- **Reliability** Reliability is critical in operations as processes that are automated are less prone to human errors. In addition, reliability in cloud is a core principle in security (*availability*). Services cannot be subject to SPOF, and all the components and controlling processes must be correct and complete. Failures and errors must be managed gracefully.

- **Operational Efficiency** Defining and following patterns is empowering: From racking individual computers to cabling them and from operations to security, savings recur and processes can be tuned and refined. In addition, a well-designed cloud infrastructure can be built and operated more effectively and more efficiently by a smaller staff per service increment then if you take the same computers and disperse them to many server rooms. And there lies a further advantage for security.

- **Resource Elasticity** Consumers of cloud resources can flex their use of computer resources (cycles, storage, bandwidth, and memory) as needed.

Doing so with traditional approaches requires over-provisioning infrastructure for occasional peak loads. With cloud computing, tiered contracts can factor into how such elastic resources are managed. By example, a tenant may pay more for the same resources with the cost differential buying them prioritized access (the "VIP" line at the nightclub).

- **Location Independence and On-demand Access** For customers of cloud, the location of the actual service should not be as important as the fact that the service is accessible over the Internet. This is more or less true, depending on such factors as the need for regulatory compliance, secrecy, and privacy.[B]
- **Technology and IT Transparency for End Users** Using a cloud-based service allows for abstracting away the technical details of building and provisioning physical infrastructure. In a sense, it does not matter as much what the underlying IT looks like if your services are delivered in a manner where opacity hides the technical details.

In considering this list of qualities, we need to point out that the economies of scale along with the elasticity qualities of the cloud both invoke concern and offer benefits for security. The fact is that security in a cloud implementation can prove to be more robust and professionally managed than in most traditional IT implementations. It is simply easier to achieve this once in a cloud model than repeatedly throughout an enterprise.

WARNING

In this book, claims or statements about cloud reliability are based on the difference between a server or even a service that is provisioned within a cloud versus a traditional implementation (with its own power and network connections, provisioning, configuration, and so forth).

With traditional one-time implementations, the process generally is manual; done at the scale of a cloud infrastructure, it's more likely to be automated, in other words, using scripts and/or specialized processes or applications. But automation only brings reliable results if it is well conceived, is correctly implemented, accounts for unanticipated circumstances, and is extensively tested. If automation is in any way flawed, if it does not account for borderline situations, or if it does not gracefully handle errors, then automation can cause far more damage than any manual process might aspire to (if it was malicious).

THE BOTTOM LINE

One aspect of estimating IT cost in typical organizations is that both the data center costs and the associated IT costs are aggregated to a degree where they are too coarse-grained. For instance, initial estimates of the operational costs of adding an

---

[B]As the focus of this book is cloud security, it should be understood that privacy protections are as essential to protect privacy information. For the purposes of this book, technical privacy controls are considered to be a subset of confidentiality and related security controls.

application to a corporate data center may fail to account for the consequent need to upgrade hardware or switches. Additional charges may be incurred by the consuming department or at the corporate level to account for unanticipated IT costs. Where public cloud computing is completely transparent in how usage is metered and charged, private cloud implementations can mimic some of that and abstract such costs and absorb the need for incrementing scale as usage increases.

Again, as we stated earlier in The IT Foundation for Cloud, the service interface/contract is a key distinguishing aspect of cloud. It is this that represents the dramatic changes in the relationship between IT and tenants/users. By abstracting what lies behind the IT organization to a contract between providers and consumers, consumers no longer can meddle in IT decisions and IT must deliver on services contracts. The impact of this should not be glossed over, it will drive a number of changes in IT organizations—starting with headcount—and it has the potential to reset the often challenging relationship between corporate IT and IT users.

There is ample evidence that the cloud model offers compelling cost efficiencies in multiple dimensions. In a traditional enterprise, one will generally find 1 systems administrator per 10 to 1,000 servers, and in a large scale cloud implementation, the systems administrator may be replaced by a systems engineer for two to three orders of magnitude more servers (1,000 to 20,000).[4]

Notably, the United States Federal Government expects that over time the savings benefit from adopting the cloud model should significantly exceed the cost of technology investment. Several other economic analyses confirm the magnitude of these savings. One study by Booz Allen Hamilton[5] estimated life cycle costs of implementing public, private, and hybrid clouds. It considered *transition costs, life cycle operations, and migration schedules* and indicated that long-term savings depend on *the scale of the data center and the amount of time required to move operations into the cloud*. In one example in this study, the benefit-to-cost ratio reached 15.4:1 after implementation, with total life cycle cost as much as 66 percent lower.

TIP

Capex is accounting speak for *Capitol Expenditure*, and Opex for *Operational Expenditure*. In cloud computing, these two terms can lead to confused business cases. There need not be a monetary advantage between treating the same server as Opex or Capex, but there are differences.

First, hardware loses value over time simply because new gear will be faster, have better features, and cost less overall. Also, aging hardware will cease being supported at some point, which has many implications. If your service or system is in the game for a long time, you will experience hardware upgrades. Second, if you buy a server, you are stuck with depreciating Capex. Or, you can lease the same gear, in which case, it's Opex. You may pay much more for it, but you can get out of the lease.

A public cloud is more like a lease. A private cloud is a different matter, but hardware upgrades are more likely going to be abstracted to another division in the organization. Having access to either a public or a private cloud has potential value for organizations. Here is the point: When a tenant bypasses organizational Capex gates, they gain the freedom to take risks, and if an organization no longer needs IT infrastructure experts, that means the IT genie is out of the bottle.

AN HISTORICAL VIEW: ROOTS OF CLOUD COMPUTING

In order to understand cloud computing, it helps to know how we got here. At the risk of being superficial, we can trace many of the themes and attributes of cloud computing to precursors over the past 40 or so years. In a sense, cloud computing is an evolution in computing with a rich family tree. Mainframes were the epitome of control and centralization in contrast to what followed in computing. This is especially so in light of the recent proliferation of computers and computer-based mobile devices. What can be unkindly described as the *tyranny* of main-frames (historical high cost to acquire coupled with fanatical operations and accounting priesthood) gave rise to minicomputers, which individual departments were more able to acquire within their budgets.

Since the era of the mainframe, the industry and computing has evolved in dramatic ways. Every aspect of the industry has seen frequent and important inno-vation and change. As depicted in Figure 1.3, these changes often had a dramatic impact on information security.

Decentralization and Proliferation

The democratization in computing accelerated with the world-changing personal computer (PC). By the 1990s, many individual departments or business units found themselves maintaining scores of identical looking PCs that were configured in laughably unidentical ways. All too often, these held copies of the same document in multiple versions which—to read or update—required multiple versions of some application. For a time, the term *PC* was almost synonymous with *chaos*.

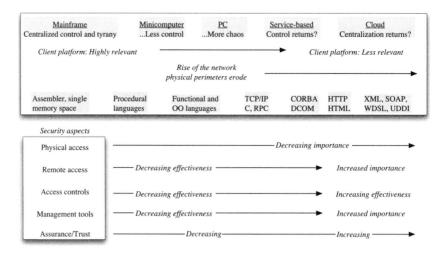

FIGURE 1.3

The impact of computing innovation on security.

During this period, you likely used either a standard commercial or a custom program in order to perform work or process data. One quality of such a *stand-alone* system was that the process was fully performed in one location without need for other connected systems. Based on the common nature of these processes, the stand-alone era and even more so the PC launched the software industry. As the software industry grew and alternative software packages arose, the cost of computing began to decrease. The software industry has on the one hand brought powerful automation to anyone who could afford a computer, and on the other hand, we produced more and more software that was developed with little regard to even basic engineering principles and with seemingly even less regard to any notion of pride in development. Software became a problem from many standpoints, notably from its poor security.

Networking, the Internet, and the Web

Transaction processing systems arose to meet the need for interaction by increasing numbers of people with a single database. In this model, a single server performed computation and data storage while simpler client machines served for input and output. Airline reservation systems took this model and pushed connected clients to the far corners of the Earth. Initially, the client had no local storage and was connected to the server via a dedicated communications link.

Similar to transaction processing systems, client/server began with the commodity PC client simply performing input/output and the server ran the custom software. But this quickly changed as the power of the underlying PC client proved to make some local computation important for overall performance and increased functionality. Now the PC was connected by a more general purpose local area network or wide area network that had other uses as well. With client/server came advances in more user-friendly interfaces.

Where we were once limited to interacting with computers via direct-connected card readers and terminals, we experienced a great untethering, first via primitive modems, later with the Internet, and more recently with pervasive high-bandwidth networking and wireless. Again, we saw erosion in security as these conveniences made life simpler for all, including those who delighted in exploiting poor software and poor implementations. More so, much infrastructure appeared to grow organically and was less planned than a garden of weeds. The consequences? Increased operating costs and insecurity were pervasive.

If the Internet brought a quiet and relatively slow revolution, the World Wide Web brought an explosive revolution. Web sites sprang up on standard servers that ran standard software. With the first Web sites and the first Web browser, it became evident that the way we were to interact with information was rapidly changing. Simple server software, simple browsers, and a common set of IPs were all it seemed to take to make it work. This interaction model expanded to include Web-based applications that let formerly stand-alone applications be expressed via Web technology.

Virtualization

With more recent advances in virtualization, computers virtually multiplied inside their own cases in the form of VMs. These are software implementations of computers—and indistinguishable over a network from a physical computer. A VM is simply an environment, typically an operating system (OS) or a program, that is created within another environment. The term *guest* is usually used to refer to the VM while we refer to the hosting environment as the *host*. A single host can support multiple guest environments in a dynamic on-demand manner. Guest VMs can execute completely different instruction sets that are foreign to the underlying physical hardware, which can be abstracted away by the host environment.

A key concept here is that we are creating a virtual version of something (be it a server, application, storage, network, client, ...) that can be separated from its underlying resources using an *execution container*, again usually an OS or a program. In some forms of virtualization, the underlying hardware layer is completely simulated, whereas in most implementations, this is not the case. In some cases, hardware may implement some virtualization support. Virtualization takes many forms (see Tom Olzak's *Microsoft Virtualization: Master Microsoft Server, Desktop, Application, and Presentation Virtualization* [ISBN: 978-1-59749-431-1, Syngress]) and can take place from bare hardware on up through applications.

Another key concept is that virtualization is used in different areas, including server, storage, or network. Virtualization can mask complexity and enable resource sharing and utilization. Virtualization also can deliver a degree of isolation and insulation from the effect of some forms of vulnerability risk. Virtualization is part of several trends in IT, including cloud computing. And that is good, because virtualization has brought important security benefits. When applications residing in VMs are subject to exploits or are subverted, it is far easier to isolate the VM and restart from an untainted copy than it would be to reprovision a server with an OS and applications.

In many ways, the collective changes in computing since the era of the mainframe are a continuing evolution into multiple directions. The progression from conventional high performance computing, such as cluster computing, to grid computing is a recent innovation in the use of existing technology that contributed to the rise of cloud computing. Likewise, the packaging of computing resources (such as storage and computation) into a metered service itself enabled both grid computing and cloud computing. Figure 1.4 depicts a selected family tree of cloud computing based on a few of the computing trends we surveyed above. In this figure, we see how individual technologies and advances led to other technologies, for instance, service-oriented architectures (SOAs) grew from Web services, which grew from the Web, which itself depended on the Internet.

Another way to view these changes and innovations is as an evolutionary spiral, corkscrewing upward in time and repeatedly passing over and revisiting familiar territory. In a sense, VMs on PCs are old hat for mainframe old-timers.

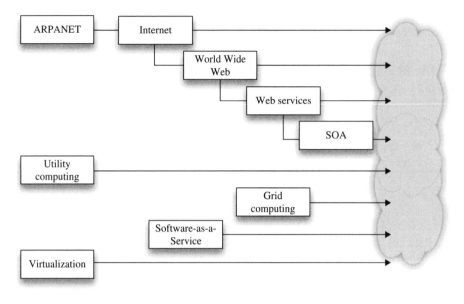

FIGURE 1.4

Simplified cloud computing family tree.

One can also view cloud computing as an across the board refactoring of many of these trends. This last point may go far in explaining the hype and allure of cloud computing. As we will describe later, a huge scale of aggregated resources and a cookie cutter approach to implementation are hallmarks of large cloud implementations. And, discipline in both process and operation is a necessity at this scale.

A BRIEF PRIMER ON SECURITY: FROM 50,000 FT

In this section, we survey just enough security to enable the non-security expert to follow the concepts and discussion in the remainder of the book, those versed in security can easily skip ahead. We read about cyber security vulnerabilities often enough that these have become a core element of our zeitgeist. But more often than not, security is an afterthought, a practice marked by the common attitude: *First we build it, then we secure it.* Equally ineffective in result, we often attempt to achieve *enough* security by relegating it to the perimeter.[C] Worse, we sometimes come to believe that the best we can do is to hope for the best, and find ourselves adopting point approaches that are ineffective. And when it comes time

---

[C]Why? Perhaps that strategy reflected our naivety about threats, or perhaps security was perceived as *secret sauce* that could be applied as a topping, or perhaps security engineers couldn't effectively communicate in a business way to decision makers and other stakeholders.

to maintain security in operation, we tend to be burdened by architectures and solutions that do not support cost-effective security practices.

Terminology and Principles

Before we consider security in the cloud arena, we should have an appreciation for the basic definitions and the fact that there are several closely related security fields:

- **Information Security** This term refers to a broad field that has to do with the protection of information and information systems. Information security has historical roots that include ciphers, subterfuge, and other practices whose goals were to protect the confidentiality of written messages. In our era, information security is generally understood to involve domains that are involved in the security of IT systems as well as with the non-IT processes that are in interaction with IT systems. The objective of information security is to protect information as well as information systems *from unauthorized access, use, disclosure, disruption, modification, or destruction.*[6]
- **Subdomains to Information Security** Among these are computer security, network security, database security, and information assurance. In cloud security, we will be drawing upon each of these as necessary to address issues that we face.
- **Confidentiality, Integrity, and Availability** The overall objective for security can largely be boiled down to the triad of security: protecting the confidentiality, integrity, and availability of information (referred to as *CIA*). The FISMA[D] defines[7]:
  - **Confidentiality** "Preserving authorized restrictions on information access and disclosure, including means for protecting personal privacy and proprietary information…. A loss of confidentiality is the unauthorized disclosure of information."
  - **Integrity** "Guarding against improper information modification or destruction, and includes ensuring information non-repudiation and authenticity…. A loss of integrity is the unauthorized modification or destruction of information."
  - **Availability** "Ensuring timely and reliable access to and use of information…. A loss of availability is the disruption of access to or use of information or an information system."
- **Least Privilege Principle** Users and processes acting on their behalf should be restricted to operate with a minimal set of privileges. This is to prevent the pervasive use of privilege or access rights within IT systems.
- **Authentication** The means to establish a user's identity, typically by presenting credentials such as a user name and password. Other means include

---

[D]Federal Information Security Management Act.

biometric or certificate-based schemes. Identity management can become very complex in many ways. Authentication data may reside in multiple systems in the same infrastructure or domain.

- **Authorization** The rights or privileges that are granted to a person, user, or process. These can be electronically represented in many ways, and access control lists (ACLs) are simple lists of users and their rights (generally simple statements such as read, write, modify, delete, or execute) against either specific resources or classes of resources. Even simpler are traditional UNIX file permissions, which are at the granularity of Owner, Group, and Others with read, write, execute, and other permissions. The problem with such authorization schemes is that they only work well enough with a very small population of users. They do not scale to large populations, and these schemes are ineffective for computing environments where underlying user IDs are recycled. They are also ineffective against problems that are more difficult to represent, such as we have with SOA services.

- **Cryptography** From the Greek word for secret *kryptos*, cryptography has two faces: One is focused on hiding or obfuscating information, and the other (*cryptoanalysis*) is dedicated to exposing secrets that are protected by cryptographic means. Encryption is the process of converting information in *plain text* into *cipher text*, with decryption serving the reverse function. Ciphers are the algorithms that are used to perform encryption and decryption, and they are dependent on the use of keys or *keying materials*. An in-depth treatment of cryptography is beyond the scope of this book, but several further points should be made. First, modern computer cryptography is measured in several dimensions. Cryptography is computationally expensive, but typically the stronger the algorithm the greater the overhead. Second, there are different kinds of algorithms; among them are key pairs (public–private) whereby an individual can safely publish their public key for anyone else to use to encrypt information that can only be decrypted using the associated private key. This has great utility in many ways. Third, cryptography has many other uses in computing; one such use is digital signatures whereby an individual or entity can authenticate data by *signing* it. Another use is to authenticate two or more communicating parties.

- **Auditing** This encompasses various activities that span the generation, collection and review of network, system, and application events to maintain a current view of security. Electronic security monitoring is based on the automated assessment of such audit data. But the term auditing is overloaded in security, and it is also used to refer to periodic manual reviews of security and security controls. These focus on security controls, security procedures, backup procedures, contingency plans, data center security, and many other areas. Sadly, the term monitoring is also overloaded, and we will find many cases where it is used to refer to activities associated with audit event assessment as well as with the periodic activities to verify security controls are appropriate and operating correctly. (We will strive to put sufficient context in our use of these terms.)

- **Accountability** This amounts to being able to retroactively establish who did what, when, and how. Accountability is dependent on identity and auditing. If accountability is important, then we need to appropriately protect all data and control information that is used to grant access as well as audit access. Since we may not discover a need to perform a forensic review of such data for relatively long periods of time, the general requirements for retaining such event data range from about 120 days and up. (At least one government organization had a requirement to retain such data indefinitely, but ran into physical media problems after 10 years!)

Depending on our needs, regulatory requirements, and other overarching demands, we will be placing more or less emphasis on security controls to enforce confidentiality, or integrity, or availability, or all three. In other words, the specific realm we work in (banking, finance, R&D, government, defense, and so on) will in part define our cloud security needs.

In many ways, security exhibits a series of qualities or characteristics that result from fundamental design and implementation decisions. Qualities such as complexity, reliability, availability, and scalability both derive security from and also may come from the environment and have a direct impact on security. Typically, we will leverage existing technology and products when we build security solutions. These components, along with *security glue,* will each and collectively exhibit qualities such as listed above. Taken together, a security solution is a composition that may be difficult or easy to verify, it may have low or high usability characteristics, and it may or may not entail constant configuration and management. Figure 1.5 depicts this relationship.

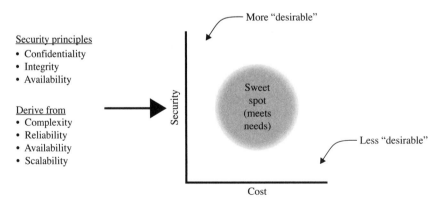

FIGURE 1.5

Security: principles and qualities.

Security entails trade-offs, by this we mean that controls should be commensurate with the value of what we seek to protect. Since not all threats and vulnerabilities will be known in advance, we sometimes describe security as having three interdependent goals: prevention, detection, and response. In operation, we will achieve cost benefits if we protect against (or protect) security risks rather than reacting over and over in response to avoidable security incidents.

Risk Management

Security approaches should be pragmatic in terms of security controls and system functionality. What we mean is that the same architecture and the same controls are generally not appropriate for both a low-risk and a high-risk environment. Making this relevant to clouds, we probably do not want to mix banking applications with social-networking applications in a public cloud! By their very nature, we would more likely find that apps that manage low-risk data can cohabitate with other apps that have similar security needs.

So, what is risk, or how do we quantify risk? In essence, we say that risk is a function of threats as they seek to exploit vulnerabilities, and in light of the countermeasures, we apply to protect our assets. This is the risk formula we use in information security:

$$\text{Risk} = \left(\frac{\text{Threats} \times \text{Vulnerabilities}}{\text{Countermeasures}} \right) \times (\text{Asset value})$$

This formula requires that we sometimes must determine tangible values for somewhat intangible assets. Since risk is expressed in terms of threats that exploit vulnerabilities and the value of assets are hanging in the balance, we want to get our security strategy right in terms of the exposure side. But we also want to get it right from the cost side as well. We have a budget for managing risk (coming from revenue-for-value decisions), and if we are going to implement cost-effective security, we need to quantify risk at an appropriate order of magnitude.

In other words: Addressing risk is a *Goldilocks* problem: Not too hot, not too cold: Just right! That's one theory anyway. Figure 1.6 depicts this relationship. The reality is that new vulnerabilities are exposed daily and that new exploits are being dreamed up as quickly. We should plan on facing some seriously bad and costly events, and thus we have insurance—or self-insure against some of the risk with more layers of security.

Security Must Become a Business Enabler

Controls must be commensurate with functionality, as too often security is seen as an impediment. Rather than having security be a business-impediment function, security must enable business. To do this, it must be integrated with broader IT plans in the earliest stages. When we take a primary security requirement, such as identification and authentication, and express it as *identity as a service*, we are

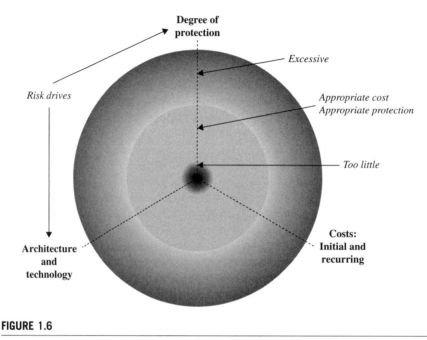

FIGURE 1.6

Appropriate security (*Goldilocks*).

creating a business and functionality enabler. This is good for security and good for business, and best of all, it can produce recurring savings. We will have a single pattern and implementation to verify and maintain, and better yet, developers no longer need to implement what should be a core security function. This view is relatively recent, and it is still not universally appreciated. However, this is a view that is far easier to promulgate with cloud implementations.

At its most elemental, security is simply a set of systems properties that are sub-definitions of *quality*. When it comes to quality, there are numerous stakeholders throughout the organization in different organizational roles. From development, operations, legal, and privacy, these stakeholders have specific goals to managing risk. They may not know it, but the opportunity is that these are all stakeholders who have an interest in security. Once IT security plans are aligned with business goals, the IT security team can enjoy broad organizational support for investment in time and cost to build better infrastructure security.

A BRIEF PRIMER ON ARCHITECTURE

If builders built buildings the way programmers wrote programs, then the first woodpecker that came along would destroy civilization.—Weinberg's second law[8]

Weinberg's quote may date from the Jurassic Age of computing, but the sentiment has applied to every subsequent period and to every practice in IT. Undisciplined systems building and cobbled together IT infrastructure gives rise to *organic* implementations that soon turn brittle. The results include:

- Ineffective and expensive operations
- Missing or broken governance
- Controls and procedures that are hard to automate
- Inaccurate information about IT components
- Poor IT security

Without a foundation of sound principles, structure, or methodology, you will get what you would expect: the IT equivalent of a shantytown. In a sense, cloud computing is the latest way out of this. Although the cloud model offers more than structured IT infrastructure, it is worthwhile to recall some relevant engineering and architectural approaches that predate cloud computing.

Systems Engineering

Systems engineering is a well-known methodology for achieving integration. James Martin described the method as viewing the entirety of components as a holistic entity rather than as an assembly of components. In his view, components should be designed in light of how they will interoperate with other components.[9] Systems engineering has grown from being an approach into an interdisciplinary engineering practice. As shown in Figure 1.7, the scope of systems engineering spans a range of activities. We need not review all these activities, but we should understand that they bring structure to the process of building complicated and

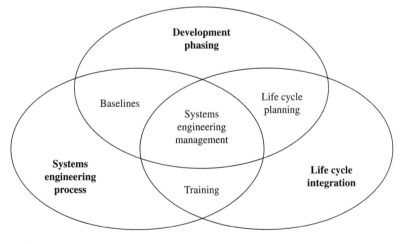

FIGURE 1.7

Systems engineering management activities.[10]

sophisticated things out of components. One cannot do justice to this topic in one paragraph, but systems engineering has been closely associated with many other engineering fields and it is a major contributor to security engineering. We will take up this theme again, after we survey IT architecture.

IT Architecture

Part blueprint and part guidance, *IT architecture* seeks to convey understanding about how an IT system or infrastructure is organized from its constituent components, how these relate to each other, and the principles that inform the choices. For IT, we might call out these three general levels:

- **Components** Individual devices, programs, applications, and so on for services, processes, tools, and governance are components.
- **Infrastructure** A functioning system or collection of components
- **Architecture** It is focused on design.

Architecture activities span from the details of individual components (or solutions levels) up to systems and infrastructure, to information architecting, and up to enterprises and beyond. In terms of breadth, it ranges across application, technical, information, and business realms. A primary objective of all architectures is to develop coherent and efficient structures that meet the needs or mission of the organization, over the long term and in a sustainable manner.

In other words, successful architecture should:

- Guide systems life cycle processes.
- Support both stability as well as continual innovation.

An understanding of business objectives and business constraints is key to achieving a viable architecture. Higher-level architectures should be strategic in how they support overall business goals and reduce costs.

SECURITY ARCHITECTURE: A BRIEF DISCUSSION

Paralleling the failures and consequences of *organic* IT implementations, *IT security* faced similar issues as it made its way toward the adoption of architectural approaches. Security architectures and models have been influenced by various process, engineering, and model efforts. Historically, a groundbreaking one was the *Capability Maturity Model* (CMM)[E] from Carnegie Mellon University. Adapted for security, this work came to a head in the late 1990s and early 2000s and is called the *System Security Engineering Capability Maturity Model* (SSE-CMM). The importance of practicing security engineering in conjunction with

---

[E]*Capability Maturity Model* and *CMM* are service marks of Carnegie Mellon University. For more on the CMM, see: www.sei.cmu.edu/cmmi/.

other engineering disciplines is core to the SSE-CMM, which states and promotes "the view that security is pervasive across all engineering disciplines (e.g., systems, software, and hardware) and defining components of the model."[11] More recently, the international standard ISO/IEC 21827 was based on the SSE-CMM.

A number of other notable engineering process, modeling, and architectural efforts have contributed to security engineering and architectures. There is a wide range of models and standards that apply to a security Software/solution/system Development Life Cycle (SDLC). Several of these can serve as reference models for security engineering, security architecture, security operations, and certainly for cloud security. But doing so is not always straightforward, as some of these are proprietary or controlled by a single entity. Furthermore, not all of the existing reference models have security architecture or security controls as their focus. Some of these models are as follows:

- **ISO 27001 through ISO 27006**[F] This series of international standards for information security covers: management, best practices, requirements, and techniques. These have important value in their potential applicability to cloud computing security.
- **European Network and Information Security Agency (ENISA)** It is the European cyber security agency. In 2009, ENISA published a *Cloud Computing Information Assurance Framework*,[G] which heavily adopts ISO 27001 and 27002 controls for cloud computing. In the same year, ENISA also published *Cloud Computing Benefits, Risks and Recommendations for Information Security*.[H] Together, these documents offer background on the security issues for organizations wishing to adopt cloud computing.
- **Information Technology Infrastructure Library (ITIL)**[I] Core to ITIL is the understanding that IT services must be aligned to business needs. Focused on IT service management, ITIL defines processes that are structured around service life cycles and practices. Security management in ITIL is based on ISO/IEC 27002. ITIL offers indirect value beyond IT service management in planning and architecture phases.
- **Control Objectives for Information and related Technology (COBIT)** It is a framework for IT management that was developed by the Information Systems Audit and Control, along with the IT Governance Institute. It is a set of generally accepted best practices, measures, and indicators for IT governance and control. COBIT is broader in scope than ISO/IEC 27002, which is focused on security.

[F]ISO27001, ISO27002, ISO27003, ISO27004, ISO27005, and ISO27006 are all from the International Organization for Standardization, www.iso.org/iso/home.html.

[G]Catteddu, D., Hogben, G., Cloud Computing Information Assurance Framework, European Network and Information Security Agency (ENISA), 2009, www.enisa.europa.eu/.

[H]Catteddu, D., Hogben, G., Cloud Computing Benefits, Risks and Recommendations for Information Security, European Network and Information Security Agency (ENISA), 2009, www.enisa.europa.eu/.

[I]ITIL is a registered trade mark of the Office of Government Commerce.

In addition, NIST has developed a deep and broad set of standards and guidelines that, although oriented for use by the US Government, have a great deal of applicability for non-government security engineering and architecture. NIST has a long and illustrious track record in producing first rate INFOSEC-related standards and guidelines. Currently, Peter Mell and Tim Grance have produced a working definition of cloud computing,[12] which has been broadly adopted. Similar to NIST, there are numerous international governmental organizations that have done complimentary work focused on their own national needs. Other organizations, companies, and individuals have made profound contributions to security engineering and architecture.

Given our earlier discussions on security, security architecture is focused on conveying understanding of security controls in several ways:

- How and where security controls support and enforce specific security qualities, notably confidentiality, integrity, and availability
- How these controls reduce complexity since complexity is counter to reliability
- How these controls relate to the larger IT architecture

Security primarily serves for protection and assurance. But as we indicated earlier, when security is strategic, it can be a business or functionality enabler. By example, a security architecture can serve to bring together a common set of service requirements from multiple stakeholder groups and recast them, addressing them collectively with a superior solution than could be afforded otherwise. Centralized or federated identity management is an example of implementing a commonly needed capability and expressing it as a common service.

Borrowing from other disciplines, security architecture has evolved from silo-like architecture to more of an integrated architecture that is broadly focused on business, information, and technology. To a large extent, this is due to the rise of SOAs, but there are other equally important contributing trends. As stated in the introduction, we can view cloud computing as an across the board refactoring of many trends in multiple parts of the IT and business landscapes.

The amount of progress in the field of security is simply remarkable, despite spotty adoption and persistently poor practices that lead to vulnerabilities, risks, and dramatic exploits. Generally, we know what should be done, but we make excuses that usually involve the words *time and money*. But worse, two trends are tightly coupled in a state of continuing tension: The first is the increasing recognition of just how disturbing and dangerously vulnerable we are to cyber threats, and the second is the powerful business drive to do more with cyber technologies. We want to go to a wild party, but we have every reason to believe it's going to end very badly.[J]

[J]There is a certain degree of suspended disbelief at work here. Perhaps we are suffering mass psychosis brought on by exposure to bit-Elves, whatever they are.

Defense in Depth

The 1996 paper *Information Warfare and Dynamic Information Defense*[13] adopted the term *defense in depth* from military operations for network security. In this domain, it has been used as a strategy to account for the fact that individual security controls are typically vulnerable and that by using multiple reinforcing controls one can present a more robust defense. Such reinforcing controls can be similar and redundant, but they should also be layered at different levels in an overall implementation—for instance, white-listed IP addresses at a network ingress, ACLs at core switches and within subnets, and access controls at individual applications or systems. With defense in depth, the goal is that if an exploit succeeds, it should be contained rather than achieving a free ride.

EPIC FAIL

A French gang known as the *gang à l'aspirateur*, or *vacuum gang*, has repeatedly found a way to extract euro notes from a chain of Monoprix French supermarket safes without opening the safes. They did this for at least 15 times over a period of 4 years as of October 2010, stealing a total of over 500,000 euros.[14]

The key to how they stole the money lies in the mechanism that Monoprix uses to transfer money from checkout stations to its safes. Cash is funneled to a store safe via a pneumatic suction tube. The thieves simply drilled a large hole into these pneumatic tubes near the safe and hooked up a powerful vacuum, allowing them to suck the money out of the safe!

The lesson here is that if your threat model is incomplete—and there is enough motivation to do so—you will pay for the oversight.

CLOUD IS DRIVING BROAD CHANGES

Despite the hype, cloud brings multiple fundamental shifts in how computing infrastructure is acquired and managed. Despite often shameless marketing by vendors and cloud providers, the opportunities with cloud computing may prove challenging to IT, business, and government. Already today, significant security concerns about cloud computing are coloring many early cloud adoption decisions. But we see cloud as a driver for better security, and we see security as an enabler and a foundation for better cloud computing.

The cloud computing approach is forcing broad changes in IT:

- **It Is Catalyst for IT Staff Changes** Cloud is altering the status quo across IT, and clearly it is having an impact on the IT workforce. In direct contrast to typical IT infrastructure, the scale of cloud computing provides the most benefit from investments in automation. However, to mitigate the (very significant) investment risk, infrastructure must be more efficiently organized and structured (recall the earlier discussion on patterns in The IT Foundation for Cloud). The combination of automation and structure means that immensely large clouds can be managed and operated by smaller staff. This, along with the technologies used in cloud computing, will drive expansion of the skill set of cloud engineers. All this—coupled with increasingly sophisticated tools—is good for security.

- **Cloud Simplifies IT** Every step required to build and operate a traditional IT solution is overhead for the underlying goal. It entails expensive skills and inefficient repeated effort. Using pooled resources in a private cloud, small departments will have access to more IT without capital commitments or traditional build overhead. The migration out of many server closets into a larger private cloud pool will bring greater reliability, lower cost, and opportunity for improved security.
- **Reliability as a Function of Architecture** Cloud enables greater reliability in computing.

Cloud computing is also enabling fundamental changes in other ways:

- **Cloud Lowers the Cost of Opportunity** Using an appropriate cloud deployment model (private, public, hybrid, or community), entrepreneurs and others will be able to take bigger bets with less capital risk than otherwise possible. Using a public cloud, anyone with a laptop and credit card will be able to prototype and deliver services at an unprecedented scale.
- **Cloud Computing Lowers the Cost of Security** By the patterns in infrastructure, greater automation, and discipline in process, cloud computing presents security advantages. But by building in security at cloud scale, better security can be presented as a cloud service. In other words, *Security-as-a Service*.

Cloud Works Today

Even as it evolves and matures, cloud computing is being adopted at a fast pace. Cloud computing is working today, and it has received investment focus by government, leading companies, and the IT vendor community. Cloud is one of the most prolific areas for startups, and it has generated incredible momentum in the few short years since it has arrived. The simple fact that cloud provider can harmonize peak loads from multiple tenants and, thereby, raise overall *server productivity* by enough percentage points makes resource sharing a cost-effective model. Utilization of cloud resources is managed by cloud providers to not only increase their profitability but by the nature of competitive market forces, lower provider costs translate into lower tenant and consumption costs.

However, customers with very large and infrastructure needs, or those who have data security, or national security needs will probably take the *build-a-private-cloud* approach. Although it makes great sense to embark on that path, it might not make as much sense to build your own enabling software. Expect to see dramatic changes and advances in cloud control, management, and security solutions.

Although the cloud model has already been shown as valuable, there are adoption issues. To begin with, many current applications that drive enterprises can't easily be migrated to the cloud. This is true for both external public and internal private clouds, but for different reasons. Each of the major public cloud providers imposes either architectures or application program interfaces (APIs) that hinder simply moving enterprise apps into these public clouds. When it comes to private clouds, the very architectural advantages of building a private cloud pose impediments; however, these are not deal breakers and can be managed.

TOOLS

The direction you take in getting started with cloud computing will depend on your need and interests. If you seek a solution for e-mail or document collaboration, then Google Apps, Huddle, Zoho, or ThinkFree Online can fit the bill. If you need a hosted virtual infrastructure, then Amazon (AWS/EC2), GoGrid, and Rackspace are three of many alternative choices. If you need to build your own private cloud, then you might start with open source such as Eucalyptus, Enomaly, or the Free Cloud Alliance.

In other words, getting started in cloud computing can be as easy as creating an account with a cloud service provider or downloading open source cloud tools. A word to the wise, regardless of the direction you take: Do your homework first. The services that are available for hosting and open source components are changing very quickly. There are enough cases of service providers who either have no experience or who are deliberately misrepresenting their abilities or commitment. Given the risk and the profits that could be made by unscrupulous providers (or sources of software for that matter), what is needed is a clearing house or review service for customers and users of these services. Sure you can google a provider and gain a great deal of understanding of what others claim about the service, but such reviews bring no real credibility to the party. Caveat emptor, user take care.

It is not entirely clear what the motivation is for why these public cloud providers insist on offering services that impose adoption impediments for potential enterprise customers. It is reasonable to expect that the *low hanging fruit* for public cloud adoption does not include large enterprises and that the typical customers who are attracted to current public cloud services are more likely to be developing apps rather than using the cloud for these enterprise-level applications. It is also worth considering that by attracting these early cloud adopters to a public cloud with unique architectural expressions or APIs, these customers are perhaps being *captured* by the providers.

Valid Concerns

But cloud computing has also raised concerns about the erosion of control when information and software move off of *organic* resources and into someone else's control sphere. Despite concerns from many security professionals, cloud computing isn't innately more or less secure. But the cloud model does force a movement toward a more robust and capable foundation of security services. The mere act of transitioning from legacy systems gives us hope that we can regain control over gaps and issues that stem from poorly integrated or *after-thought security*. With cloud, greater investment for in-common security services has great potential for return on investment (ROI) given cloud scale.

Some advocates almost instinctively see the benefits of cloud computing, whereas others are painfully skeptical. As Bernard Golden, writing at www.cio.com stated:

> *Significant elements of IT organizations dismissed the PC at its introduction as a "toy." I well remember running an engineering organization in 1995, when someone in the group put an article up on the communal bulletin board that proclaimed "The Internet will never be used for important applications."*[15]

The real question is whether the aggregate benefits of cloud computing are significant enough to overcome their present day shortcomings. Based on the product developments coming out of the IT industry, it is clear that all the major vendors have embraced cloud computing. It appears that all the major vendors IBM, HP, Microsoft, and Oracle have concluded that at the very least, cloud is a certainty for the IT future.

SUMMARY

In this chapter, we introduced the qualities and characteristics of cloud computing in order to understand this model of computing and to allow us to address the broad area of cloud security in the remainder of the book. We surveyed the technologies that cloud infrastructure is built on, and we defined a series of terms that we will use in the remainder of the book. We also started to look at security for cloud computing, but we will address that topic in greater depth in the remainder of the book.

Endnotes

1. William *"Bill"* Meine, in private communication; 2010.
2. Butzer D. As Interviewed on NPR. Transcript available from: http://www.npr.org/templates/story/story.php?storyId=102112026; 2009 [accessed 19.03.09].
3. Aristotle. *Metaphysica*.
4. Marsan C. *The Google-ization of Bechtel, Network World*. http://www.networkworld.com/news/2008/102908-bechtel.html?page=1; 2008 [accessed 29.10.08].
5. Morton G, Alford T. *The economics of cloud computing: Addressing the benefits of infrastructure in the cloud*. Booz Allen Hamilton, Inc.; 2009. Available from: http://www.boozallen.com/media/file/Economics-of-Cloud-Computing.pdf [accessed 21.03.11].
6. Federal Information Security Management Act (FISMA) TITLE-III—INFORMATION SECURITY SEC. 301. INFORMATION SECURITY.SEC. 3542. Definitions.
7. Ibid.

8. Weinberg GM. http://www.geraldmweinberg.com [accessed 21.03.11].

9. Martin J, Martin M, Martin P. *Systems engineering guidebook: A process for developing systems and products.* Taylor & Francis, Inc.; 1997.

10. Adapted from: *System engineering fundamentals.* Fort Belvoir, Virginia: Defense Acquisition University Press; 2001.

11. *System Security Engineering Capability Maturity Model and SSE-CMM are ® Service Marks of Carnegie Mellon University.* http://www.sse-cmm.org/index.html.

12. Mell P, Grance T. *The NIST definition of cloud computing,* Version 15; 2009. National Institute of Standards and Technology, Information Technology Laboratory.

13. Winkler J, O'Shea C, Stokrp M. Information Warfare And Dynamic Information Defense, 1996, Proceedings: 1996 Command and Control Symposium, Naval Postgraduate School, Monterey CA.

14. http://frenchtribune.com/teneur/101083-french-thieves-vacuum-money-supermarkets-safe [accessed 21.03.11].

15 Golden B. *Cloud Computing: The Dangers of Irrational Economics.* CIO.COM http://www.cio.com/article/print/596401; 2010 [accessed 09.06.10].

Cloud Computing Architecture

2

INFORMATION IN THIS CHAPTER

- Cloud Reference Architecture
- Control over Security in the Cloud Model
- Making Sense of Cloud Deployment
- Making Sense of Services Models
- How Clouds Are Formed and Key Examples
- Real-world Cloud Usage Scenarios

In Chapter 1, we developed an introductory background to cloud computing and examined several characteristics of cloud computing. We focused specifically on those that are related to economies of scale and flexibility. In doing so, we stated that these can both offer security benefits and can raise security concerns. Chapter 1 covered important concepts and terminology that we will now use to explore the cloud model in greater detail. Working from a commonly accepted view of what constitutes cloud computing will allow us to narrow our focus when we identify or select best practices for cloud security and when we design or evaluate the security for a cloud.

CLOUD REFERENCE ARCHITECTURE

In this section, we will revisit what we described in Chapter 1 as *Cloud Computing Qualities*. Next, we will look at cloud service models (SaaS, PaaS, and IaaS), and finally, we will look at the different cloud deployment models.

As a general model for delivering Information Technology (IT) services, cloud computing has broad applicability for adopters who may have diverse needs. As we adopt the cloud model to meet various requirements, you will see clouds implemented in different ways using different technologies and expressing new and different services. Some cloud advocates adhere to rigorous definitions of what a *true* cloud must include, stating with certainty that one technology or characteristic is critical to the definition. Others have offered less limiting definitions and list characteristics and common qualities that are typically associated with the overall model.

> **TIP**
>
> Some cloud advocates have argued that virtualization is a necessary technology component of cloud computing, whereas others argue that it is not always necessary.
>
> In a Google Groups Cloud computing post, Paul Robinson put it this way: "The quickest and cheapest method to providing the necessary level of abstraction in terms of server resource is currently virtualization. So, yes, it's possible to run a cloud without virtualization, but you need to do a lot of work in order for it to still offer all the core attributes and values of a cloud service that virtualization gives you."[1]
>
> There are several points that should be made about this:
>
> - There is a difference between enabling technologies (such as virtualization) and the capabilities or features that are required for a given cloud.
> - A specific capability may be achieved by alternative technologies or approaches.
> - Technology and innovation do not stand still.

By example, some advocates claim that multitenancy is a necessary cloud capability. But there are implementations where this is not the case, are these then not clouds? Such arguments or discussions can become pointlessly reductionist, so it may be more reasonable to approach the situation from a practical perspective.

Revisiting Essential Characteristics

In a broadly accepted working paper,[A] Peter Mell and Tim Grance of the National Institute of Science and Technology (NIST) have developed a set of definitions around cloud computing. In that paper, they state that cloud computing is a still-evolving paradigm, and they describe cloud computing as:

> ... a model for enabling convenient, on-demand network access to a shared pool of configurable computing resources (e.g., networks, servers, storage, applications, and services) that can be rapidly provisioned and released with minimal management effort or service provider interaction. This cloud model promotes availability and is composed of five essential **characteristics**, three **service models**, and four **deployment models**.[2]

Mell and Grance identify the five *essential characteristics* as:

On-demand self-service. *A consumer can unilaterally provision computing capabilities, such as server time and network storage, as needed automatically without requiring human interaction with each service's provider.*

Broad network access. *Capabilities are available over the network and accessed through standard mechanisms that promote use by heterogeneous thin or thick client platforms (e.g., mobile phones, laptops, and PDAs).*

[A]Mell P, Grance, T. The NIST Definition of Cloud Computing Version 15, 10-7-09, National Institute of Standards and Technology, Information Technology Laboratory.

Resource pooling. *The provider's computing resources are pooled to serve multiple consumers using a multi-tenant model, with different physical and virtual resources dynamically assigned and reassigned according to consumer demand. There is a sense of location independence in that the customer generally has no control or knowledge over the exact location of the provided resources but may be able to specify location at a higher level of abstraction (e.g., country, state, or data center). Examples of resources include storage, processing, memory, network bandwidth, and virtual machines.*

Rapid elasticity. *Capabilities can be rapidly and elastically provisioned, in some cases automatically, to quickly scale out and rapidly released to quickly scale in. To the consumer, the capabilities available for provisioning often appear to be unlimited and can be purchased in any quantity at any time.*

Measured Service. *Cloud systems automatically control and optimize resource use by leveraging a metering capability at some level of abstraction appropriate to the type of service (e.g., storage, processing, bandwidth, and active user accounts). Resource usage can be monitored, controlled, and reported providing transparency for both the provider and consumer of the utilized service.*[3]

One can agree that the NIST-defined characteristics are important, but one can also have a somewhat different perspective having been on a seasoned team that designed, built, and operated several large-sized cloud infrastructures. Such an experience will likely convince you that it is the service interface between the provider and the consumer that is a key defining characteristic of cloud services. As Bill Meine put it: "It is represented by a contract that enforces the value proposition with guarantees (SLA) and terms (price). Everything that happens to make clouds stand out as something new is due to this interface. It enables competition, drives the cost behavior of the seller, and the value choices of the buyer. Without it, you just have enterprise IT at work."[4] This service interface does not necessarily require full software automation or even instantaneous response. What this direct service interface does is to offer an authorized tenant a SLA response and performance that is not generally found in the world of IT services.

WARNING

A central concern with the cloud services model is that it is completely dependent on network connectivity. Although dependency on network connectivity is hardly new with other IT models, networking is central to functionality in every aspect of the cloud.

Furthermore, as cloud adoption accelerates and as more critical business functions are recast as cloud services, network connectivity and bandwidth must become comprehensively reliable.

Driven by cloud, computing is undergoing an evolution and is becoming a broadly available utility—not unlike the electric grid and its ubiquitous power outlets. The problem with this dependency on connectivity is that due to the number of discrete links between

(Continued)

> (*Continued*)
> the cloud service and the cloud consumers—even with a private cloud—there are many different failure modes. Minimizing such risks starts with the CSP, who is responsible for assuring that reliable and redundant connectivity will provide needed bandwidth even when a primary data center Internet connection is lost. The CSP is also responsible for verifying that the network provider has reliable and redundant links to Internet backbone providers. Likewise, the consumer or tenant of cloud services has similar responsibilities if they are to have highly available Internet connectivity.

In Chapter 1, we listed the following as *essential cloud computing qualities*: pooling resources at massive scale, repeated patterns, greater automation, reliability, operational efficiency, resource elasticity, location independence, and on-demand access, as well as technology and IT transparency. If you build infrastructure at a huge scale and you want to operate it on a shoestring budget, your design must be based on repeating patterns that enable automation, reliability, and operational efficiency. Delivering IT to customers in a manner that abstracts the technology via a service interface brings IT transparency for customers. This also will benefit the provider's operation and competitiveness by driving down costs. In part, the agility of on-demand self-serve interfaces will both insulate the provider's IT staff and free them to cost effectively deliver against the SLA. This in turn enables service delivery at the speed that customers need and without traditional IT interaction.

But as we pointed out in Chapter 1, there is an elephant in the room: The cloud model won't work for the consumer without reliable network connectivity and without the right bandwidth. For the few minutes where there may be no network connectivity to the cloud, it does not matter that your network reliability is 99.99999 percent. This is as true for an internal private cloud as it is for an external public cloud. In security terms, reliability is a sibling of availability. We might say that delivering cloud services in an agile and a cost-effective manner depends on many factors, but to be useful all the time, cloud *demands* network connectivity and cloud service security *must* meet security requirements.

EPIC FAIL

There are several classic examples of connectivity failure that were largely beyond the control of a consuming organization. Even in the past few years, there have been many cases of severed undersea cables leading to disruption of transnational communication services. In December 2008, a severed underwater fiber optic cable in the Mediterranean Sea disrupted 70 percent of internet and telephone traffic to the Middle East for 2 days. This traffic was rerouted through the United States and Asia to maintain connectivity. Earlier the same year, ship anchors had disrupted communications through the same cables between Europe, Africa, and Asia. This scenario was again repeated in April 2010 when the SEA-ME-WE 4 undersea cable was severed, again requiring traffic to be rerouted. Users reported that their effective bandwidth was severely affected. In the same year, an Oceanic Time Warner cable in the Hawaiian Islands was severed, disrupting television, telephone, and Internet.

> But disruptions of service have also occurred in terrestrial links as well. There are numerous examples of a data center or an enterprise losing communications due to a backhoe or similar construction gear ripping up the computer era's fiber optic umbilical cord. These outages are generally short lived, but they can lead to huge costs in lost business. The common themes in these events are that the severed link is either an only link, the best backup link is often colocated with the lost link, or when the loss of bandwidth from the primary link cannot be compensated for.
>
> One of the more interesting disruptions was the Howard Street Tunnel fire, which is also known as the Baltimore Freight Rail Crash of 2001. A 60 car CSX freight train derailed in tunnel under Howard Street in Baltimore, MD. A chemical fire resulted and lasted for 6 days. Not only did this force evacuation of downtown Baltimore, but the accident also severed fiber optic cables that ran through the tunnel. These cables carried a major portion of the east coast Internet traffic for WorldCom. The disruption of this link slowed Internet service throughout many portions of the United States for many hours. Adding insult to injury, the accident also caused a water main break, which itself caused further damage to the communications cables. The effects of the disruption were felt for up to 36 hours.

By now, it should be clearer that cloud computing is still an evolving model and that describing it is sometimes akin to weather reporting. There are different perspectives, as one might well expect with such a convergence of enabling technologies and innovative approaches. The cloud model abstracts and manages IT resources to deliver a range of IT services in new and more efficient ways, resulting in further innovation and opportunity.

Cloud Service Models

We have already used the terms SaaS, PaaS, and IaaS in Chapter 1, but what do we really mean by these? These are the three service models for cloud computing. As Mell and Grance define them[5]:

> Cloud Software-as-a-Service (SaaS). *The capability provided to the consumer is to use the provider's applications running on a cloud infrastructure. The applications are accessible from various client devices through a thin client interface such as a Web browser (e.g., Web-based e-mail). The consumer does not manage or control the underlying cloud infrastructure including network, servers, operating systems, storage, or even individual application capabilities, with the possible exception of limited user-specific application configuration settings.*

> Cloud Platform-as-a-Service (PaaS). *The capability provided to the consumer is to deploy onto the cloud infrastructure consumer-created or acquired applications created using programming languages and tools supported by the provider. The consumer does not manage or control the underlying cloud infrastructure including network, servers, operating systems, or storage, but has control over the deployed applications and possibly application hosting environment configurations.*

Cloud Infrastructure-as-a-Service (IaaS). *The capability provided to the consumer is to provision processing, storage, networks, and other fundamental computing resources where the consumer is able to deploy and run arbitrary software, which can include operating systems and applications. The consumer does not manage or control the underlying cloud infrastructure but has control over operating systems, storage, deployed applications, and possibly limited control of select networking components (e.g., host firewalls).*

We refer to these three as the *SPI* model. What we are really describing are three broad classes of capabilities that reside on top of physical cloud infrastructure, as depicted in Figures 2.1 and 2.2. These can be layered—IaaS as

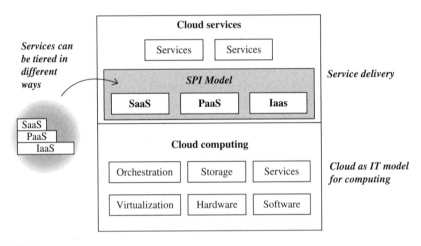

FIGURE 2.1

The SPI model: software, platform, and infrastructure as a service.

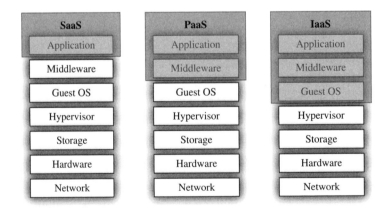

FIGURE 2.2

The SPI model: relating services to infrastructure.

a foundation for PaaS, and PaaS as a foundation for SaaS—or they can stand-alone. How services are implemented will depend on the provider. The case can be made that "IaaS and PaaS are special purpose versions of SaaS that enable new cloud services."[6] The Cloud Security Alliance has taken the following view:

> IaaS is the foundation of all cloud services, with PaaS building upon IaaS, and SaaS in turn building upon PaaS .... In this way, just as capabilities are inherited, so are information security issues and risk. It is important to note that commercial cloud providers may not neatly fit into the layered service models. Nevertheless, the reference model is important for relating real-world services to an architectural framework and understanding the resources and services requiring security analysis.[7]

Their position is well taken as it certainly would be more *agile* for a cloud provider to express SaaS as a service of PaaS, and PaaS as a service of IaaS. However, most cloud providers do not implement services delivery in that manner. The point is that infrastructure, platform, and software are three forms of cloud service delivery and that they can be delivered independently—or as layered services. But these services classes are also quite similar; each offers a container with specific interfaces, capabilities, and limitations. Some of the containers provide interfaces that act like a whole operating system, and some are so application specific that they can't be generically programmed. These definitions are really just examples of interesting points on a continuum of offered services.

Beyond SaaS, PaaS, and IaaS, several other service delivery models have been proposed, these include Data center-as-a-Service, Security-as-a-Service, Monitoring-as-a-Service, and Identity-as-a-Service, but these should be seen as specialized cases of the SPI model. While many new and innovative products and services have been enabled because of the cloud model, many marketing organizations have had a field day in representing anything as a service. But the increase in fine-grained as-a-service definitions is evidence that the SPI model is not necessarily universal and that we are rapidly evolving toward more useful definitions of overall cloud services models.

Cloud Deployment Models

Mell and Grance next define the four Cloud Deployment models[8]:

> Private cloud. *The cloud infrastructure is operated solely for an organization. It may be managed by the organization or a third party and may exist on premise or off premise.*

> Community cloud. *The cloud infrastructure is shared by several organizations and supports a specific community that has shared concerns (e.g., mission, security requirements, policy, and compliance considerations). It may be managed by the organizations or a third party and may exist on premise or off premise.*

> Public cloud. *The cloud infrastructure is made available to the general public or a large industry group and is owned by an organization selling cloud services.*

Hybrid cloud. *The cloud infrastructure is a composition of two or more clouds (private, community, or public) that remain unique entities but are bound together by standardized or proprietary technology that enables data and application portability (e.g., cloud bursting for load-balancing between clouds).*

These four deployment models can see significant variation depending on other factors that we will discuss in the next section, but they serve to address the broad questions as to how one can deploy pooled cloud resources. Before we move on, it is important to make two points about the NIST Cloud Model:

- A customer or *tenant* can have greater security control over more resources as one moves from SaaS to PaaS and again from PaaS to the IaaS service model.
- A customer or *tenant* can achieve greater security control over more resources when moving from a Public cloud to a community cloud and again from a community cloud to a Private cloud.

Figure 2.3 is an adaption of the NIST Cloud Computing Model, which has been annotated to reflect the discussion in this section on customer and tenant control. We will examine the issue of control in greater detail in the next section.

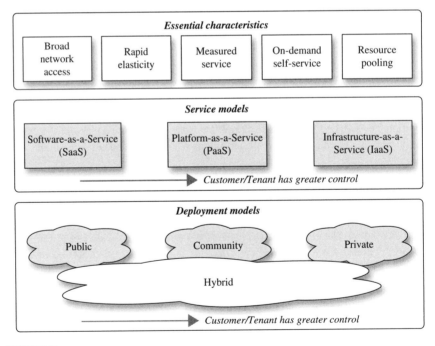

FIGURE 2.3

The annotated NIST cloud model.

CONTROL OVER SECURITY IN THE CLOUD MODEL

In part, the SPI service model represents increasing abstraction from complex underlying IT infrastructure. As depicted in Figure 2.4, cloud-based IaaS does not typically expose actual hardware or networking layers to the tenant of the service, rather these underlying resources are abstracted for the consumer. PaaS abstracts infrastructure to a greater extent and generally presents middleware containers that are tailored for categories of usage—such as development. These containers provide tools to simplify application development and limit application interactions with the underlying systems. SaaS abstracts even further and generally exposes narrow-functionality software-based services such as Customer Relationship Management (CRM) or e-mail. At every step up the SPI continuum, there are increasing limitations on lower-level computing functions. In other words, from IaaS to SaaS underlying computing functions are more and more abstracted.

With SaaS, the burden of security lies with the cloud provider. In part, this is because of the degree of abstraction, but the SaaS model is based on a high degree of integrated functionality with minimal customer control or extensibility. By contrast, the PaaS model offers greater extensibility and greater customer control but fewer higher-level features. Largely because of the relatively lower degree of abstraction, IaaS offers greater tenant or customer control over security than do PaaS or SaaS.

Another way to consider this is that with SaaS the provider is responsible for most aspects of security, compliance, and liability, but with these responsibilities,

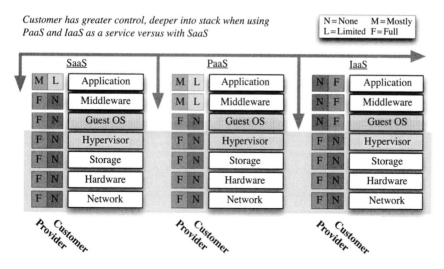

FIGURE 2.4

Extent of control over security in SaaS, PaaS, and IaaS.

the provider is more apt to change important aspects of the service or associated service contracts (that is, SLAs).

Given this discussion of service models and security, we should consider how cloud deployment impacts the degree of owner data/application control over security. Clearly, the degree of control that a tenant or customer has in a public cloud is minimal, whereas the tenant organization has maximum control with a private cloud. The degree of control will vary for community and hybrid clouds and may not be relevant depending on what such external computing resources are used for.

But the public and private deployment vector is not the only aspect of this discussion. For a private cloud especially, we should also consider where the cloud infrastructure resides and who operates it.

NOTE

By internal, we mean that the cloud is within your own physical boundary, and by external, we mean that it is outside your physical boundary.

By insourced, we mean that your own staff provides the IT services, and by outsourced, we mean that someone else provides those services.

But this is not necessarily true as a private cloud can benefit greatly from the physical security that a hosting facility can offer. Likewise, outsourcing operations can be just as secure and potentially less expensive than having ample 24×7 IT personnel on staff. This last point is especially true for security monitoring services as there is true benefit to using a security monitoring staff that sees more incidents and issues than a single cloud may present. Knowledge does scale, and it can be expensive to develop.

When considering how to secure public versus private cloud architectures, the security concerns are more different than common. If a cloud is private, internal on a customer premises, and owned/managed/maintained exclusively by the organization utilizing it, the principles in securing it vary greatly from those of a public cloud hosted externally by a third party. A private cloud doesn't have the data confidentiality and legality concerns that a public cloud might. This book dedicates several chapters to the security of these two types of clouds. Chapter 4, Securing the Cloud: Architecture, discusses the underlying architectural issues for both public and private clouds. Chapter 5, Securing the Cloud: Data Security, surveys the security issues specific to data in both public and private clouds. Chapter 6, Securing the Cloud: Key Strategies and Best Practices, also applies equally to public and private clouds. Chapter 7, Security Criteria: Building an Internal Cloud, and Chapter 8, Security Criteria: Selecting an External Cloud Provider, both cover much of what should be considered for either securing an internal or selecting a public/external cloud. Hybrid clouds end up having both public and private cloud security concerns. For the remainder of this book, we will tend to view community clouds as special cases of private clouds where organizational control is delegated to a community proxy.

Cloud Application Programming Interfaces

From the standpoint of the tenant and consumer, different cloud providers may vary how the provider of a service and a consumer interface with it. There are several factors that come to play here, and things are evolving quickly. A service can be provided at the SaaS, PaaS, or IaaS level. New services can be developed as standalone, or they can be composed by leveraging existing services.

Cloud Application Programming Interfaces (APIs) are mechanisms or abstractions that define an interface between a cloud service and other entities. Cloud services APIs vary from provider to provider, with both proprietary APIs and standards-based APIs. Where proprietary APIs are used, possible lock-in benefits the provider by making it difficult to switch service providers. Proprietary APIs can have their advantages, but open and standards-based APIs can more readily lead to an ecosystem of services built up by customers across cloud providers. In addition, the case can be made that proprietary APIs may have security advantages, but such claims have been hotly contested. Clearly, the uncertainty and incompatibility with proprietary APIs and the partial emergence of standards-based APIs make for concern for both tenants and consumers.

Cloud APIs are typically written using SOAP[B] or following REST[C] principles. Since most Public Clouds are Web based, they tend to use RESTful APIs. There are *Cross Platform*–based APIs that abstract cloud provider implementation details, allowing an application to use a single API regardless of the back-end cloud. There are also infrastructure APIs that provide the means to manage or configure virtual infrastructure. These APIs allow operations to perform a series of operational functions including provisioning components (for instance, virtual machines) and configuring attributes (for instance, memory, storage, network controls, and CPU).

Cloud provider APIs are specific to a provider and often have proprietary provider calls, which are intended to enable control. Cloud provider APIs use authentication mechanisms to enforce that only authorized API calls are allowed. Such Cloud provider APIs use an ID or Authentication Key to provide authorization and authentication, typically over HTTPS. These APIs may also create a hash-based token or a password to authenticate, thereby providing further security (such as with Public Key Infrastructure).

MAKING SENSE OF CLOUD DEPLOYMENT

In this section and the next, we will look at how clouds are used by surveying some example offerings. In doing so, our focus will be on security. This will serve as background in later sections of this chapter. Readers who are familiar

---

[B]*Simple Object Access Protocol*, or SOAP, is based on XML and defines an envelope format and a number of rules for describing the contents. Along with WDSL and UDDI, SOAP is one of the foundation standards of web services.
[C]*Representational State Transfer*, or REST, is a software architecture style for distributed systems such as the World Wide Web.

with examples of public, private, community, and hybrid clouds may wish to skip this section. We begin with the four cloud deployment models.

Public Clouds

In its simplest definition, a public cloud exists externally to its end user and is generally available with little restriction as to who may pay to use it. As a result, the most common forms of public clouds are ones that are accessed via the Internet. There has been tremendous development in the public cloud space, resulting in very sophisticated Infrastructure-as-a-Service offerings from companies like Amazon, with their Elastic Compute Cloud (EC2), Rackspace's Cloud Offerings, and IBM's BlueCloud. Other forms of public cloud offerings can take the form at more of the application layer, or Platform-as-a-Service, like Google's AppEngine and Windows' Azure Services platform, as well as Amazon's service-specific cloud hosting SimpleDB, Cloud Front, and S3 Simple Storage.

At a basic level, public clouds have unique security components and evaluation criteria when compared with private clouds. Public clouds can be formed by service providers wishing to build out a high-capacity infrastructure and *lease* pieces of it to a variety of clients. As a result, data might become comingled on common storage devices, making identity, access control, and encryption very important. There is a certain amount of inherent trust (albeit it should be a measured, tested, and verified) by subscribers with their public cloud providers.

Private Clouds

In contrast to a public cloud, a private cloud is internally hosted. The hallmark of a private cloud is that it is usually dedicated to an organization. Although there is no comingling of data or sharing of resources with external entities, different departments within the organization may have strong requirements to maintain data isolation within their shared private cloud. Organizations deploying private clouds often do so utilizing virtualization technology within their own data centers. A word of caution here: "Describing private cloud as releasing you from the constraints of public cloud only does damage to the cloud model. It's the discipline in cloud implementations that makes them more interesting (and less costly) than conventional IT. Private clouds could very well be more constrained than their public counterparts and probably will be to meet those needs that public clouds cannot address."[9]

Since private clouds are, well, private, some of the security concerns of a public cloud may not apply. However, just because they are private does not mean that they are necessarily more secure. In a private cloud, considerations such as securing the virtualization environment itself (that is, hypervisor level security, physical hardware, software, and firmware, and so on) must still be addressed, whereas in a public cloud, you would rely on the provider to do so. As a result, when comparing public to private clouds, it may be difficult to make generalizations as to which is inherently more secure. But as we pointed out earlier in this chapter in the section on Control over Security in the Cloud Model, a private cloud offers the potential to achieve greater security over your cloud-based assets. However, between the potential for better security and the achievement of better security lie many ongoing activities. The true advantage of a private cloud is that "the provider has a vested interest in making the service interface more perfectly matched to the tenant needs."[10] However, it should also be pointed out that many of the sins of enterprise security have to do with the fact that the enterprise itself implements and manages its own IT security—which would be perfectly fine except security is generally not a core investment nor is it measured as though it were.

Community Clouds

The promise of community clouds is that they allow multiple independent entities to gain the cost benefits of a shared nonpublic cloud while avoiding security and regulatory concerns that might be associated with using a generic public cloud that did not address such concerns in its SLA. This model has tremendous potential for entities or companies that are subject to identical regulatory, compliance, or legal restrictions. Different kinds of community clouds are being considered in the United States and the European Union by governments at the national and local levels. This makes great sense since there are multiple benefits to both the individual entities as well as collectively. For instance, when multiple government agencies that transact business with each other have their processing colocated in a single facility, they can achieve both savings and increased security in terms of reducing the amount of traffic that would otherwise need to traverse the Internet. Continuity of operations can also be enhanced at a lower overall cost to all parties when multiple data centers are used to implement such a community cloud.

Hybrid Clouds

In the previous sections, we took a closer look at public, private, and community clouds. Next, we refer to Figure 2.5 in which we depict two examples of how an organization might leverage a public cloud or community cloud to expand the capabilities of its private cloud and thereby implement a hybrid model.

Hybrid clouds are just as the name implies. They are formed when an organization builds out a private cloud and wishes to leverage public or community clouds in conjunction with its private cloud for a particular purpose; the linking of the two clouds is what would be called a hybrid cloud. (Actually, a hybrid cloud could be formed by any combination of the three cloud types: public, private, and community.)

Many organizations deploy an internal private cloud for their critical infrastructure but find certain needs that just aren't economical to build out internally.

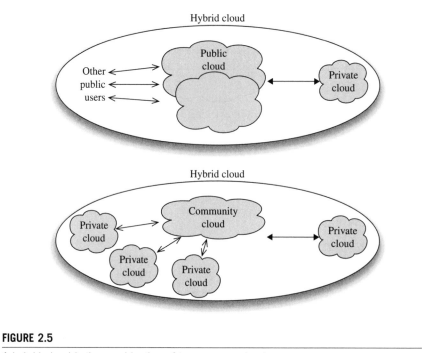

FIGURE 2.5

A hybrid cloud is the combination of two or more clouds.

A common example would be for testing or quality assurance purposes. For instance, an internal cloud might be used to run the infrastructure of a business, but the business may need to test an upgrade or roll out of a new system. It might be advantageous to pay for capacity of a public cloud for a few months to complete the testing, and when their own private cloud is upgraded, discontinue the public cloud usage.

Another example of a hybrid cloud would be a Web site where its core infrastructure is private to the company, but certain components of the Web site are hosted externally—that is, heavily trafficked media such as streaming video or image caching.

If an organization has already built out an internal cloud, additional advantages of public cloud–based architectures may be too great to ignore. As a result, many organizations may consider the benefits of adopting a public–private hybrid model. However, certain requirements can prevent hybrid clouds from being fully adopted by an organization. For instance, financial services organizations might not be able to meet specific compliance regulations if customer data is externally hosted at a third party, no matter how well it may be secured. Governments might not be able to take the risk of the compromise (political, malicious, or otherwise) if their cloud-based data is attacked. Yet all these organizations might still have specific use cases for public clouds.

MAKING SENSE OF SERVICES MODELS

As we saw in the earlier discussion on Control over Security in the Cloud Model, there are various tradeoffs across the three services models. In this section, we take a closer look at the three services models. Compared to traditional IT services models, the SPI model allows for greater agility and makes IT accessible to more potential consumers. With traditional models, one might need to acquire and assemble IT hardware components before considering implementing a software service, whereas with SPI model, all that *scaffolding* already exists and is simply provisioned before the new service is developed, tested, and put into production. There are also licensing advantages with the SPI model versus other models. Licensing costs with SPI can be charged on a subscription or a consumption model. Taken together, SPI reduced startup costs and the startup timeframe.

Cloud Software-as-a-Service

In its most common form, a SaaS cloud implementation delivers software or, more generally described, an application to its end user. The end user doesn't usually need to understand or be concerned with the supporting infrastructure and simply utilizes an application. All the back office details of the application are masked and provided *as-a-service* behind the scenes of that application.

Web sites accessed via the Internet that provide the end user an application or a service can be considered SaaS. For instance, Salesforce.com provides a CRM SaaS, Google's GMAIL or Yahoo Mail provide email services, and even former premise-based software-only solutions like Microsoft Share Point are available as SaaS online, via a Web browser.

Cloud Platform-as-a-Service

PaaS providers usually deliver a bundling of software and infrastructure in the form of a programmable container and provide a cloud for an end user to host their own developed applications or services. PaaS is similar to SaaS, but with PaaS, the service is the entire application environment—typically, PaaS includes the computing platform as well as the development and solution stack.

Google's Google App Engine is an excellent example of a PaaS architecture. So is Salesforce.com's Force.com platform. In both cases, the end user receives an environment from the provider (also called a *container*) that is ready to host a particular application or service that the end user requires. The end user does not need to worry about lower-level services such as the infrastructure; these are provided for them within the *service*.

Cloud Infrastructure-as-a-Service

In general, IaaS clouds deliver virtualized resources, such as guest virtual machines (ready to load an operating system), storage, or database services. The tenant interacts with IaaS clouds in a similar way as giving a systems architecture to an IT department to provide the necessary systems (although usually with very formal descriptions). This is the virtual equivalent to physically deploying servers, storage, or database.

Amazon's Web Services or RackSpace's Cloud Services are both prime examples of IaaS providers. In their most common form, end users choose to still have the ability to manage their infrastructure at the operating system level but outsource *as-a-service* the details of managing and maintaining the servers, switching, routing, firewalling, and connectivity concerns. They basically purchase this bundled from the IaaS provider.

NOTE

Examples of Infrastructure-as-a-Service providers include Amazon's EC2 service or RackSpace's Cloud Hosting. The end user receives access to a platform (that is, the virtual machine and all of the abstracted infrastructure that enables it—routers, switches, firewalls, data centers, and so on—that it *bundles* or expresses as a service). However, providers such as Amazon have evolved their infrastructure to the point that it is presented as a platform. Amazon provides a more than just a virtual server instance for development or deployment of a custom service. Today, Amazon provides database, payment processing, queue services, and storage services for a customer application.

Salesforce.com began as a Software-as-a-Service provider, and through its own software maturation and several feature progressions, it added the ability for third parties to write applications for it. As a result, Salesforce.com now describes itself as a Platform-as-a-Service provider with its Force.com platform. Using Force.com, third-party applications can be entirely created, hosted, and deployed, fully integrated with Salesforce.com's software as a service.

HOW CLOUDS ARE FORMED AND KEY EXAMPLES

In this section, we will briefly survey how clouds are formed along with some real-world cloud scenarios, but first we will build some context. Throughout this chapter, we have discussed different aspects of clouds. But what do vendors provide in these spaces? Figure 2.6 lists classes of offerings that are currently available.[11]

As we can see, the range of offerings in the cloud world is quite large given the short history of cloud computing. So, how are these offerings actually formed? For the purposes of this book, we are going to cover the most common and generally accepted ways of forming clouds.

1. **Virtualization Formed Clouds** Clouds that are formed using virtualization technology such as from VMWare, the open source community (Xen, Virtualbox), Citrix, and Microsoft
2. **Application/Service Formed Clouds** Clouds that are formed not necessarily using virtualization or virtual machines—the application or service they provide was written inherently to be cloud based

Infrastructure services	Cloud platforms
Storage	Public clouds
Compute	Private colds
Services management	Open clouds
Networking, firewalls,	Custom clouds
load balancers, and so on.	
	Platform services
Software services	General purpose
Billing	Business intelligence
Financials	Integration
Legal	Development and testing
Sales	Database
Desktop productivity	
Human resources	**Cloud software**
Content management	Data
Collaboration	Appliances
Social networks	Compute
Backup and recovery	Cloud management
CRM	File storage
Document management	

FIGURE 2.6

Categories of cloud vendor offerings.

Using Virtualization to Form Clouds

Virtualization by its very nature takes the operating systems/software and abstracts it from the physical hardware on which it is running. As a result, virtualization has several key attributes, which also happen to be key attributes of cloud computing:

- **Sharing of Infrastructure** The physical hardware running the software no longer has a 1:1 mapping, meaning a single physical server can run multiple virtual servers, allowing for economies of scale to be captured. Users can run more with less hardware and fewer expenditures—and, it is up to the provider to sell the server fractions that are not needed by a particular user.
- **Scalability and Elasticity** If physical infrastructure is abstracted and made available as virtual resources, the ability to add or release capacity can be performed quickly and in an automated manner. Additionally, because physical infrastructure is being shared among virtualized servers during a period of heavy load, one virtualized server can consume far more resources than it could have if it existed only within a single physical server.
- **Resiliency and Redundancy** Because the applications/operating systems are not physically married to a physical server, they are by their very nature portable. A virtual server, with properly designed infrastructure, does not even need to exist at one physical location. It can move on demand and dynamically among physical sites or even be mirrored in real time to another site for redundancy.

- **Agility** Virtual servers can literally be created in a matter of seconds. Because the hardware is abstracted from the software, it's literally a simple matter of copying files to create new virtual servers.
- **Location Independence** A server that is virtualized doesn't have to exist only within a single data center and can be copied or moved to other data centers very quickly.

These key virtualization attributes contribute immensely to the implementation of clouds. However, the tradeoff to all of these benefits is the fact that with more abstraction can come greater complication. Greater complexity both challenges and requires increased security as the attack surface is generally wider. In general, complex interactions require more complicated security. For example, the historical effort in the field of computer security to abstract security functionality into a single common implementation within an OS resulted in the concept of a security kernel—which has had a positive benefit for OS security. Fortunately, with virtualization, we gain a strong degree of isolation between VMs, so the tradeoff between the complexity of virtualization mechanisms and the resulting security for VMs seems to favor security.

NOTE

It's important to note that the term virtualization doesn't just apply to a relationship between hardware (that is, servers) and operating systems (for example, Windows, Linux). Virtualization can apply to components of a server—storage being the most common application. The data being written to the physical hard drives doesn't exist within a single physical drive and is shared among many (that is, a storage area network or SAN). Most serious virtualized cloud computing architectures take advantage of not just a single form of virtualization. Because virtualization shares the same basic attributes of any cloud, it can be said that the more virtualized the more *cloud like* the environment is.

Virtualization is also used for networking. Network virtualization can take numerous forms, but at the heart of this, lies the advantage of deploying and managing network resources as logical services rather than physical ones. This improves agility and network efficiency, and it can greatly reduce operational costs.

Server/OS Virtualization for Clouds

Virtualization can be implemented at the server or OS level. Without virtualization, there is a relationship of 1:1 of servers to operating systems. At the time of publishing, virtualization is one of the most mature components of cloud architecture that is thought to have been first described all the way back in 1959 by Christopher Strachey, who presented at the International Conference on Information Processing at UNESCO. Used in mainframes, it was not until late 2004 and early 2005 that virtualization became a mainstream technology. Companies such as VMware (1998/1999) entered the space, and dozens of others followed. Unfortunately, because the basic virtualization attributes are also the basic attributes of clouds, the two terms are often used synonymously. Virtualization technologies are what enable the forming of most modern cloud computing architectures.

When talking about operating system virtualization (separating the hardware or server from the OS), the most important enabling component is called a hypervisor. When looking at the threat surface for clouds, often the hypervisor is viewed with some concern. In terms of security research and development, securing the hypervisor is one of the most actively investigated areas of cloud security.

In a manner similar to how virtualized servers work (that is, virtual machines or VMs), rootkits, or malicious software that gets installed above the operating system, can be implemented via hypervisors as well. It is outside the scope of this book to discuss hypervisor concerns in depth, but we will cover hypervisor security and outline some key related security concerns in Chapters 4 and 5.

Desktop Virtualization for Clouds

Virtualization can exist not only at the server level but all the way down to the desktop level. As an implementation of this, the end user can use a *thin-client* that basically provides input (keyboard/mouse) and output (monitor) to the *cloud* hosting the virtual desktop. The servers hosting the virtual desktop can themselves be virtualized, but this isn't a requirement. Similar principles for securing clouds apply for desktop virtualization. In fact, public virtual desktop clouds exist today for organizations that just can't get enough virtualization. The industry even has an *as-a-service* term for this—DaaS or Desktop-as-a-Service.

NOTE

One of the leading vendors in this space is a company called Desktone, who provides DaaS services. Both VMware with its Virtual Desktop Infrastructure (VDI) and Citrix's XenDesktop are vendor technologies playing in this space.

Sun Microsystems was a pioneer in this space that started with the JavaStation and culminated with various releases of the Sun Ray thin client. In the Sun Ray product line, a single workgroup server had ample power to drive dozens to hundreds of thin clients. In a sense, the Sun Ray model for desktop virtualization was yet another precursor to the cloud computing model. All processing and data resided at the server, with the Internet representing a very long combined keyboard, mouse, and display cable.

Storage Virtualization for Clouds

Finally, when discussing cloud computing architectures, the virtualization of storage is also worth mentioning. The same principles of operating system/server virtualization apply. In general, storage virtualization means that the data being stored does not have a 1:1 relationship with the drives that it is written to.

Storage-based clouds still share the same merits of all clouds, including sharing of infrastructure, scalability and elasticity, resiliency and redundancy, agility, and location independence.

Using Applications or Services to Form Clouds

Although virtualization is commonly deployed to create a cloud, it is not necessarily the only way to do so. Applications can, by their very nature, be developed to create or form a cloud. Applications can be developed to leverage the cloud simply by forming a cloud within their software architecture and not by simply running in a virtualized environment.

An application can form a cloud simply by applying the same concepts of virtualization to its own internal software architecture—sharing of infrastructure, scalability and elasticity, and resiliency and redundancy. This can be as simple as creating an application that can run multiple instances of itself as it seamlessly supports multiple clients—thus forming a very simplified sort of cloud. But it can also be much more complicated, and the line between a cloud application and a cloud in general can get quite blurry when an application is designed to leverage virtualized cloud computing resources.

An application created to run on a provider's Platform-as-a-Service, such as Google's AppEngine or Salesforce's Force.com, is inherently very cloud-like. The platforms provided are usually virtualized, true clouds; therefore, any applications running within them are clouds as well.

Also worth mentioning is that there are applications that appear to create clouds within clouds. For example, any application that supports peer-to-peer technology usually will form a cloud. There is no reason why such a network cannot operate as a service within another enabling service that is implemented as a cloud. Another example of a cloud service was offered by Sun Microsystems as a private part of its public cloud service: Hardware-as-a-Service for internal Sun tenants. In this example, tenants leased actual physical servers from within the same public cloud infrastructure. Tenants could then virtualize the server for their IaaS users.

TOOLS

Many enterprises would love to ban the use of insecure protocols but are stymied by internal users who insist that their applications depend on insecure telnet, ftp, or similarly insecure protocols and applications. Practically speaking, these protocols have been obsolete since they are insecure and there are safer alternatives.

What makes these protocols insecure is their use of plaintext authentication. In other words, when you authenticate yourself to a telnet or ftp server you send your credentials (login ID and password) *in the clear* or unencrypted. In addition, the data or payload that is subsequently sent is also communicated unencrypted. This exposes credentials and transmitted data at every intermediate link between the client and the server.

Alternatives to such insecure protocols are widely available. SSH (secure shell) is a replacement for telnet, and SFTP (FTP over SSH) is a safer replacement for FTP. Both encrypt login credentials as well as the payload.

REAL-WORLD CLOUD USAGE SCENARIOS

In this section, we will briefly survey some real-world cloud scenarios that illustrate various types of practical cloud usage. We will do that in context of the outline we used in the previous section. In addition, we will also offer examples of hybrid clouds.

Virtualization Formed Clouds

When talking about forming clouds using virtualization, it is useful to review examples. We do that below, based on the type of cloud.

Public

One of the most common forms of a public cloud at the virtualization level would be any company that purchases a virtual server running on the Amazon EC2 platform (or any other cloud hosting provider). The public cloud offering from Amazon actually has a private cloud origin. Amazon, in an ingenious business development, decided to capitalize on the excess capacity of a private cloud that they had already built out to support the Amazon.com site. Already very scalable and highly resilient, they did this by building out a Platform-as-a-Service offering called Amazon Web Services and then basically allowed subscribers to purchase excess capacity of their private cloud in the form of a public cloud.

One major advantage of adopting a public cloud is that most providers charge for the service in a *pay for consumption* model. Subscribers can purchase this service and pay for only what they actually consume—whether it is hours running a virtual server or actual amount of disk space consumed (both with prices measured in cents and no long-term commitment required). This also enables public clouds to often *scale on demand*—if you need more infrastructure you can dynamically spin up or down virtual servers depending on demand, without the need to pay for them when they are not needed.

As a result, an organization can today purchase a (public cloud) virtualized Windows, Linux, or other virtual server running completely virtualized within Amazon's environment. Why would someone use such a service? There are several compelling scenarios in which using a cloud-based virtual server (or servers) is advantageous:

- **Testing and Quality Assurance** An organization might have a need for server instances that are temporary in nature and also might also require an abnormal amount of capacity. Needing to test an application under load or test software upgrade cycles without affecting performance are all projects that make the cloud more than ideal. Organizations can *rent* time on an existing cloud and discontinue use when it's not needed.
- **Web-based Application Hosting** Since Web applications are already accessed from the cloud, it can be a natural fit to hosting them in the cloud. Additionally,

Web applications (especially, popular ones) suffer from peak demand issues. A Web site might normally have a small amount of load, say 100K visitors a day, but because of some compelling event, they may experience a sudden peak load, say 1M visitors a day, and then return back to a normal load after a day or two. The difference in the amount of physical infrastructure required to handle 100K users a day versus 1M users a day is monumental and can be cost prohibitive when it's not the normal every day usage for the site. As a result, public cloud–based virtual hosting can be an ideal solution, as servers can be dynamically added and removed depending on load, while only paying for the time that you actually need them.

- **Outsourcing Needs** Many organizations don't necessarily want to get into the business of building, managing, and maintaining data centers and all the complications surrounding them, so public cloud hosting allows them to basically outsource that part of their business, which allows them to focus on whatever reason they are in business—that is, their core competencies. Information technology can often just be a cost of doing business.
- **High-performance Computing** Any organization or application that specifically needs a lot of computational horsepower that is impossible to achieve without a massive amount of infrastructure may want to access a cloud service.
- **Small Organizations** With an extremely low barrier to entry (that is, costs measuring in cents per hour), even small organizations with limited budgets can take advantage of a massively resilient and scalable infrastructure for a fraction of what they would have to pay to build it themselves.

Private

It's not uncommon for organizations to have already deployed virtualization products from companies such as VMware for the simple fact of when they do, they can capture multiple economies of scale. It is very common to use simple virtualization if you have particular applications that consume server capacity at different times of day or applications that require the operating system in which they run to be dedicated but consume very little overall system resources to operate.

As more and more applications and resources become virtualized, the needs of this virtualized infrastructure will likely evolve as well. Below is a list of some of the most common needs that might evolve, that, in essence, end up creating private clouds within such an organization:

- **High Availability/Business Continuity** As more applications and resources become virtualized, the virtualized environment itself needs to become highly available. A common scenario would be to replicate the virtualized infrastructure at a second data center and interconnect the two, in essence, forming a private cloud.
- **Scale Required** As information technology continues to modernize business and become more and more an essential part of operations, the demand on the

infrastructure can become great. New business acquisitions might demand an infrastructure that can scale on demand. Private clouds are ideally suited to address these needs.

Application/Service Formed Clouds

When talking about forming clouds using applications or services, several examples are mentioned below, based on the type of cloud.

Public

There are many applications that exist today that are considered a *cloud* service, which doesn't necessarily mean that they are running on a cloud-based infrastructure. They might be or they might not be, but that is irrelevant to the fact that, to the end user, the service is a *cloud*. How the application's internal infrastructure is architected can be something as simple as a properly designed application that allows for the sharing of infrastructure, scalability and elasticity, and resiliency and redundancy. Or, the application might do all the above and still be layered onto a virtualized cloud hosting environment. However, that specific note is beside the point when talking about an application or a service-based cloud. Some examples of cloud-based applications or services:

- **Google App Engine** The Google App Engine lets the user run their Web applications on Google's infrastructure. Google App Engine applications are easy to build and easy to maintain. They can scale as traffic and data storage needs grow. Google App Engine is ideally suited for public application-formed clouds. Entire applications can be written to exist entirely within Google App Engine. One of the more popular examples would be a site called Jaiku, a Twitter-like microblogging application that was developed entirely on top of Google's Engine.
- **Web 2.0 Applications** Although they may or may not use virtualization, most modern Web 2.0 applications are developed to function as clouds. Any time you have a site or service that exists across multiple servers (and therefore usually multiple locations), and the application has been developed to adopt the same attributes of clouds providing the sharing of infrastructure, scalability and elasticity, resiliency and redundancy, agility, and location independence, it functions as a cloud. Facebook.com, Twitter.com, and so on are all examples of application-formed clouds. The application itself has layers of front end server to back end server interaction, Web, database, load balancing, multiple data centers, and so on.

Private

From the viewpoint of the service consumer, any internally developed or deployed business application that was developed with the same principals of a cloud could be classified as a private, application-formed cloud.

Hybrid Cloud Models

There are a number of hybrid clouds in existence. Below are two common ways public clouds end up becoming interconnected to a private cloud:

- **Security** An organization that has deployed a private cloud might have certain data that may need to exist on organization-owned assets and could never be stored at a third party provider. However, that same organization might have certain applications that could take advantage of a larger cloud (that is, a public cloud that might simply have far more resources and capacities than its own private cloud). The carefully considered internetworking of these two clouds would result in a hybrid cloud. A bank might not ever be able to allow its customer financial data to be stored on Amazon's EC2 infrastructure but might have the need to utilize Amazon's infrastructure to crunch numbers or test new system development.
- **Scalability** With the smaller absolute scale of a cloud with very few tenants, there are limited opportunities to derive the cost benefits of larger-scale clouds. Thus, by mixing in the use of public or community clouds, the overall application deployment cost may be improved considerably. A private cloud might consist of two dozen systems interconnected, where often public clouds consist of thousands of systems.

SUMMARY

In this chapter, we examined cloud computing and offered some additional perspectives in order to better understand what constitutes cloud computing. We presented the NIST Cloud Computing Model and revisited our essential characteristics of clouds. In doing so, we dissected the three SPI cloud service models along with the four cloud delivery models. We also looked at the relative degree of control a tenant or consumer has with the different models. We then looked at the cloud deployment models and the cloud services models from a different set of perspectives, leading to a discussion of how clouds are formed and how clouds are used. In the next chapter, we will take a closer look at the security concerns and issues with clouds, along with surveying the legal and regulatory considerations of different clouds.

Endnotes

1. Robinson P. cloud-computing@googlegroups.com, [Cloud Computing] Cloud without Virtualization. August 20, 2010 12:53:39 PM EDT; 2010.
2. Mell P, Grance T. The NIST Definition of Cloud Computing Version 15; 2009, National Institute of Standards and Technology, Information Technology Laboratory.
3. Ibid.

4. William "Bill" Meine, in private communication; 2010.

5. Mell P, Grance T. The NIST Definition of Cloud Computing Version 15, 10-7-2009, National Institute of Standards and Technology, Information Technology Laboratory.

6. William "Bill" Meine, in private communication; 2010.

7. Brunette G, Mogull R. Security Guidance for Critical Areas of Focus in Cloud Computing V2.1; Prepared by the Cloud Security Alliance; 2009.

8. Mell P, Grance T. The NIST Definition of Cloud Computing Version 15, 10-7-09, National Institute of Standards and Technology, Information Technology Laboratory.

9. William "Bill" Meine, in private communication; 2010.

10. Ibid.

11. Adapted from http://cloudtaxonomy.opencrowd.com/ [accessed March 21, 2011].

Security Concerns, Risk Issues, and Legal Aspects

3

INFORMATION IN THIS CHAPTER

- Cloud Computing: Security Concerns
- Assessing Your Risk Tolerance in Cloud Computing
- Legal and Regulatory Issues

In Chapters 1 and 2, we covered many of the qualities and promises of cloud computing. In addition, we examined the three models for cloud services (SPI) and the four models for cloud deployment (public, private, community and hybrid). While developing a background in cloud computing, we also discussed many security aspects of clouds. In this chapter, we are going to investigate some of those security issues more closely. In subsequent chapters, we will draw upon this material when we offer guidance on how to deliver secure cloud services (Chapters 4, 5, and 10). We will also add structure to this same material in Chapters 6 and 9 to identify best practices and to produce a set of evaluation criteria for cloud security.

While some might find the cloud inappropriate from a security standpoint, we will attempt to show that this amounts to a wrong conclusion. As we stated frequently, by its inherent qualities (see Chapter 1), cloud computing has tremendous potential for organizations to improve their overall information security posture. There are many reasons for this, but the best way to sum up the argument is to state that the cloud model enables the return of effective control and professional operation over Information Technology (IT) resources, processing, and information. By virtue of public cloud scale, tenants and users can get better security since the provider's investment in achieving better security costs less per consumer. For the same reasons, a private cloud can obtain significant advantages for security. But there are wrinkles: You won't get the benefit without investment, and not every model is appropriate for all consumers. But, regardless of which services delivery model or deployment model you select, you will transfer some degree of control to the cloud provider—which would be completely reasonable if control is managed in a manner and at a cost that meets your needs.

CLOUD COMPUTING: SECURITY CONCERNS

To begin with, we will recall some security concerns we identified in Chapters 1 and 2:

- **Network Availability** The value of cloud computing can only be realized when your network connectivity and bandwidth meet your minimum needs: The cloud must be available whenever you need it. If it is not, then the consequences are no different than a denial-of-service situation.
- **Cloud Provider Viability** Since cloud providers are relatively new to the business, there are questions about provider viability and commitment. This concern deepens when a provider requires tenants to use proprietary interfaces, thus leading to tenant lock-in.
- **Disaster Recovery and Business Continuity** Tenants and users require confidence that their operations and services will continue if the cloud provider's production environment is subject to a disaster.
- **Security Incidents** Tenants and users need to be appropriately informed by the provider when an incident occurs. Tenants or users may require provider support to respond to audit or assessment findings. Also, a provider may not offer sufficient support to tenants or users for resolving investigations.
- **Transparency** When a cloud provider does not expose details of their internal policy or technology implementation, tenants or users must trust the cloud provider's security claims. Even so, tenants and users require some transparency by providers as to provider cloud security, privacy, and how incidents are managed.
- **Loss of Physical Control** Since tenants and users lose physical control over their data and applications, this results in a range of concerns:
    - **Privacy and Data** With public or community clouds, data may not remain in the same system, raising multiple legal concerns.
    - **Control over Data** User or organization data may be comingled in various ways with data belonging to others.
    - A tenant administrator has limited control scope and accountability within a Public infrastructure-as-a-service (IaaS) implementation, and even less with a platform-as-a-service (PaaS) one. Tenants need confidence that the provider will offer appropriate control, while recognizing that tenants will simply need to adapt their expectations for how much control is reasonable within these models.
- **New Risks, New Vulnerabilities** There is some concern that cloud computing brings new classes of risks and vulnerabilities. Although we can postulate various hypothetical new risks, actual exploits will largely be a function of a provider's implementation. Although all software, hardware, and networking equipment are subject to unearthing of new vulnerabilities, by applying layered security and well-conceived operational processes, a cloud may be protected from common types of attack even if some of its components are inherently vulnerable.

- **Legal and Regulatory Compliance** It may be difficult or unrealistic to utilize public clouds if the data you need to process is subject to legal restrictions or regulatory compliance. While we should expect providers to build and certify cloud to address the needs of regulated markets, achieving certifications may be challenging due to the many nontechnical factors including the current stage of general cloud knowledge. As best practices for cloud computing encompass greater scope, this concern should largely become a historical one. The second half of this chapter is devoted to legal and regulatory issues.

WARNING

Although the public cloud model is appropriate for many nonsensitive needs, the fact is that moving sensitive information into any cloud that is *not* certified for such processing introduces inappropriate risk.

Let's be completely clear:

- It is at best unwise to use a public cloud for processing sensitive, mission critical, or proprietary data.
- It is expensive and excessive to burden nonsensitive and low-impact systems with high assurance security.
- It is irresponsible to either dismiss cloud computing as being inherently insecure or claim it to be more secure than alternatives.
- Selection of a cloud deployment model along with ensuring that you have appropriate security controls should follow a reasonable assessment of risks.

To begin, listing security concerns has benefit if we can either dismiss them or validate them and counter them with compensating controls. We will revisit some of these concerns further throughout this chapter.

A Closer Examination: Virtualization

Before we consider some of the security concerns around the use of virtualization in cloud computing, we need to understand how virtualization is implemented. Starting at the level of our objective, a virtual machine (VM) is typically a standard operating system (OS) instance *captured* in a fully configured and operationally ready system image. This image essentially amounts to a snapshot of a running system including space in the image for virtualized disk storage. Supporting the operation of this VM, we need some form of enabling function, typically called a hypervisor that represents itself to the VM as the underlying hardware. Vendor implementations of virtualization will vary, but in general terms, there are several types of virtualization:

- Type 1 also *native* or *bare metal* virtualization is implemented by a hypervisor that runs directly on bare hardware. Guest OSs run on top of the hypervisor. Examples include Microsoft Hyper-V, Oracle VM, LynxSecure, VMware ESX, and IBM z/VM.

- Type 2 or *hosted* virtualization has a hypervisor running as an application within a host OS. VMs also run above the hypervisor. Examples include Oracle VirtualBox, Parallels, Virtual PC, VMware Fusion, VMware Server, Xen, and XenServer.
- OS implemented virtualization is implemented by the OS itself taking the place of the hypervisor. Examples of this include Solaris Containers, BSDjails, OpenVZ, Linux-VServer, and Parallels Virtuozzo Containers.

The topic of virtualization is far more complex than we can represent in this book; therefore, the interested reader should avail themselves of any of a number of excellent resources on the topic, beginning with vendor materials from the above examples.

Figure 3.1 depicts type 1 and type 2 hypervisor examples; in both cases, there are two VMs hosted on a single hardware server.

There are many interesting security concerns around the use of virtualization even before we consider using it for clouds. First, by adding each new VM, you are adding an additional OS—which itself entails security risk. Every OS should be appropriately patched, maintained, and monitored as appropriate per its intended use. Second, typical network-based intrusion detection does not work well with virtual servers that are colocated on the same host, consequently advanced techniques are needed to monitor traffic between VMs. When data and applications are moved between multiple physical servers for load balancing or failover, network monitoring systems cannot yet assess and reflect these operations for what they are. This is even more the case when clustering is used in

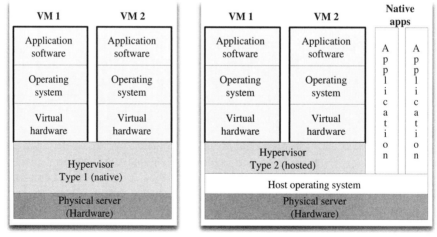

Type 1 hypervisor   *Type 2 hypervisor*

FIGURE 3.1

Type 1 and Type 2 hypervisors.

conjunction with virtualization. Third, the use of virtualization demands the adoption of different management approaches for many functions, including configuration management to VM placement and capacity management. Likewise, resource allocation problems can quickly become performance issues; thus, performance management is critical to run an effective virtualized environment.

Virtualization Concerns with Cloud Computing

As we transition from using virtualization for server consolidation to using virtualization to produce a flexible on-demand infrastructure, we approach the realm of cloud computing. But so far, we have only mentioned some of the issues one faces when adopting virtualization; we have yet to consider the further security issues of virtualization in a cloud.

In adopting virtualization for cloud computing, it will become evident to the cloud builder that the management tools used in a physical server-based deployment will not suffice in a highly dynamic virtualized one. To begin, in a physical server deployment model, provisioning automation is generally not heavily used unless the number of server OSs to be provisioned is significant and warrants the overhead of implementing automated provisioning strategies. The typical strategy for provisioning physical servers involves repetitive steps by a systems administrator. In a heavily virtualized environment, whether it be a cloud or not, OS provisioning will rapidly transition toward being highly automated. Figure 3.2 depicts these differences in management tools along with several related qualities as we move from a physical realm to a virtualized one or to a cloud realm.

Virtualization has altered the relationship between the OS and hardware. In itself, this challenges traditional security perspectives as it undermines the *comfort* that you might feel when you provision an OS and application on a server that you can see. But, some of us already believe that this sense of comfort is misplaced for most situations. The actual security posture of even a PC with an Internet connection is very hard to realistically discern for the average user. Virtualization complicates the picture, but it does not necessarily make security better or worse.

There are several important security concerns we need to address in considering the use of virtualization for cloud computing. One potential new risk area has to do with the potential to compromise a virtual machine hypervisor itself. If the hypervisor is vulnerable to being exploited, it will become a primary target. At the scale of a cloud, such a risk would have broad impact if not otherwise mitigated with network isolation and if it is not detected by security monitoring.

In examining this concern, we first should consider the nature of a hypervisor. As Andreas Antonopoulos observed[2]:

> ...hypervisors are purpose-build software with a small and specific set of functions. A hypervisor is smaller, more focused than a general purpose operating system, and less exposed, having fewer or no externally accessible

Management function	Physical servers	Virtualized servers	Cloud realm
Performance management, fault management	Point solution approaches that use manual or rule-based approaches to monitor and manage resource usage in an event-driven manner.	Greater use of automation, model-based view focused on services and applications.	Completely automated with operator adjustment, integrated or coordinated with other management functions. Sophisticated usage trends and analysis.
Control infrastructure: Change control, configuration management	Manual processes in conjunction with ticketing approaches to request and implement changes to the control plane.	Control infrastructure changes may not require faster change implementation. CMDB is used to enable better control through better information (reflected architecture).	Control infrastructure changes require faster change implementation. CMDB is tightly coupled with change process.
Server: Change control, configuration Management	Manual processes in conjunction with ticketing approaches to request and implement changes to the control plane.	Virtualized server changes require faster change implementation. CMDB is used to enable better control through better information and automation.	Virtualized cloud server changes require automated change implementation. CMDB is integral to change process and overall process is integrated with other control operations.

FIGURE 3.2

Representative management activities in a physical versus virtual environment.[1]

network ports. A hypervisor does not undergo frequent change and does not run third-party applications. The guest operating systems, which may be vulnerable, do not have direct access to the hypervisor. In fact, the hypervisor is completely transparent (invisible) to network traffic with the exception of traffic to/from a dedicated hypervisor management interface. Furthermore, at present there are no documented attacks against hypervisors, reducing the likelihood of attack.

So, although the impact of a hypervisor compromise is great (compromise of all guests), the probability is low because both the vulnerability of the hypervisor and the probability of an attack are low.

Another area of concern with virtualization has to do with the nature of allocating and deallocating resources such as the local storage associated with VMs. If during the deployment and operation of a VM, data is written to physical media—or to memory—and it is not cleared before those information resources are reallocated to the next VM, then there is a potential for information exposure. However, these problems are certainly not unique to virtualization and they have been addressed by every recent commonly used general purpose OS. Two points should be noted, the initial OS may terminate in error before resources are zeroes. Second, not all OSs manage the clearing of data the same way, some may clear data upon release, whereas others may do so upon allocation. Hence, it is conceivable for two different OSs to have an opportunity to experience this circumstance. The bottom line? Assume control over your use of storage and memory when using a public cloud. How? By clearing data yourself and treating operations against sensitive data as warranting careful handling,[A] and those against privilege controls as *atomic*[B] ones. Verifying that a released resource was cleared is an excellent practice for security as well.

A further area of concern with virtualization has to do with the potential for undetected network attacks between VMs that are colocated on a physical server. The problem is that unless the traffic from each VM can be monitored, you cannot verify that traffic is not possible between VMs. There are several possible approaches here, the first is that the VM user can simply invoke OS-based traffic filtering or firewalling. One potential complication that can be faced by a customer who needs multiple communicating and cooperating VMs is that these VMs may be dynamically moved around by the service provider to load balance their cloud. If VM Internet Protocol (IP) addresses change during this relocation (unlikely, but possible between VM instantiations) and absolute addressing is used for firewall rules, then firewall filtering will fail.

In essence, network virtualization must deliver an appropriate network interface to the VM. That interface might just be a multiplexed channel with all of the switching and routing handled in the network interconnect hardware. Most fully featured hypervisors (for example, VMware) have virtual switches (and firewalls) that sit between the server physical interfaces and the virtual interfaces provided to the VMs. All of these facilities have to be managed as changes are made to VM locations and the allowable communication paths between them.

Another, although theoretical, technique that may have potential for limiting traffic flow between VMs would be to use segregation to gather and isolate different classes of VMs from each other. In this strategy, we propose that VMs would be traced to their owners throughout the life cycle and would only be colocated on physical servers with other VMs that meet the requirements for colocation. This approach could include some form of VM tagging or labeling that is akin to

---

[A]When sensitive data is processed in any environment where data remnants of the operation (such as buffers or temp files) may become exposed to other parties, you ought to invest more effort to properly handle this data. For instance, when a piece of code receives a clear text password from a user, the buffers that are used to receive the password and transmit the clear text password for authentication really must be cleared out as part of the authentication process. Otherwise, the risk of exposure is extended for longer than is necessary to complete the operation.

[B]An atomic operation is one that must be performed in entirety or not at all, i.e., if the operation fails you must roll back to the previous state.

labeling within multilevel OSs (such as Trusted Solaris or SE-Linux). Or, the configuration management database could be used to track tenant requests for application isolation. But in all these examples, the problem is "when the tenant also needs the application components to have maximal separation from common mode failures for availability (e.g., server failure and all of the contained VM's). It's not that such a scheme couldn't be made to work, it's that the cost of all the incompatible and underutilized server fragments (which can't be sold to someone else) has to be carried in the service cost."[3]

One actual practice for managing traffic flows between VMs is the use of virtual local area networks (VLANs) to isolate traffic from one customer's VMs from other customer's VMs. However, to be completely effective, this technique requires extending support for VLANs beyond the core switching infrastructure and down onto physical servers that host VMs. This support is almost universal with VM technology now. The next problem is scaling VLAN-like capabilities beyond their current limits to support much larger clouds. That support will also need to be standardized to allow multivendor solutions, and it will also need to be tied in with network management and hypervisors.

Finally, in considering the security issues with VMs, it is important to recognize that this technology is not new and that several products have undergone formal security evaluations and received certification. What this means in practical terms is that several vendors of VM technology have taken pains for obtaining independent and recognized security certifications of their technology.

Virtualization absolutely complicates infrastructure management, but with cloud, this simply must be automated if the technology is used at cloud scale and cloud elasticity. The bottom line with virtualization risk is that the use of this technology must be better planned and managed with cloud than with noncloud uses. And by automating the management of virtualization with cloud computing, we achieve multiple benefits, better security included. Further, the end of ad hoc use of virtualization itself is good for security and it represents a return to control over infrastructure.

A Closer Examination: Provisioning

The prime advantage of automated provisioning in clouds is quite simply the automation, predictability, and speed of constituting a resource for a customer. Resources can span the range of a virtual data center (IaaS), a VM with or without a software stack (PaaS), or hosted application software (software-as-a-service [SaaS]). Figure 3.3 depicts the services models (IaaS, PaaS, and SaaS) as they relate to the service stack that spans the data center up to the service consumer. But there are other advantages to provisioning, and these include enhancing availability by provisioning multiple instances of a service or provisioning a service across multiple data centers.

Since provisioning represents a delivery stage that must have integrity and that is only useful if the service that is provisioned has integrity in deployment.

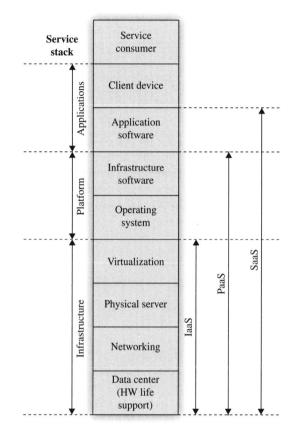

FIGURE 3.3

Service stack elements.

The security of provisioning depends on the ability to protect master images and deploying them intact and in a secure manner. Challenges with this include the reliance on hypervisors as well as the need for process isolation at every stage of provisioning and deprovisioning. At this point in time, there is greater concern for potential compromise of a provisioning service than for the security of a hypervisor. And it is certainly true that after a service or VM is provisioned, it must be protected and isolated from other tenants and services belonging to others. Here too we have greater current concern for security than with underlying VM technologies.

Although a tenant or customer may have on-demand access to security controls such as virtual firewalls, authentication services, and security logging, these services may undergo change as the underlying implementation is patched or updated. Firewall rules and other security configuration data may become operationally incorrect as VM images are reprovisioned in an updated or reconfigured infrastructure. Although this is typically handled by public cloud implementations, there is a need for fundamental improvement in areas such as version control and configuration management for cloud implementations.

There are other risks, including unintended interactions or information transfer when on-demand security controls are integrated with a customer application. Recycled user IDs and IP addresses also represent concern if recycling an IP or UID makes it possible for a user to inadvertently gain access to an information resource that is not theirs. The essential issue here has to do with the correctness and completeness of the process that implements allocation and deallocation of any VMs, information resources or enabling elements.

Finally, the concerns that exist with provisioning have an analog when the service or VM is deprovisioned. This process can have identical consequences if it fails or is compromised as at any other stage.

A Closer Examination: Cloud Storage

There are several concerns around cloud data storage, and these include the following:

- Since clouds tend to implement storage as centralized facilities, some view storage as having the potential to be an attractive target for criminals or hackers. This has always been the case for any valuable resource and can be mitigated by the application of appropriate security controls.
- Multitenancy again presents concerns, this time with the potential for data isolation mechanisms that may either fail in operation or in a rollback operation from a backup system.
- Storage systems are complex hardware and software implementations. There are always questions as to the potential for catastrophic failure modes that might either destroy the data or expose the data from one customer to another customer.

You may note that these concerns are largely hypothetical although not outside the realm of reason. A cloud consumer would be well served to select a provider based on how they represent their approach to mitigate or avoid these risks. But we should expect that if cloud providers are aware of such risks, they will likely seek to address them to avoid damaging their reputations.

There are other storage security concerns that may warrant greater attention, and we listed several that have to do with data privacy and control in the introduction to this section. As we mentioned above, there is a possibility that a cloud provider may store data in multiple jurisdictions. Hence, the potential exists for data to become accessed by foreign governments. There are several concerns here, notably the opportunity for a hosting nation to flex its legal rights to obtain a copy of transiting or stored data via a warrant. But this is likely to become a *self-correcting* situation as providers will likely avoid the risk to their reputations as data custodians by transferring data from a source nation to another one where data may be accessed by another nation's authorities.

But perhaps the greater concern for most customers is the possibility that a customer's data may be comingled in various ways with data belonging to others. This is generally not a risk unless one encounters a failure mode that results in information exposure. Realistically, the underlying controls that are built into file systems, disk partitioning, raid schemes, and hardware controllers that implement or otherwise support data separation are very reliable. When failures occur, they tend to be detected at low levels rendering the storage unit unavailable. But rather than comingling data belonging to multiple users in a single logical file system, the use of VMs allows for further isolation by how a VM can use virtual storage within the VM. There are many ways that one user's data can be isolated from data belonging to other users, and it is likely the norm that with cloud storage multiple means of isolation will be mutually reinforcing from the VM up to file system permissions to disk partitioning and even to physical devices. Again, jurisdictional and comingling concerns warrant investigation by prospective cloud consumers.

Cloud providers generally address many of these storage concerns. Although implementation of cloud storage is dependent on provider choices, the inherent characteristics of the model invite better data storage security than traditional infrastructure typically provides. Since storage in a cloud tends to be centralized, implementing data protection and encryption across the board in a public cloud is fairly straightforward. Thus, the use of encryption for data at rest and in transit is typical for public cloud offerings. Centralization of storage also makes it easier to implement monitoring, most likely at a level that can't be implemented in a cost-effective manner in a decentralized infrastructure.

But data does not only exist within the bounds of the cloud itself, the typical data center continuously backs up data for disaster recovery or retention purposes. Often, these backups are stored off-site at an offline facility that is operated by a third party. Although these providers are more likely to act within the bounds of their contract and preserve the confidentiality of these data copies, they are subject to error and certainly they are subject to arm twisting by a jurisdiction that may not have the best interests of the data owner in mind.

We have already mentioned the need for encryption for data storage in this section, but encryption has numerous other uses in a cloud. These include:

- Controlling access to the control interfaces for resources
- Controlling access for administrators to VMs and OS images
- Controlling access to applications

We will examine data security, data ownership, and privacy at various points in this chapter, and throughout this book. In Chapter 5, Securing the Cloud: Data Security, we will examine that topic in far greater detail.

A Closer Examination: Cloud Operation, Security, and Networking

As we have mentioned several times in Chapters 1 and 2, the cloud model brings benefits for the IT operations and support teams. Every step required to build and operate a traditional IT solution is overhead for the underlying goal. It entails expensive skills and often times inefficient repeated effort. Furthermore, traditional IT infrastructure can be dwarfed by the scale of cloud computing. Infrastructure at massive cloud scale demands automation. But even with a small cloud, automation is critical if IT processes (such as provisioning and deprovisioning) are to be performed in a cost- and time-effective manner.

Cloud infrastructure demands efficient structure and organization. By defining and following patterns, at every step from racking individual computers to cabling them, from operations to security, savings recur and processes can be tuned and refined. An intelligently planned and organized cloud infrastructure can be more effectively and more efficiently built and operated by a smaller staff then if you take the same computers and disperse them to many server rooms.

The aggregation of components into patterns is not limited to computers, storage, and network. Power and network cabling also benefit from regular patterns, this includes their labeling or nomenclature and it is empowering to the configuration management and change management processes. These patterns have value when they are optimized to eek even small margins in the build stage of a cloud, but they have recurring benefit at every stage afterward: from provisioning VMs to managing and operating cloud infrastructure. Objectives such as *lights out management*, *remote operations*, and *fail in place* contribute to the further refinement of patterns.

Has security come up yet in this discussion on scale, structure, and organization? The combination of automation and structure also means that immensely large clouds can be managed and operated by smaller staff. This, along with the technologies used in cloud computing, will drive expansion of the skill set of cloud engineers. Simply put, you gain the advantage of graduating from a series of systems administrators associated with typical infrastructure or server closets to a dedicated team of cloud administrators and a dedicated security team.

Even with a private cloud implementation, the aggregated scale of a private cloud implementation accrues benefits. The benefits of intelligently conceived patterns and automation can include fault tolerance and reliability, along with greater resiliency. There is little question that a well conceived and correctly implemented cloud network can offer a tenant or other customer better networking security than many could otherwise achieve if they instead attempted to build, configure, and operate a traditional network infrastructure. First, the implementation patterns we discussed in Chapters 1 and 2 make for a more predictable and disciplined network than the typical infrastructure network or data center network. Second, most enterprises cannot afford the level of networking expertise that a cloud provider can deliver indirectly when they hire their staff. There is no question that the cloud customer benefits from this. Third, maintaining the security of a network involves constant learning and intelligent response to new and emerging threats.

It is simply more cost effective to benefit indirectly from the work that the cloud provider performs on behalf of countless customers beside yourself.

This aggregation also brings other advantages, and in the next section, we will discuss networking but every aspect of cloud infrastructure benefits from the scale and the need for professional grade gear and operations. The investment in security infrastructure quite simply needs to be greater with the cloud model, and given the scale it can be so and affordably so especially when you consider the benefits of repeating patterns and one-time cost associated with identity solutions or security development.

Among the many advantages of a cloud provider delivering network security is the tendency for a provider to employ carrier grade network gear that has more sophisticated capabilities than typical enterprise networking gear. Sure you can buy the same gear, but its cost will likely exceed the cost of all your other data center costs! Such carrier grade gear requires expertise to install, configure, and operate. But the benefits are truly substantial since the security functionality will afford greater resilience to dedicated attacks, better automated traffic inspection among many other capabilities. Besides strong perimeter security, benefits include protection against a distributed denial of service along with sophisticated VLAN capabilities.

A deep discussion on the topic of networking is beyond the scope of this book; if this is of interest, then the reader is encouraged to invest the time to gain a better understanding of this complex area by taking advantage of the many books and online references on the subject.

ASSESSING YOUR RISK TOLERANCE IN CLOUD COMPUTING

A frequent question about cloud computing goes like this: *Is it safe to use a public cloud?* This is a fair question that is begging for information. But answering it depends on a clear understanding of your acceptance of risk. And understanding how much risk you can tolerate depends on assessing your security requirements and how you value your information assets (data, applications, and processes). Only when we understand these issues can we make an informed decision as to which deployment models and which service delivery models are appropriate for our needs and risk tolerance.

A full risk evaluation is an involved process that is beyond the scope of this book. In this section, we are presenting a high-level treatment of the subject with the goal of presenting reasonable guidance to general questions like the one we posed above (*Is it safe for me to use a public cloud*). The interested reader is encouraged to refer to several excellent references on the topic.[c]

Identifying information assets is important before we adopt a public or hybrid model because these will involve at least some degree of ceding control over how

---

[c]NIST is an excellent source for information on many security topics, risk assessment included. Two of particular value to this topic are: SP 800-115 "Technical Guide to Information Security Testing and Assessment" and 800-30 "Risk Management Guide for Information Technology Systems" See: http://csrc.nist.gov/publications/PubsSPs.html

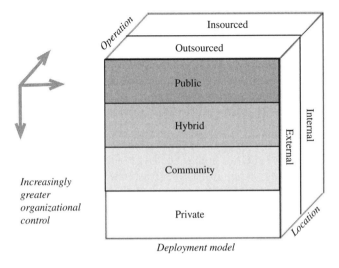

FIGURE 3.4

Organizational control varies according to model.

that information will be protected and where it might reside (location/jurisdiction). Figure 3.4 depicts these relationships and roughly shows that there is increased organizational control for an internally hosted and internally operated private cloud versus for other combinations.

But let's not forget that the sum total of our information assets is not limited to information or data. Our applications and processes can easily be as sensitive or proprietary as our information is. In fact, in many realms, including intelligence and finance, the algorithms or programs that are used are often proprietary and highly secret to the organization. Their exposure can constitute a dramatic loss to the organization.

Assessing the Risk

In Chapter 1, we introduced the concept of information security risk (*Risk Management*) and now we will build on that by briefly examining risk analysis. To begin with, we might ask the following questions[D]:

- **Threat Categorization** What can happen to your information assets?
- **Threat Impact** How severe could that be?
- **Threat Frequency** How often might that happen?
- **Uncertainty Factor** How certain are you in answering these three questions?

The central issue with risk is uncertainty that is expressed in terms of probability. But what we really want to know is what to do about it (countermeasures or

---

[D]Modeled after: Tipton, H., Information Security Management Handbook, page 247–286.

risk mitigation). So, once you analyze and address risks, you can ask several further questions[E]:

- **Mitigation** What can you do to reduce the risk?
- **Mitigation Cost** What does risk mitigation incur?
- **Mitigation Cost/Benefit** Is mitigation cost effective?

To be clear, these three questions are more rhetorical for a public cloud than for a private or hybrid one. In a public cloud you get what you pay for, and the cloud provider is the party that is responsible for answering these three questions above. Similarly, these questions are also less relevant for SaaS than they are for PaaS, but they are more relevant yet for IaaS.

Information Assets and Risk

We stated above that the central issue with risk is uncertainty, and applying that to our question, we must examine our information assets a bit more. Identifying information assets can be elusive, especially so with the create-once, copy-often aspect of digital systems. The typical organization rarely has sufficient control over its information in terms of assurance that if we control a given copy we can rest assured there are no other copies. From the standpoint of protecting digital data (a leaky sieve in the ocean?), that may be the worst of it. But organizations have many other problems managing their information assets.

So, when we are looking at moving our information assets to a cloud and we seek to identify our information assets, we may need to be satisfied in answering the question in terms of classes or categories of information versus specific bits of information in databases or individual files. Unfortunately, here too we generally have a problem with how we categorize our information. This might not be so bad if our computing systems enforced information labeling, but they usually do not. Information labeling in computer systems is based on real world processes of individuals having a *need to know* and the appropriate *clearance* for information. In the real world, this is organizationally controlled along the lines of information classification[F] and additional handling caveats (such as *Project X Only*). In the world of computers, the appropriate controls are usually insufficient to prevent digital duplication and intended or unintended information hemorrhaging.

Remembering the security triad (confidentiality, integrity, and availability), we can ask a series of targeted questions around information assets along the lines of what would the consequence be if[G]:

- The information asset was exposed?
- The information asset was modified by an external entity?

[E]Modeled after: Tipton, H., Information Security Management Handbook, page 247–286.
[F]By example: "Top Secret" for national security, and "Marketing Plans" for a corporation.
[G]For a similar line of information asset evaluation, see "Security Guidance for Critical Areas of Focus in Cloud Computing V2.1."

- The information asset was manipulated?
- The information asset became unavailable?

If these questions raise concern about unacceptable risk, we might approach the overall problem by limiting risk-sensitive processing to a private cloud (avoiding the introduction of new risk) and by adopting use of a public cloud for non-risk-sensitive data. But adopting a private cloud does not obviate the need for appropriate controls.

In that regard, let's consider what we might get:

- By mixing outsourcing in a public cloud for nonsensitive data and reserving internal systems for sensitive data we might gain some cost advantages without assuming new risk.
- Where use of a private cloud would pose no new risks to your information assets, use of a hybrid or public cloud model may.
- Switching from a traditional IT model for internal processing to a private cloud model may reduce risk.

These are reasonable statements that constitute a start toward aligning the importance of our information assets toward both deployment models and service models.

In the next few sections, we will look at the problem from the standpoint of various operational security issues.

Privacy and Confidentiality Concerns

Beyond the information asset risks we discussed above, we may be processing, storing, or transmitting data that is subject to regulatory and compliance requirements. When data falls under regulatory or compliance restrictions, our choice of cloud deployment (be it private, hybrid, or public) hinges on an understanding that the provider is fully compliant. Otherwise one will risk violating privacy, regulatory, or other legal requirements. This obligation usually falls on the tenant or user. It should go without saying that the implications for maintaining the security of information are significant when it comes to privacy, business, and national security information.

Privacy violations occur often enough outside cloud computing for us to be concerned about any system—cloud-based or traditional—storing, processing, or transmitting such sensitive information. In 2010, several cloud privacy information exposures occurred with a number of cloud-based services, including Facebook, Twitter, and Google.[H]

[H]On July 15, 2010 Twitter disclosed that a hacker had exploited a Microsoft Hotmail feature to hijack a Twitter employee's work e-mail account, and with that gained access to sensitive documents at Google Apps. While this incident is not a cloud-specific vulnerability, the fact that the sensitive data was stored outside an enterprise is a key element to consider.

Privacy concerns with the cloud model are not fundamentally new. As a tenant with legal privacy obligations, your handling of privacy information is not going to be different if you use a cloud. Just as you would not store such information on a server that lacked adequate controls, you wouldn't select any cloud provider without verifying that they meet the same benchmarks for how they protect data at rest, in transmission, or while it is processed. That is not to say that your policy may quite reasonably shun the use of *any external provider* managing such information for you, cloud included. It also bears pointing out that while there may be a perception that the computer on your desk is safer than one that is in a public cloud, unless you are taking unusual technical and procedural precautions with your desktop computer, it is more apt to be the one with the weaker security. But safety and governance are two separate issues, and as part of due diligence, you will need to fully understand a provider's privacy governance along with their security practices and guidelines.

As with personal information subject to privacy laws, classes of business information, and national security information are also subject to regulation and law. National security information and processes benefit from a strong and developed corpus of law, regulation, and guidance. There derive from public law and flow downward through each individual agency or officially responsible entity. Although cloud is a relatively new model, a studied examination of the available guidance should be ample to absolutely restrict any classified information from residing in a public cloud. The area of probable concern lies with other government functions that do not process sensitive or classified data. Suffice it to say, when you examine the opportunity for use of public clouds there are many distinct and separate lines of business between a national government down to a local jurisdiction. Given the size of government and the number of levels and jurisdictions, it seems as though government itself could operate a series of community clouds for its exclusive use thereby obtaining the benefits and avoiding the issues with cohabitation in a public cloud. On the other hand, if government is to use a public cloud, then that service must fully meet the interests of the tenant and all applicable regulations and laws. It is possible that a tenant can implement additional security controls that meet regulatory or legal requirements even when an underlying public IaaS or PaaS that does not fully meet those same requirements. However, it must be understood that the range of additional controls that can be added by a tenant are limited and cannot overcome many gaps in some public cloud services.

Data Ownership and Locale Concerns

In addition to privacy and confidentiality concerns, further concern arises with ownership of information assets. The problem is that there is potential for erosion of information asset ownership when moving such resources to any external system. There is a fundamental difference between data ownership and having responsibility as a data custodian. Although the legal ownership of data will remain with the originating data owner, one potential area for concern with a public cloud is that the cloud provider may become responsible for both roles. There is no better example of this as when a law enforcement entity serves a warrant to a cloud provider for access to a tenant's information assets.

Related to ownership concerns are concerns with where data resides and what jurisdictions it may traverse. The Internet presents a grand opportunity for the nosey and the wicked when it comes to the opportunity for surreptitiously examining someone else's secrets.[1] In response to this, the European Union (EU) directive on Data Protection[4] stipulated in which countries EU private and personal data may or may not traverse or reside. This has profound implications for all computing by EU member states.

From the standpoint of cloud computing, the impact of this directive is likely shaping how public cloud providers, along with SPI service providers implement their services. This is a perfectly reasonable model for limiting the jurisdictional footprint of data to minimize the mischief that data is subject to in extraterritorial traversal, processing or storage. All tenants or end users of cloud services should be concerned by the potential that a public cloud or SPI service may push data or applications out of the jurisdiction in which the tenant resides or has legal obligations.

Auditing and Forensics

Auditing is an overloaded term in security, in our present use we are referring to those activities when we evaluate security policy, procedures, practices, and the technical controls for correctness and completeness. This is necessary to assess whether controls and procedures are adequate to meet all operational aspects of security, including compliance, protection, detection, and forensics. For cloud, such audits have great value for tenants and customers as they convey a sense of trust about the cloud provider's diligence in assuring security.

As the owner of information assets, a tenant must perform informed due diligence on the provider. Since due diligence by customers generally does not scale for the provider's business model, the provider must be transparent in their security policy, governance, and procedures, and as a result, tenants are in a better position to make informed decisions.

There are several issues around the responsibilities and limits that affect tenants and providers with regard to collecting legally admissible evidence for prosecution. Understanding who did what and how is hard enough with an evidence chain where responsibility for collecting data is shared between the provider and tenant. One party may be the lawful owner of the data, while the other is the custodian.

---

[1]To understand this at a superficial level you can review which systems your e-mail traversed on its way to you. To do this, select a single e-mail in your inbox and select the view option to see the "full header." What you will see is a list of all the stops or servers that had a hand in transmitting your e-mail on its path from the point of origin to the one hosting your e-mail client. If that e-mail wasn't encrypted, anyone with access to any of those systems could have seen it.

Given the nature of how some SPI services may be accessed, it is not unlikely that it may be very difficult to authoritatively represent or even understand the trail that represents the actions leading to and following a compromise or penetration. To begin with, having a tenant obtain access to a provider's records may compromise the privacy of other tenants. Second, events in the two sets of logs may not track if system clocks are not identical. Further, it may be difficult to prove that a tenant's forensics data that is gathered and stored in a public cloud has not been tampered with. To be clear, this situation represents a set of excellent opportunities for cloud providers to distinguish themselves by offering advanced services. We will pursue this more in Chapter 4 where we examine security monitoring in the cloud.

Emerging Threats

Some of the oldest programs are sometimes found to have vulnerabilities that have been undiscovered for years. In other words, we should always expect that what we thought was safe may be found to have been vulnerable by a hacker before we become aware of it. In addition, some of the technologies and certainly many of the software components that cloud computing is comprised from are still quite new and have yet to engender a high degree of trust for experienced security professionals. Some components are built on top of what can only be described as layers upon layers of software and protocol scaffolding. Is the sum of these parts secure? The answer is probably no. Complexity and interaction between components are two realms from which vulnerabilities spring forth. It also bears to mention that some of that scaffolding continues to enjoy refactoring and changes by both vendors and the open source community, so it really is an unstable set of scaffolding layers we are increasingly dependent upon.

So, Is It Safe?

Although cloud is still new, the push for effective controls over the protection of information in clouds is nascent. In general, there may presently be fewer security solutions for clouds than there are for securing physical devices in traditional infrastructure, and while the cost of instantiating virtual security appliances is lower in clouds, the technology is newer. But, we should also remember that security is no stranger to virtualization, as there is a strong history of getting virtualization security right going all the way back to mainframes. What is new is the highly dynamic nature of on-demand cloud computing.

To be fair, much of the present action in adopting public clouds is in the realm of early adopters, and it is difficult to ascertain if any data or processing is being done in violation of legal requirements or compliance. The U.S. federal government has launched an effort called *FedRAMP*,[J] which is oriented toward enabling

---

[J]http://www.govinfosecurity.com/articles.php?art_id=2350.

the entire process of assuring cloud instances are appropriate for individual agency applications.

Two organizations that are actively pursuing the improvement of data protection and security controls in clouds are the Cloud Security Alliance[K] and the Cloud Computing Interoperability Group. Another group, the Jericho Forum,[L] has approached the problem from a different perspective, namely that de-perimeterization has already taken place due to a variety of services that penetrate the perimeter of infrastructure largely by tunneling through firewalls to provide access to critical services. One problem with most certifications is that they are focused more on facility and process than they are on the de-perimeterized service-oriented world we have largely already transitioned to. A second issue is that many of the systems we are already using have virtualized servers running on them. If these servers have conflicting security requirements, we already have a problem in practice.

In the author's opinion, most of the security issues with cloud computing are neither unique to the cloud computing model nor very difficult to address. And, as stated frequently in this book, the cloud model represents a golden opportunity to achieve better security based on the model itself. However, we do need to recognize that there are differences in the model and that we can't be cavalier about security with the cloud model.

LEGAL AND REGULATORY ISSUES

This section of the chapter is an informal survey of the legal and regulatory landscape that cloud operates in; by no means should this material be considered *legal advice*. Readers are encouraged to explore this topic more extensively by reviewing other sources as well.[M] The legal and regulatory landscape is not static, new laws are being proposed that may change the responsibilities of tenants and providers.

Cloud computing which employs a hybrid, community, or public cloud model "creates new dynamics in the relationship between an organization and its information, involving the presence of a third party: the cloud provider. This creates new challenges in understanding how laws apply to a wide variety of information management scenarios."[5] The impact of this is that it creates practical challenges in understanding how laws apply to the different parties under various scenarios. Regardless of which computing model you use, cloud or otherwise, you need to consider the legal issues, specifically those around any data you may collect, store, and process. There will likely be state, national, or international laws that

---

[K]http://www.cloudsecurityalliance.org/.
[L]http://www.opengroup.org/jericho/.
[M]An excellent source of information on cloud privacy issues is "Cloud Security and Privacy," by Tim Mather, a friend Subra Kumaraswamy and Shahed Latif. Published by O'Reilly, 2009.

you (or preferably, your lawyers) will need to consider to ensure that you are in legal compliance.

If the tenant or cloud customer operates in the United States, Canada, or the EU, then they are subject to numerous regulatory requirements. These include Control Objectives for Information and related Technology and Safe Harbor. These laws may relate to where the data is stored or transferred to, as well as how well this data is protected from a confidential aspect. Some of these laws will apply to specific markets only, such as the Health Insurance Portability and Accountability Act (HIPAA) for the health care industry. However, often companies may store health-related information about individual employees, which means that the company may have to comply with HIPPA even if they are not operating in that market.

The failure to adequately protect your data can have a number of consequences, including the potential for fines by one or more government or industry regulatory bodies. Such fines can be substantial and potentially crippling for a small- or medium-sized business. For example, the Payment Card Industry (PCI) can impose fines up to $100,000 per month for violations to their compliance. Although these fines will be levied onto the acquiring bank, they are as likely to impact the merchant as well.

Laws or regulations will typically specify who within an enterprise should be responsible and held accountable for the accuracy and security of the data involved. If you are collecting and holding HIPAA data, then you must have a security position designated to ensure compliance. The Sarbanes–Oxley Act designates the Chief Financial Officer (CFO) and Chief Executive Officer (CEO) to have joint responsibility for the financial data. The Gramm–Leach–Bliley Act (GLBA) is broader, specifying the responsibility for security with the entire board of directors. Less specific is the Federal Trade Commission (FTC), who just require a specific individual to be accountable for the information security program within a company.

This section will look at some of the laws and issues that can arise as they apply to cloud computing. Primarily this will look at laws for the United States and the European Economic Union (EEU), but similar laws will often be in force in other countries.

Third Parties

If you use a cloud infrastructure that is sourced from a cloud service provider, all legal or regulatory requirements that apply to your enterprise must be imposed on this supplier as well—this is your responsibility, not the providers. Taking the HIPAA regulations as an example, any subcontractors that you employ (for example, a cloud service provider) must have a clause in the contract that they will use reasonable security controls and also comply with any data privacy provisions. In the United States, both federal and state government agencies such as the FTC and various Attorney Generals have made enterprises accountable for the actions of their subcontractors. This has been replicated in other countries, such as the Data Protection Agencies in the EU. As the use of cloud infrastructure becomes more prevalent, the risks of a third party accessing the data illegally will rise as well. Even with the data being encrypted, the third party may have access to keys and therefore have access to the underlying data. Often the risks may magnify, as there may be a number of third parties involved—the cloud provider, cloud support, operations and management teams, along with others who may manage and support applications. Contractors who work for any of those organizations may further compound the dissipation in control.

Contractual Issues

In the previous section, we touched on contractual aspects. As this is a large topic, we will expand on it in this subsection, outlining some of the issues that need to be considered at all stages of the contractual process:

- Initial due diligence
- Contract negotiation
- Implementation
- Termination (end of term or abnormal)
- Supplier transfer

Initial Due Diligence

Prior to entering into a contract with a cloud supplier, an enterprise should evaluate its specific needs and requirements. You should define the scope of the services you are looking for, along with any restrictions, regulations, or compliance issues that need to be satisfied. For instance, if you are going to collect and/or store employee HIPAA data in the cloud, then you must ensure that any supplier will meet the guidelines defined by the HIPAA regulations. Assessing the different laws and regulations your enterprise needs to abide by, may well define what you can deploy in a cloud or which type of service you can use.

Any services you deploy to the cloud should also be rated as to their criticality to your business. If you want to deploy a service that is critical to the business or would cause a major disruption if it became unavailable, then you will need to factor this into your supplier evaluation. As a number of suppliers are entering this market, it is inevitable that some will fail or simply stop providing the service if they deem it is not profitable for them. Often, large companies will enter the market but leave it once the expected profit does not materialize. If this is the core business of the cloud supplier, it may be willing to continue operating for longer with a smaller profit.

Questions that you should consider prior to evaluating cloud service providers are:

- Is this cloud service a true core business of the provider?
- How financially stable is the provider?
- Are they outsourcing any aspect of the service to a third party, and if so does the third party have the appropriate arrangements with the provider?

- Does the physical security of their data centers meet your legal, regulatory, and business needs?
- Are their business continuity and disaster recovery plans consistent with your business needs?
- What is their level of technical expertise within their operations team?
- How long have they been offering the service and do they have a track record with verifiable customers?
- Does the provider offer any indemnification?

Once your enterprise has performed such due diligence you can begin serious evaluation of providers. This will reduce the time you will spend overall in the negotiations and ensure that the correct level of security is in place for your particular needs. The cloud supplier cannot be expected to know your business requirements in detail and may well be unaware of the regulations that need to be adhered to. If there is a breach in regulations, it will be your enterprise that is penalized and not the cloud supplier you have selected.

Contract Negotiation

Once you have narrowed your selection of cloud service providers, the actual contract needs to be agreed to. Depending upon the service you are contracting for, this may not be negotiable at all, and your contract may be limited to an online click-through agreement which you can either accept or not. The results of the due diligence will obviously play a part in deciding what you need in the form of a contract. If you need to have a tailored contract, you can immediately eliminate a number of suppliers. But to be clear, the bulk of cloud services are less likely to involve tailored contracts than traditional hosting or outsourcing contracts—the economics of the model (for both provider and client) make that the case.

There will be many scenarios where you will accept a click-through agreement from a supplier due to either the financial savings (both in terms of minimal contract negotiations and ongoing costs from the supplier) or the low risk you have deemed your application and/or data to be at. However, you should also look at the bigger picture and define a strategy and procedure for future applications that your company may need to deploy. Often one part of the business may see that you are using a cloud infrastructure and may deploy other applications in the same way without going through the rigor of determining if the solution is appropriate for the new applications. Having in place well-defined corporate standards and procedures will ensure that *rogue* applications are not deployed that breach your security model, or worse that do not comply with one or more regulations that your company is bound by.

Where you can and want to negotiate the contract, ensure that your requirements are defined in a way that the provider can understand and agree to. Specifying that data is to be held according to HIPAA regulations, for example, may be meaningful to your company, but the cloud provider may not fully understand the law or its implications. If you know you want the supplier to ensure segregation of duties, personnel screening, data privacy, or other security measures, these need to be fully defined.

TIP

Client requirements are onerous for cloud providers to manage when each client presents their requirements in a nonstandard and unique manner. For a provider, wading through numerous requests from multiple prospective clients eats into profitability. The cloud model favors on-demand resource allocation, not on-demand contract negotiations!

Rather than have a cloud service provider respond to numerous prospective client contract requests, there are a number of external accreditations that providers can obtain that will provide evidence that they have both implemented appropriate security and follow sound security practices. One of these is the Statement on Auditing Standards (SAS) number 70, commonly known as an SAS 70 audit, which was originally published by the American Institute of Certified Public Accountants (AICPA). Their website can be found at www.aicpa.org. The audit is for service organizations and is designed to ensure that the company has adequate controls and safeguards when they are hosting or processing data belonging to one of their customers. The Sarbanes–Oxley Act Section 404 relates to the process of reporting on the effectiveness of the internal controls over its financial reporting. A company that has a SAS 70 certificate has been audited by an external auditor and the control objectives and activities have been found to be acceptable per SAS 70 requirements.

Implementation

The life cycle of the contractual process does not end when the contract is signed, but has to be continually evaluated throughout the term of the agreement. This will obviously be less rigorous with a click-through agreement as opposed to a negotiated contract. However, even with a click-through agreement, the cloud supplier needs to be assessed to ensure that the contracted services are in fact being delivered. For instance, if the supplier is contracted to perform updates to an operating system, this needs to be checked to ensure that it is undertaken in the specified time and manner. Checks to ensure that all policies and procedures that have been contracted for are being followed is important, even though this may be difficult as the cloud provider and enterprise may be in different states or countries.

Throughout the length of the contract, the enterprise needs to re-evaluate its needs and the risks that will continually change. This may be due to the need or desire to deploy different applications or data in the cloud, or perhaps changes in laws and regulations that the enterprise has to abide by. Also, any external accreditation such as an SAS 70 certificate that the supplier has at the start of the contract needs to be checked to ensure that it is renewed or not revoked due to noncompliance.

Termination (End of Term or Abnormal)

The end of the contract, whether due to reaching full term or abnormal termination, needs to be considered carefully as this is the time when data is at most risk. Abnormal termination can occur due to a number of factors such as:

- Cloud provider ceasing activities
- Breach of contract by one party
- Bankruptcy

During this time, your efforts may be directed more towards sourcing a replacement vendor rather than spending time and effort with the current supplier. The data will still be on the supplier's systems and in their backups, which you may wish to be removed depending upon its confidentiality. Obviously, as the contract is terminated for whatever reason, the cloud supplier may be less than willing to assist in the cleaning up of your data. If you can define what you require in the event of termination in the original contract, you will have a good legal basis to ensure that data is removed and cleansed as required. As the cloud provider may be in a different jurisdiction to your enterprise and the data may be elsewhere, this may be an enhanced risk you will have to accept or ensure it is well defined in your contract.

Supplier Transfer

If you transfer services from one supplier to another, either at the termination of the contract or during the contract, you will have to consider the same factors as discussed in the section above. However, you will need to define a plan on how to transfer the data securely between vendors. Depending on the amount of data involved, you may just move it back to your organization and then upload it to the new supplier or you may look at transferring it directly between the two vendors. Whichever method you use, you will need to ensure that the data is secure for each of the transfers, perhaps using encryption for the data whilst it is in transit.

Data Privacy

As we intimated earlier in this chapter (Privacy and Confidentiality Concerns), the issue of data privacy is very much to the forefront of everybody's mind, with many television commercials advertising products and news programs describing another data breach. Any organization has a legal obligation to ensure that the privacy of their employees and clients is protected. Laws prohibit some of this data to be used for secondary purposes other than for what it was collected. You cannot surreptitiously collect data on say, the health of your employees, and then use this to charge smokers with higher insurance premiums. In addition, you cannot share this data with third parties. In the world of cloud computing, this becomes much harder as you now have a third party operating and managing your infrastructure, and hence by inference will have access to your data.

If your organization is collecting and storing data in the cloud and this is subject to the legal requirements of one or more regulations (for instance, HIPAA or GLBA), then you must ensure that the cloud provider protects the privacy of the data in the appropriate manner. In the same way as data collected within your organization, data collected in the cloud must only be used for the purpose that it was collected for. If the individual specified that the data collected be used for one purpose, then that must be upheld.

Often, privacy notices specify that individuals can have access to their data and to have this data deleted or modified. If this data is in a cloud provider's environment, privacy requirements still apply and the enterprise must ensure that this is allowed within a similar timeframe as if the data were held within a traditional IT implementation. If this can only be accomplished by personnel in the cloud provider's enterprise, you must be satisfied that they can undertake the task as you need.

If you have entered into a click-wrap contract, you will be constrained to what the cloud provider has set out in these terms. Even with a tailored contract, the cloud provider may try to limit the control over your data to ensure that all its clients have a unified approach, hence reducing their overhead and the need to have specialist staff on hand. If complete control over your data is a necessity, then you need to ensure upfront that this can be accomplished and not try to bend to the cloud provider's terms.

There are a number of cloud provider companies that specialize in distinct markets and tailor their services to those markets. This is likely to become more prevalent in the upcoming years and there will also likely be niche cloud providers. For instance, cloud providers that offer services in the health care marketplace would be bound by the relevant regulations for that market (HIPAA in this case)—and we would expect them to charge for the special handling and controls that are needed.

Data Location

Over a few short years, the Internet has become an essential tool for businesses of all sizes. Any business with a Web presence or individuals who post on social networking sites are recording data on one or more servers that could actually be located anywhere. Whether you are posting personal information to Facebook, or updating your business links on LinkedIn, this data will be stored somewhere. As businesses move towards the using and embracing of cloud providers, the location of the data will become more and more important due to data privacy, legal, or regulatory demands.

Global companies need to ensure that any services it deploys to the cloud are used according to laws and regulations that are in place for the employees, foreign subsidiaries, or third parties who need to use it. As we have stated previously, U.S. law will be markedly different from that in certain other countries, so even if it is your own employees who are using the service, you need to be aware of the laws that pertain to them in their location.

Subsidiaries in other countries may all have slightly differing laws that you have to account for, even if they are in the same general area. Also, some foreign subsidiaries may have no problems in sharing data with one country, but will not be able or willing to share it with another. Adding in a cloud provider will add another complexity to this. The primary location of the data and any backup locations will need to be known to ensure that all these laws and regulations can be adhered to. Often, it is the backup locations that need to be determined. Amazon, for instance, has large data centers in both the UnitedStates and Ireland, which could cause problems if they were used as backup centers for some types of data.

The data protection laws of the EU member states, as well as other countries, are extremely complex and have a number of definitive requirements. The transfer of personal data outside these countries needs to be handled in very specific ways. For instance, the EU requires that the collector of the data, or data controller, must inform individuals that the data will be sent and processed in a country outside of the EU. The data controller and end processor must also have contracts approved by the Data Protection Authority before this can be undertaken. This will have different levels of difficulty depending on the country that is processing the data. The United States and the EU have a reciprocal agreement and the U.S. recipient only has to self-certify its data procedures by registering with U.S. Department of Commerce.

Obviously, you would also need to ensure that any cloud providers you use outside if your jurisdiction have adequate security measures in place, including their primary and backup locations as well as any intermediate locations if data is being transferred between jurisdictions.

In putting your data onto a third party server, whether a cloud provider or otherwise, you are entrusting your data to them. You need to ensure that the security is adequate for your needs and meets all the regulatory and legal requirements. Provider controls and procedures must also comply with the local laws of the country where the server is located. Thus, if you have entered into an agreement with a company in the United States but they host the data on a server in the EU, then it is likely that you will have to abide by the laws of the EU if you want to transfer data into and out of the system.

These laws may be more onerous if the server is hosted in certain countries, such as China, where the local laws may allow the local government to have unlimited access to the data regardless of its sensitivity. You may even be limited (or prohibited) from encrypting the data without ensuring the local authorities can decrypt it when they require.

The cloud provider market is expanding, but there are still only a limited number of players who can offer large scale hosting of applications and data. This may lead companies that subcontract some or all of the hosting to another company, possibly in another country. Before entering into any agreement, you should be aware of any subcontracts that may be placed and then perform appropriate security checks on these as well.

> **NOTE**
>
> Even large companies can be known to subcontract services or use data centers not owned or operated by themselves. There are many examples of companies who market themselves as providing a service such as hosting their application for customers and then using a third-party data center to house and manage their servers.

Some cloud providers will inevitably go bankrupt or cease operating as a cloud provider and the access to your data could become an issue. Depending on where the server resides, this may cause you to go through another country's jurisdiction to get the data back and it may be subject to completely different access rules to what you are used to.

Secondary Use of Data

Depending on the type of cloud provider you contract to, you will have to consider if your data is going to be mined by the supplier or others. The use of your data may occur unbeknownst to you or by virtue of a configuration error on the provider's part. Based on the sensitivity of your data, you may wish to ensure that your contract prohibits or at least limits the access the cloud provider has to use this data. This may be especially hard when you enter into a click-wrap agreement—and as we all know, very few of us will read the fine print at all and just click the *I agree* box when it appears. In 2009, when Facebook (www.facebook.com) changed its terms around security of data, many people complained, but the majority of users carried on using the service because they found it useful. It is likely that your users will react in the same way, which may well give you security issues.

> **EPIC FAIL**
>
> On April 1, 2010 the online gaming store GameStation changed their online terms and conditions to read[6]:
>
> > By placing an order via this Web site on the first day of the fourth month of the year 2010 Anno Domini, you agree to grant Us a non transferable option to claim, for now and for ever more, your immortal soul. Should We wish to exercise this option, you agree to surrender your immortal soul, and any claim you may have on it, within 5 (five) working days of receiving written notification from gamesation.co.uk or one of its duly authorized minions.
>
> Apparently over 7,500 souls voluntarily agreed to this *immortal soul clause*. According to newslite, only 12 percent of purchasers noticed the clause.[7] This begs the question: Will you carefully read the terms and conditions and other click-through licenses that your cloud service provider presents?

The data you are storing in the cloud may be confidential or hold personal data which you want to ensure is secure. The cloud provider is likely to have full access to this data to maintain and manage the servers for you. You will need to ensure that this access is not abused in any way. Although a contract may protect you legally, you will also need to ensure you are confident that the security in place at the provider will detect any unauthorized access to your data.

Disaster Recovery

The importance of the issue of business continuity and disaster recovery needs to be stressed. In terms of disaster recovery, you need to consider some possible scenarios: a provider may go out of business or their data center may become inoperable. The main issues with the first scenario is getting your data back and relocating your cloud applications to another supplier. These should be thought out before deploying to the cloud and further protecting your interests by ensuring regular backups of your data. Some form of plan should be set out when you move to the cloud and that plan should be revisited on a regular basis as the market and circumstances may change quite rapidly.

There have been a number of instances where a data center has suffered a catastrophic outage, and consequently loss or disruption to many websites and businesses, such as:

- Fire in a data center in Green Bay, Wisconsin in 2009 with up to 10 days of outages for some hosted websites.
- Fisher Plaza (Seattle) outage in July 2009. Bing Travel being one of the affected sites.
- An explosion in *The Plant* data center in Houston in 2008 took nearly 9,000 customers offline, some for a few days.
- Rackspace had an outage in their Dallas center in 2009, which lasted just under an hour.
- In 2007, the 365 Main data center had outages, which affected Craigslist and Yelp among others.
- Google suffered a data center *rolling blackout* during February of 2009, causing the loss of mail service for many customers. This was due to software upgrade error.

Depending on your level of preparedness, any of these could be an inconvenience or a threat to your business. While smaller companies are more likely to be hit harder as they will have less expertise to call upon, an outage could seriously disrupt any business. As can be seen from the list above, it is not just physical issues due to power or cooling failures but also software errors that can take a data center down. Hackers have used denial of service attacks against Web sites which if located in the same data center, may also affect your site by virtue of bandwidth issues.

Breaches of Security

The security of your application may be breached, or your data compromised, while it is in the cloud. Initially, however, you have to be notified of the breach through the cloud provider's systems or other means (hopefully not by a customer complaining their identity has been stolen). You need to be clear about the disclosure policy of the cloud provider and understand how quickly they will disclose the breach to you. The majority of U.S. states have security breach disclosure laws in place that require the data owner to notify individuals if their personal data has been compromised in any way. These laws will therefore require you to ensure that you are informed promptly of any breach, preferably defined in the initial contract.

Alternatively, if you find that your data has been breached, you may need to inform the cloud provider of the breach in case this has implications for its other clients. You are likely to be sharing an environment with one or more enterprises, and depending on the breach, this may affect some of them. Having defined measures in place in the contract or an agreed incident response plan will ensure that both parties have defined actions that will help mitigate the consequences of the breach.

Litigation

Litigation may affect either the cloud service provider or client, where your data needs to be accessed or given to a government agency or a lawyer. You will need to be satisfied that if you are asked to deliver specific data, your cloud provider can access and deliver the necessary data to the depth required. As the data owner, you will be held responsible if you cannot deliver it. If you, as the cloud service client, are in litigation with a third party, you must know how your cloud provider will react to requests for data, and in what timeframe. There are a number of compliance regulations related to e-discovery that will need to be met and will apply to both the provider and client.

There may be occasions when a cloud provider is contacted directly to provide data to a third party, via a court order or subpoena. The cloud provider needs to be made aware of, preferably in the contract, what actions to take in this event. You may well want to contest the request due to the confidentiality of the data or due to the unreasonable request. You will therefore need to be assured that the cloud service provider informs you in a timely manner and before it complies with the request.

> ### TOOLS
>
> Several different groups have approached the issues of what should be covered by cloud customer rights. For instance, the Gartner Global IT Council for Cloud Services report *Rights and Responsibilities for Consumers of Cloud Computing Services* identifies the seven rights and responsibilities of cloud service consumers as[8]:
>
> 1. The right to retain ownership, use, and control of one's own data.
> 2. The right to service-level agreements that address liabilities, remediation, and business outcomes.
> 3. The right to notification and choice about changes that affect the service consumer's business processes.
> 4. The right to understand the technical limitations or requirements of the service up front.

5. The right to understand the legal requirements of jurisdictions in which the provider operates.
6. The right to know what security processes the provider follows.
7. The responsibility to understand and adhere to software license requirements.

Taking a different tack for a proposed cloud customer *bill of rights*, the Information Law Group lists the following[9]:

1. Data Location Transparency
2. Security Transparency
3. Subcontractor Transparency
4. Subcontractor Due Diligence and Contractual Obligations
5. Customer Data Ownership and Use Limited to Services
6. Response to Legal Process
7. Data Retention and Access, Incident Response
8. Indemnification and Limits of Liability

There is a great deal of overlap between these two approaches in the *fine print*, and these can serve as a model for cloud consumers to identify possible legal or data ownership concerns. But it is interesting that the Gartner list is worded more from a business-of-IT perspective, whereas the Information Law Group's list is more legally oriented.

SUMMARY

As systems, clouds are massively complex in terms of scale and orchestration of resources. But as we stated in Chapter 1 (section Cloud Scale, Patterns, and Operational Efficiency), massive scale, a disciplined appearance, and repeated patterns are three qualities of successful cloud implementations. The complexity of clouds is in part an illusion, as much of a cloud amounts to repeated patterns at massive scale, or in other words, multiplied simplification: The security benefits of this are significant. Likewise, security achieves additional operational advantages as all management is done using common functional units.

The resulting homogeneity contributes to simplified security testing and security assessment. It also makes for simplified auditing and monitoring, except that these functions now need to incorporate additional information sources if the monitoring in a highly dynamic cloud is to both correctly reflect the relationship between entities and if automated analysis is to be accurate and complete in its indications and warnings.

In contrast to traditional IT implementations, with cloud we have multitenancy combined with elasticity and abstraction away from physical infrastructure. The most significant consequence is that when we use a public cloud we can no longer have a sense of comfort that we know where our data and applications are located. Although this may raise concern, the fact is that with the cloud model, and even with our use of public clouds for nonsensitive data, we can actually achieve greater security and better IT management of our information resources at a lower overall cost. The cloud model also enables redundancy and disaster recovery.

We also discussed that an organization can improve security when it segregates public data from internal sensitive data. By removing associated external access or interactions, this reduces the potential for exposing internal sensitive data. Using a public or external cloud to segregate public from private data is but one strategy for achieving this, but with the rise of public clouds this strategy is easier to achieve.

In Chapter 2 we discussed the differences between the four deployment models, Figure 3.5 revisits that series of discussions in light of the legal and regulatory issues we discussed in this chapter, specifically that a consuming organization has greater control and responsibility when using a private or community cloud than with a public cloud—but the organization does not transfer all risk with a public cloud adoption.

Figure 3.6 depicts the other aspect of control with different service delivery models, namely the ownership over data and applications.

Laws can be complex and hard to interpret accurately, and this is no different when it comes to the laws that apply to the use of a cloud. This chapter has tried to give an overview of some of issues that you may encounter in this area but, as is commonly said, it is best to seek a lawyer if you need any specific legal advice.

The privacy of data is very important and breaches can lead to heavy fines and loss of confidence in your company. Most countries have laws governing privacy,

Cloud deployment

	Private	Community	Public
Compliance	Organization	Organization or community	Cloud provider
Governance	Organization	Organization or community	Cloud provider
Security	Organization	Organization or community	Cloud provider
Operations	Organization	Organization or community	Cloud provider
Risk	Organization	Shared	Shared
Cloud owner	Organization or "leased"	CMTY or "leased"	Cloud provider
Use limited to	Organization	Organization or community	Public

The consuming organization has greater control, and greater responsibility when using a Private or Community cloud, but the organization does not transfer all risk with a Public cloud.

FIGURE 3.5

Organizational responsibility in different deployment modes.

Service delivery by provider

	IaaS	PaaS	SaaS
Data	Organization	Organization	Organization
Applications	Organization	Shared	Service provider
Systems	Service provider	Service provider	Service provider
Storage	Service provider	Service provider	Service provider
Network	Service provider	Service provider	Service provider

Data: The consuming organization retains ownership of data for all service delivery models (IaaS, PaaS, and SaaS).

Applications: The consuming organization retains ownership of applications for IaaS, and to some extent for PaaS but not for SaaS.

FIGURE 3.6

Organizational ownership of data across different deployment modes.

and they vary. If you are undertaking business internationally or even across states, you need to be aware of the legislation that surrounds the data in all of the jurisdictions.

The last section of this chapter dealt with litigation, something you hopefully will not have to contend with. If you are unfortunate enough to need a lawyer, you need to know how the law will affect you in this area. As with other parts of this section, national, international, and state laws will need to be adhered to; due to the complexity of this area, it is likely you will need to call into service a lawyer who is knowledgeable in this area.

In the next chapter, we will address the cloud security from the standpoint of security architecture. In the remaining chapters, we will offer guidance for implementing cloud security. In addition, we will also develop an information security assurance framework that can be used to evaluate the security of public, hybrid, community, and private clouds.

Endnotes

1. Mann A. Five Steps on the Journey from Virtualization to Private Cloud, CA Community site. http://community.ca.com/blogs/automation/archive/2010/08/02/five-steps-on-the-journey-from-virtualization-to-private-cloud.aspx; 2010 [Adapted] [accessed 21.03.11].
2. Antonopoulos A. A risk analysis of large-scaled and dynamic virtual server environments, Nemertes Research. http://www.nemertes.com/issue_papers/virtualization_risk_analysis.
3. William "Bill" Meine, in private communication; 2010.
4. EU Directive 95/46/EC – The Data Protection Directive; 1995.

5. Brunette G, Mogull R. The Cloud Security Alliance, Security Guidance for Critical Areas of Focus in Cloud Computing V2.1, p. 35; 2009.
6. http://newslite.tv/2010/04/06/7500-shoppers-unknowingly-sold.html; 2010 [accessed 21.03.11].
7. Ibid.
8. Plummer D. Rights and Responsibilities for Consumers of Cloud Computing Services, Gartner Global IT Council for Cloud Services; 2010.
9. http://www.infolawgroup.com/2010/10/articles/cloud-computing-1/cloud-computing-customers-bill-of-rights/[Abstracted]; 2010 [accessed 21.03.11].

Securing the Cloud: Architecture

INFORMATION IN THIS CHAPTER

- Security Requirements for the Architecture
- Security Patterns and Architectural Elements
- Cloud Security Architecture
- Planning Key Strategies for Secure Operation

Chapter 2 presented the National Institute of Standards and Technology (NIST) definition of cloud computing as an Information Technology (IT) model for "enabling convenient, on-demand network access to a shared pool of configurable computing resources that can be rapidly provisioned and released with minimal management effort or service provider interaction."[1] But what does that translate to when you are building a cloud? At a high level: A data center (a.k.a. infrastructure life support), hardware (servers, storage, and networking), a broad set of enabling software, a staff with broad and deep experience, and process to make it work. Figure 4.1 depicts a high-level view of these components.

Operating a cloud securely and efficiently entails a great deal of advance planning. At a high level, we start with a data center and redundant Internet connections that connect to a cloud ingress. This ingress constitutes the technology portion of an information security boundary[A] that is comprised of some combination of network devices that serve to safely enable communication. NIST defines it as "the process of uniquely assigning information resources to an information system defines the security boundary for that system."[2]

Inside this boundary we have a massive amount of gear that is racked and cabled following defined patterns. There will also need to be some infrastructure that is used to manage the cloud and its resources as it operates. Going further, each component—server, storage, and network—requires some degree of configuration. This overall picture is one of numerous components that are organized in part according to visually evident patterns.

When designing or planning any complex system, it is important to look ahead and consider the processes and procedures that will be necessary for operation. Although it is possible to build a small cloud without much planning,

---

[A]A security boundary can be defined by a set of systems and components that come under a single administrative control.

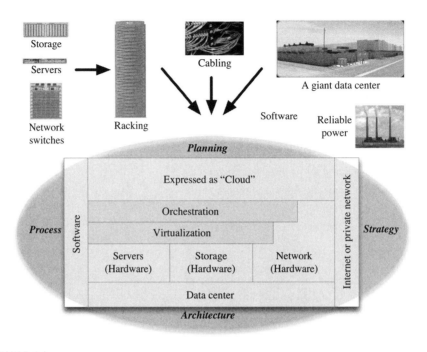

FIGURE 4.1

Cloud architecture and cloud implementation.

anything more substantial entails significant planning and design. Failing to plan appropriately will typically lead to higher ongoing costs due to inefficiencies in design and process and with operations that are not up to the time domain needs of managing a highly dynamic cloud. But what constitutes appropriate planning? Overplanning often entails misreading the future and doing so can result in significant rework and excessive cost. But failing to anticipate any change will result in a dead end and halted work. A better approach entails prudent architecture that accepts the need for inevitable evolution and reserves flexibility for such adaption as you face it.

Remember, in Chapter 1 (in the section Cloud is Driving Broad Changes), we introduced the notion that cloud offers advantages toward simplifying IT; in Chapter 2 (in the section Cloud Reference Architecture), we discussed the on-demand and self-service aspects of accessing cloud services. If cloud is to deliver on these promises, then the architecture must be designed and planned accordingly.

In this chapter, we will take a close look at the architectural components that can be used to build a cloud with an eye on security. We begin by identifying requirements for a secure cloud architecture along with key patterns and architectural elements. With that as a background, we will present and discuss several different cloud architectures. We will finish off the chapter with a brief discussion on key strategies for secure operation. Although this material is focused on work that will be undertaken by the CSP, tenants are often in the role of service providers for other users and hence this material will also apply to them.

SECURITY REQUIREMENTS FOR THE ARCHITECTURE

One goal for architecture is that it should be appropriate in meeting needs. This section surveys key architectural requirements for a typical cloud implementation. Several factors serve as the underlying motivation for requirements; these include:

- **Costs and Resources** The cloud provider's financial resources will act to constrain investment in technology, security controls included. But it is important to recognize that the absence of unlimited resources can be very motivating to how one designs, architects, and builds. For instance, if you know that your staff will be small, then this can force you toward process improvement and greater automation. Likewise, cost is also a motivation for the consumer of cloud services. The nature of these constraints tends toward the development of services with operating characteristics that are not ideal for all consumers.
- **Reliability** This is a quality that refers to the degree you can depend on a system to deliver its stated services. Reliability can be described as a guarantee that the underlying technology can provide delivery of services.
- **Performance** A measure of one or more qualities that have to do with the usefulness of a system. By example, common measures include responsiveness to input and the amount of throughput the system can handle.
- **The Security Triad** The essential security principles of confidentiality, integrity, and availability apply to most systems; the responsibility of a security architect is to match security controls with security requirements that sometimes must be derived from the need to assure the other three drivers (reliability, performance, and cost).
- **Legal and regulatory constraints** (we have covered these to some extent in Chapter 3) Legal and regulatory constraints can lead to the need for many additional requirements having to do with technical security controls, access policies, and retention of data among many others.

We begin with an unusual area of requirements for system security requirements: Physical security. But, by the time we are done you will see what motivates this.

Physical Security

Beginning with the facility that the cloud data center is hosted in, physical security is as important as any other security controls that seek to protect the security and operation of the cloud. Physical facilities are subjected to various threats, including natural hazards, human actions, and disaster. Building your cloud data center on a floodplain is as unwise as granting privileged access to all users.

The scope of issues in physical security is significant, and it involves a range of measures to avoid, prevent, detect, and respond to unauthorized access to the facility or to resources or information in the facility. Physical security for a facility should itself be viewed as a system for protection, with the individual security elements complementing each other in a multifaceted and layered defense. These elements will include aspects of environmental design, access control (including mechanical, electronical, and procedural), monitoring (including video, thermal, proximity along with environmental sensors), personnel identification and access controls, and intrusion detection in conjunction with response systems (lights, gates, and locking zones).

EPIC FAIL

In 2005, the author was involved in a substantial build of a public-facing grid computing data center. The site was in London in a former brewery (very thick walls) in a neighborhood that was at the edge of a wild bar and club scene.

On Monday mornings, the build team would arrive at the site being careful to avoid countless broken beer bottles at the entrance of the facility. The street entrance to the facility consisted of regular unreinforced glass that ran from floor to ceiling with an automatically locking glass door that operated very unreliably. Inside this space sat a regular office desk with an unarmed guard sitting behind it. The guard had two buttons to push, one unlocked the street door and the second button unlocked the door to the interior of the building. On the wall next to the guard was an unlocked cage key case; on the desk was a computer that was used to program the tenant's access cards to various floors, rooms, and cages in the building. The restrooms in the building were located to the rear, and each had a tilt-out window that an adult could easily climb through. A ladder tall enough to reach the second floor restroom window casually lay nearby.

The moral of this story is that this facility looked like it had physical security, but it was paper thin and ineffectively layered. On one occasion, the author's access card did not work for the correct zones and the guard was new to his role. After watching that the guard fails to navigate the process of using his computer console to grant correct access privileges, the author asked the guard if he might try driving the card security access software program. The answer was an astonishing *yes*...

The moral of this story was that because security control was undermined from the physical facility up, writing SLAs for tenants in this place was nearly impossible.

Physical security for a facility should be layered with each element integrated within an overall automated control and monitoring center. Planning for effective physical security entails deep consideration of circumstances that will be faced, these will include regular activities and unanticipated situations. Layered physical security elements must be supported by procedures that are appropriate and best implemented by a trained and professional staff. This physical security staff must be dedicated to the mission of protecting the assets and maintaining physical security procedures and processes even when a disaster unfolds. Given the scope and complexity of planning for physical security, a best practice is to engage experienced and recognized experts from the planning stage onward.

As stated in the introduction to this section, including physical security requirements in a section on requirements for security architecture may raise some eyebrows.

However, we live in a world where the boundaries between physical and virtual security are being increasingly blurred. There are obvious reasons why we should be concerned about the physical security of our cloud, but there are also virtual security reasons. As we will discuss later in the book (Chapter 6 in the section Security Monitoring), environmental sensors, physical security sensors, and camera imagery all represent information sources that can help resolve system security events and illuminate security situations that might otherwise raise alarm. In other words, security monitoring greatly benefits from such physical security sensor data.

Cloud Security Standards and Policies

Although some security requirements may be unique to the cloud implementation, it is important that requirements for cloud security should be consistent with appropriate standards, such as International Organization for Standardization (ISO) 27001 and ISO 27002—if one is to leverage a large body of practical experience, best practices, and review. Further, all aspects of security should be captured in a cloud security policy, which is best to develop as a formal document that has the complete approval and blessing of management. A security policy should be seen as the foundation from which all security requirements derive. Security policy should not detail technical or architectural approaches (as these may change more frequently than the policy) rather the policy should set forth the underlying requirements from an organizational or business standpoint. For instance, policy should explain the need for the use of standard-based encryption via use of a formally evaluated commercial product, rather than spelling out the use of Transport Layer Security, Secure Sockets Layer, or other specific means for communication security.

The security policy should also call for the development of several supporting documents, these should include:

- A set of guidelines for enabling security in development of infrastructure software, infrastructure management processes, and operational procedures.
- An acceptable use policy for each category of user, from internal operations, administrative, and other staff to tenants and end users. This policy should identify categories of use that are prohibited, why they are prohibited, and what the consequences for infractions are.
- A set of security standards for all aspects of the cloud, from development to operation. Security standards for a cloud should include:
    - **Access Controls** These should be at a granularity necessary to guide implementation of physical access to facilities and logical access to systems and applications.
    - **Incident Response and Management** This shall detail all roles and responsibilities of various parties along with procedures and timelines from detection through postmortem reporting.
    - **System and Network Configuration Backups** It is important to have a current and authoritative copy of all configurations including infrastructure components, servers, and switches as well as for all hosted systems.

- **Security Testing** The cloud provider must perform and document the results of initial and periodic security testing. This standard should include roles and responsibilities as well as detailing when third-party testing or reviews should be performed.
- **Data and Communications Encryption** This standard should detail functional areas (such as web server traffic), the approved cryptographic algorithms and the required key lengths.
- **Password Standards** This standard should detail the qualities that acceptable passwords must comply with (notably length and composition) and how the cloud provider will test compliance.
- **Continuous Monitoring** This standard should detail how configuration management and change control are performed to support ongoing security of the baseline as it evolves and is updated.

There are several other areas under the control of the cloud provider that benefit from the development of formal standards. Some of these include Termination of inactive sessions; Definition of roles and responsibilities for cloud personnel; Rotation of duties and vacation schedules; Magnetic and electronic media handling, including assured destruction procedures for media that can no longer be erased; Off-premises removal or use of equipment; The timely removal of user privileges; and Disaster recovery and continuity of operations.

Cloud Security Requirements

The security architecture of the cloud should be consistent with the intent of the security policy. Thus, the first security requirement is to develop a security policy for the cloud. An appropriate second requirement is the development of placeholders for each of the documents and standards listed in the previous section. At some point, a separate set of activities will revolve around identifying granular requirements that are preliminary in developing the cloud security architecture. Representative security requirements that are likely to apply to your cloud architecture are listed in the remainder of this section.

Cloud-wide Time Service

Since the correct operation of systems and authoritative system logs depend on the correct time, all systems must be synchronized to the same time source. Typically, this will be achieved by use of Network Time Protocol (NTP), which is one of the oldest Internet Protocols (IPs) that is still in use. Correct and synchronized time becomes especially important when you have communicating computers that reside in different locations, but which need to have their record and event time-stamps synchronized to a single source. Once clocks drift between network devices and/or computers, a cloud infrastructure is subjected to all manner of errors and made difficult to diagnose failures.

In overview, correct time information comes from authoritative national time standards via multiple paths, including radio, cellular, satellite, and hard-wired transmissions to primary time servers. From these it is distributed via NTP subnets to literally millions of secondary servers and from there to end-clients. NTP provides Coordinated Universal Time (UTC), all time zone or daylight saving time information must be provided separately.

WARNING

Physical cloud infrastructure should include accurate, reliable, and verifiable time sources, such as WWV and GPS. The time system should be based on at least two reliable time source paths and devices for resilient and secure operation. All computers and network devices must obtain their time information for correct synchronization and reliable cloud operations. Best practices for managing NTP are the following:

- Configure clients to reference at least two time servers to provide redundant time.
- Accurate time synchronization depends on how frequently clients update their time from time servers.
- Limit input network or radio broadcast signals to authoritative and *legal* ones.

Identity Management

Identity is a key element in the security of an operating cloud. This information must be correct and available to cloud components that have a validated need for access. Requirements include as follows:

- Controls must be implemented to protect the confidentiality, integrity, and availability of identity information.
- Implement an identity management system that will support the needs for authenticating cloud personnel.
- Implement an identity management system that will support the larger scale needs for authenticating cloud tenants and users.
- Consider using a federated identity system to allow for identity portability for the user population and to present a single mechanism for internal access as well as tenant and user access. A federated identity management system will allow for interoperability with customer and third-party identity providers or realms as may be appropriate.
- Verify identities of users at registration time in accordance with policy and legal requirements.
- Assure that when identities are deprovisioned, historical information for users is maintained to allow for future legal investigations.
- Assure that when user identities are deprovisioned and identities are recycled, access by a new user is not granted to a previous users data, contexts, or other private information resources. This amounts to assure that at the appropriate level in the identity system, user identities are never actually reused thus preventing future conflicts or confusion.
- Implement the means for customers to verify assertions of identity by cloud provider personnel.

Access Management

Access controls use identity information to enable and constrain access to an operating cloud and its supporting infrastructure. Requirements include as follows:

- Cloud personnel shall have restricted access to customer data in general. Cloud personnel may require access to a hypervisor on a customer-allocated machine or to storage devices that host customer VMs or customer data, but such access shall be tightly constrained and limited to specific operations that are well defined by the security policy and SLAs. Implement need-to-know procedures for cloud personnel to prevent unnecessary opportunity for access to customer data.
- Implement multifactor authentication for highly privileged operations. Apply additional security controls for highly privileged operations. Assure that authorization mechanisms for cloud management are constrained and do not allow for cloud-wide access.
- Do not allow the use of accounts that are shared (such as administrator), instead use *sudo* or the equivalent to gain auditable privilege and only allow such access for users who are members of the appropriate role.
- Implement the least privilege principal (LPP) when assigning permissions. Implement role-based access controls (RBAC) to appropriately constrain access by authorized users on the basis of their role.
- Implement whitelisted source IP addresses for all remote control or remote access by operations personnel. Where whitelisted IPs are not feasible, require access to proceed through additional mechanisms, such as hardened jump hosts or gateways.

TIP

Under unusual circumstances, it may become necessary for the cloud provider to gain emergency access to certain cloud control functions or to tenant VMs. In anticipation of this sort of circumstance, you should consider the use of alarmed *break glass* strategy. With break glass (the name derives from breaking the glass to pull a fire alarm), security controls that are always in place can be bypassed in the event of an emergency.

A break glass procedure must be clearly defined and well understood, it should be well documented and tested. Such a strategy can be based on prestaged emergency-only privileged accounts that should only be used under specifically defined circumstances.

However, the consequences of doing so must be severe if the circumstances are found to not warrant having done so. Part of the procedure should include formal reporting on the circumstances that lead to the need to invoke break glass. These procedures should also include steps to cleanup after such emergency accounts or procedures are used.

Key Management Requirements

In a cloud, encryption is a primary means to protect data at rest (storage) and between storage and processing phases. Requirements for key management include as follows:

- Ensure that appropriate controls are in place to limit access to keying material that the cloud provider maintains control over.
- Ensure that root level and signing keys are managed appropriately.

- For multiple site cloud infrastructure, ensure that key revocation is performed without side effects or undue delay.
- Ensure that procedures are effective for recovering from compromised keys.
- Protect and encrypt all customer data and VM images at all appropriate phases of their life cycle.

System and Network Auditing

System and network security event logs are a keystone for managing the ongoing security of any system. In a cloud, audit events will be generated in fundamentally different trust zones; these range from highly secured network and security components to systems where the CSP grants significant control to tenants or users. Thus, security events should be recognized as having different degrees of integrity. The following are key requirements for the generation and management of audit events:

- Auditing is required for all operational systems, from infrastructure system and network components up to but not necessarily including customer VMs. Tenant confidentiality agreements along with service contracts may set the boundary for what data can be collected within a tenant VM, and in many cases tenant virtual networks.
- All security-relevant events must be recorded with all relevant information that is necessary to analyze the event; this shall include the correct time, resolvable system, and user IDs and appropriate event codes and supporting information.
- Generated audit events must be logged in a near-real-time manner. The correct operation of auditing and logging shall be verified on an ongoing basis using means such as heartbeat or call-and-respond.
- All audit events and logs shall be continually and centrally collected to ensure their integrity and to support timely alerting and monitoring.
- All audit events and logs shall be retained and securely archived for at least as long as the security policy requires, preferably indefinitely to support retroactive long-term analysis to either support legal action or to improve security and security monitoring.
- As necessary to support the validated legal or operational needs of tenants or customers, audit records will be sanitized to allow sharing with tenants and customers—either as a part of a security service or as needed.
- Controls must be implemented to protect the confidentiality, integrity, and availability of audit events, audit log collection, log centralization, archiving, processing, and reporting.

Security Monitoring

Security monitoring is predicated on audit logs, network security monitoring (using traffic inspection such as snort, and so on), and environmental data (see section Physical Security, above). Requirements for security monitoring include as follows:

- Security monitoring shall be a highly available and hardened service that is accessible internally or remotely in a secure manner.
- Security monitoring shall include.

- The generation of alerts based on automated recognition that a critical security event or situation has taken place or is detected.
- The delivery of critical alerts via various means in order that security and management are made aware in a timely manner.
- The means for security personnel to investigate and prosecute an unfolding incident or simply to review logs to improve alerting mechanisms or to manually identify security incidents.
- Implement a cloud-wide intrusion and anomaly detection capability and consider expressing this as a service for tenants or users (see Figure 4.2 for an overview of security event management and how it relates to security monitoring).
- Consider functionality to allow customers to implement intrusion/anomaly detection for platform-as-a-service (PaaS) or infrastructure-as-a-service (IaaS) and further to allow them to send appropriate event sets or alerts to the cloud provider's security monitoring system. (This is discussed further in the Security Monitoring section in Chapter 6.)
- Ensure that security monitoring is implemented to be reliable and correct even under circumstances of failure in the pathway of event generation and collection through reporting. Security logs must be retained in a manner that is compliant with law, applicable regulation, and the security policy.

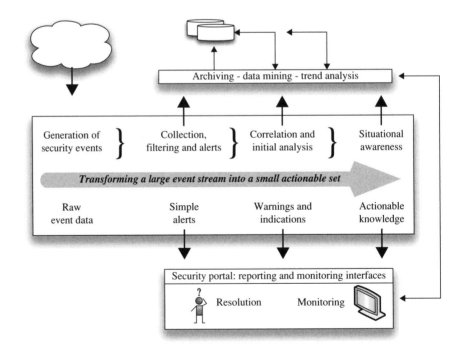

FIGURE 4.2

Overview of security event management and its role in monitoring.

Incident Management

Ensure that incident management and response will be inline with SLAs and the security policy:

- Ensure that incidents can reliably be managed and their impact contained. There must be a formal process in place to detect, identify, assess, and respond to incidents. This should be detailed in a standard or formal process, and it must be tested on a periodic basis.
- Ensure that incident management includes clear and reliable means for customers and tenants to report situations or events to the provider.
- The incident management process should include periodic reviews and reporting.

Security Testing and Vulnerability Remediation

Security testing shall be performed for all software before approval is granted for production. It is important to implement a vulnerability and penetration testing capability for near continual operation. To be most effective, this capability should be coordinated with monitoring and configuration management changes to prevent false alarms and incident response. Specific requirements include the following:

- Separate environments shall be used for development, testing, staging, and production of all cloud provider software and systems, including the fielding of patches into production.
- Patch management procedures must be defined for all infrastructure components, servers, storage, virtualization software, applications, and security components. Although the term patching typically refers to *live systems*, this dangerous practice can largely be avoided in cloud because of the faster allocation and provisioning mechanisms that are necessary to begin with.
- Define an integrated strategy for vulnerability remediation or compensating controls that can be used for a range of circumstances from responding to immediate or eminent threats, to less critical patching to improve the security or reliable operation of the cloud. Some vulnerabilities will come from vendor software and will require either vendor patches, a vendor-identified work around or in-house development of compensating controls. Other vulnerabilities can be introduced by the cloud provider through custom software, insecure design elements that result in security flaws or controls that are simply misconfigured. Figure 4.3 represents an example process that can be implemented to fix provider realm security flaws.

System and Network Controls

These should be implemented for infrastructure systems, systems that host customer data and applications and all networking gear. This should include all physical and virtualized components or services. Specific requirements include as follows:

- Ensure proper isolation, configuration, and security for security components.
- Implement network isolation between different functional areas in the cloud infrastructure, begin by implementing completely separate networks—including

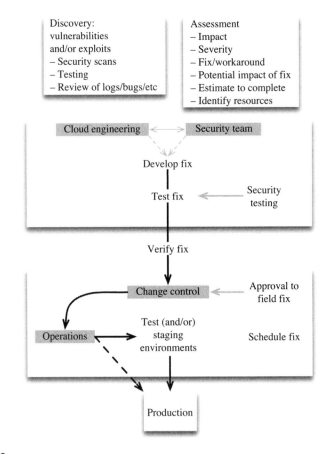

FIGURE 4.3

Security patch/fix process.

use of physical separation and network virtualization—for public accessible components (VM hosts or storage interfaces in a public cloud), infrastructure management components, and security and network administration. Reinforce this by use of other network controls and by use of software firewalls on machines.

- Hardware platform access separation from operating system (OS) (or VM) access to prevent a user with management access to the hardware from gaining access to the VM or publically accessible side. Access from the reverse (VM to platform) should also be prevented.
- These same controls should also serve to reinforce the isolation between executing VMs belonging to different customers.
- Appropriate controls will be implemented to assure the integrity of OSes, VM images, infrastructure applications, network configurations, and all customer platform software and data.

- The cloud provider shall implement the means to vet software and system upgrade releases before placing any into production. Code vulnerability checking shall be used along with malicious code scanners and other means.

TOOLS

Among several common uses, whitelisting is used in networking to identify trusted IP source addresses and in systems to identify permitted applications. As used in networking, constraining source IP addresses to those that are on a whitelist, you can effectively shun all nontrusted traffic from any other IP addresses. In a similar manner, one can constrain the allowed set of applications that can be run by use of a whitelisting product. When a whitelisted application is run by a user, the system checks the list and verifies its execution. Applications can be listed with their characteristics, including size, location, and so on, and all others will be explicitly denied. Examples of companies that are operating in this space include CoreTrace (www.coretrace.com/) with their Bouncer product and Bit9 (www.bit9.com/) with their Parity product.

The downside of using a whitelisting product is that you have to ensure that all the applications that you are going to execute on that system are authorized in the whitelisting product, and you will have to update that list whenever you upgrade any applications. (Note that such information can also be maintained by a CMDB and subsequently verified by a script or application.)

The use of whitelisting products has increased over the last couple of years and should be considered as a potential tool to be used when you deploy a cloud infrastructure, especially if you wish to minimize the number of upgrades you have to perform on an ongoing basis.

Configuration Information

With a highly dynamic cloud infrastructure and VM provisioning/deprovisioning, it is critical that one maintain a current list of all cloud assets to include hardware, systems, software, configurations, allocations, and any cloud asset that is managed or monitored in operation. Requirements for this include as follows:

- A best practice is to use a CMDB, which we will discuss further in this chapter in the section The Importance of a CMDB.
- Classify all assets and cloud components in terms of their function, sensitivity, criticality, and other characteristics that have a material impact on managing their security or understanding the security impact if they fail or are compromised.

General Infrastructure Security Requirements

In addition to the other cloud security requirements discussed in this section, there are numerous more general requirements for infrastructure security; these include as follows:

- Seek to leverage vendor and community best practices, which are the distillation of experience. If a best practice isn't applicable, we can still gain benefit from that knowledge as well.
- VMs should be hardened and minimized by default.

- Open ports should be the minimum needed for initial provisioning and allocation to a customer. When an operational process requires a port to be opened, it should be done only as needed and only for as long as needed.
- Implement the means to assure continuity of operations inline with service level agreements. Periodically verify that the recovery point objective (RPO) and recovery time objective (RTO) are reliably met.
- Ensure that network connectivity is maintained by use of multiple pathways to the cloud services. Ensure the use of diverse and redundant physical and logical network connectivity. Verify that redundant connectivity does not resolve to the same physical or logical backbone or service that is simply rebranded by a second provider. Ensure to the extent possible that physical links which enter the facility (and from there to the cloud infrastructure) are not subjected to a single point of failure under some catastrophic event.
- Ensure that the facility has ample power recovery capabilities and that power is distributed to the infrastructure in a manner that allows for redundant key infrastructure in the event that power is lost to some part of the facility. In other words, there should be ample power for the cloud provider to maintain some core capability either in support of remote continuity of operations or in support over maintaining security of the facility until it is restored to fully operational status.
- Ensure that deprovisioned internal cloud IP addresses, such as one previously assigned to a tenant for a VM, are sufficiently aged before being recycled for use by another user to prevent access by the new user to the previous user's resources.
- Expect continued innovation and changes in cloud computing and underlying technologies, and plan to modify, adapt, or extend infrastructure in ways that you may not be able to fully anticipate in advance.

SECURITY PATTERNS AND ARCHITECTURAL ELEMENTS

This section examines several patterns and elements that support or contribute to cloud security. Investing effort to develop such patterns will pay dividends during the build process, during operations and will often contribute to better security.

Defense In-depth

The term *Defense in-depth* in computer and network security was first documented in a 1996 paper *Information Warfare and Dynamic Information Defense*,[3] and was adopted from military operations. This approach has been used for system and network security under a number of names, including *layered defense*. Essentially, this is a strategy that accounts for the fact that individual security controls are typically incomplete or otherwise not sufficient, and that multiple reinforcing mechanisms or controls will compose a more complete and robust security solution. Such reinforcing controls can be similar and redundant, but can also be implemented or layered at different levels throughout the implementation. When using a series of layers consisting of even the same type of mechanism, residual risk can be significantly reduced.

From an architectural standpoint, it is wise to design for mutually reinforcing controls to increase assurance. By example, defense in-depth for access control mechanisms might first require the use of a virtual private network (VPN) (defense layer 1) for remote administrative access. Second, a VPN connection attempt may be shunned by the ingress router for any non-whitelisted source IP (defense layer 2). In this manner, only traffic for a single port (or service) is allowed to connect to an internal VPN termination point and only if the source address is whitelisted—thus, the amount of random Internet *door knocking* is greatly reduced at the edge of the infrastructure, reducing all manner of associated consequences compared to otherwise passing such traffic deeper into the network before it is identified as undesired. As a third level, the use of access control for remote administrative users could require use of a dynamically changing code that is generated by a device owned by the remote administrator. Such security tokens are used to offer greater assurance in verifying the identity of an administrative user (defense layer 3).

NOTE

The concept of defense in-depth has been around for thousands of years and was applied to castles long before it was applied to computer systems. Castles built throughout Europe during the Medieval period are a classic example of a defense in-depth. These were typically surrounded by a moat, which is a large trench usually filled with water. The castle was accessed by one of two entrances that provided a drawbridge over this moat. Attackers would find it difficult to cross the moat other than via the drawbridges as wading or swimming through water is not easy and makes anyone undertaking it a clear target for the defenders. The drawbridges could be raised or lowered acting as a double barrier. When they were raised, they covered the entrance door blocking the attackers from coming in and removing the passage way across the moat.

The entrance to the castle was usually through a small enclosed area, which was often further protected by a portcullis—a latticed gate made of metal or wood—which could be lowered down from above to block the entrance. Any attacker, should they get past the drawbridge, would have another defense to get through. The defenders would usually have additional defenses in this entrance way to further delay the attackers—often times holes where hot or burning oil or water could be poured onto the attackers or small slits in the floor where arrows could be fired down from.

Although all this was occurring, the defenders would be behind the walls of the castle, which were thick and built to withstand the attackers. These walls had numerous slits in them known as murder holes, which allowed the defenders to fire arrows at the attackers while being relatively safe. Castle walls were also built high so allowing defenders to rain arrows down.

The design of the castles had a twofold result—the castle was difficult to penetrate and could be defended by a small force. A similar principal applies when you design and implement a cloud.

Honeypots

A honey pot is a well-known and sophisticated network decoy technique. In an enterprise network, the goal of a honeypot is to create a false or nonproduction system that appears enticing for an attacker to target. After the attacker is lured to that target, the honeypot is used to observe, distract, and potentially alarm on the attacker's network penetration. In any event, the objective is that if the attacker is wasting time in the honeypot, they aren't in your production systems.

The same technique can apply to cloud computing. It can be used in network zones that are controlled by the CSP, and it can be used by tenants within zones that they control. A honeypot virtual machine can be deployed and then used to monitor and report on any attempt to access it, which would generally indicate *exploratory* snooping at the least. Honeypots could also be used by the CSP in a CSP honeypot VM for each hardware server. In this scenario, if there is a hypervisor level threat, then there is a good chance that changes are going to be made on the honeypot VM. This can serve as a form of intrusion detection at the hypervisor.

Sandboxes

Sandboxing, at the software layer, by its very definition uses a form of virtualization or abstraction between the software or code being executed from the OS in which it is running. As a result, it's very similar to hypervisor-based virtualization, running one layer up between the OS and the hardware, instead of between the OS and the application.

One of the goals of the defense in-depth model is to add layers of security. Without a doubt, a sandboxed environment adds such a layer of security between the applications running within a guest virtual machine and the hypervisor.

Network Patterns

Cloud infrastructure deviates from traditional IT infrastructure at many levels, including networking. Public clouds face several challenges in terms of ensuring sufficient network isolation between tenants, especially when VMs that are assigned to different tenants are colocated on a physical server.

Isolation of VMs

Switching infrastructure in the cloud can't isolate traffic between VMs that reside on a single hardware platform because this traffic is limited to a shared physical machine and does not enter the cloud network. Without use of encryption for this traffic, VMs could observe traffic that belongs to an adjacent VM—but the ability to do this will be a function of how the hypervisor implements networking. The use of encryption for VM network traffic can result in effective network isolation between adjacent VMs. The overall security in this case heavily depends on the security controls of each VM and on the isolation between VMs that the hypervisor affords. Thus, the security architecture patterns here are as follows:

- Select VM technology that affords network isolation between adjacent VMs.
- Encrypt communication traffic into VMs.

- Harden and tighten the security controls on VMs, especially ports and associated services.
- Filter traffic to a VM by using a software firewall or similar mechanisms to shun traffic that is not whitelisted.

Isolation of Subnets

There are other network patterns that can be followed for cloud architecture. By segregating the network into physically separate networks, you can improve isolation between public-accessed subnets and infrastructure control subnets (as depicted in Figure 4.4). Network isolation can be achieved to a point by use of network virtualization, but this is subjected to vulnerabilities and misconfiguration. Physical separation is also prone to error, but process controls can be used to minimize the probability.

Isolation really should be physically separate for administrative and operational traffic, for security and network operations traffic, for storage networks, and for public accessible components (user and tenant access to SaaS, PaaS, and IaaS). But such isolation is only effective if traffic is not routed between these separate networks. Thus, network isolation should be reinforced by additional layers of security. Firewalls are a traditional means of achieving this, and when used in conjunction with network controls, a firewall can act as an additional reinforcing layer; this is especially useful when multiple subnets would benefit from a common service, such as directory. It should be pointed out that having multiple networks to support isolation may drive up infrastructure costs, which is a point of tension between security and overall cloud costs.

Impact of Isolation Strategies on Network Device Selection

There are several cost aspects associated with multiple networks or a higher port count, the most notable ones are the cost to implement and the operational costs

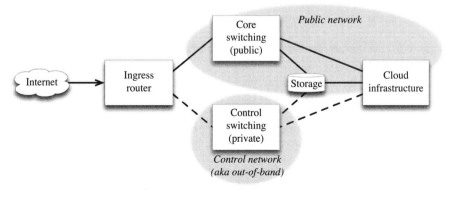

FIGURE 4.4

Basic network isolation of control and public traffic.

to manage them. Port count can be reduced through aggregation strategies, but there are trade-offs as well. For the purpose of this book, this discussion around networks and ports really comes down to several qualities that go to the security of the infrastructure.

As background, a typical rack has 42 rack units (RU), servers will require one or several RUs. Each server needs at least one Ethernet (or fiber, Infiniband, so on) port for communications. One of those ports will be for *public* traffic, and another one will likely be dedicated to directly access the hardware platform itself (power on, hardware health, so on). Servers can be extended with additional network cards to support a variety of networking strategies.

There are many possible approaches to create a networked infrastructure, but one of the points of decision is the use of in-rack switches to consolidate the traffic within a single rack of servers. In general, there are several aspects to this. First, the introduction of additional hardware introduces a potential point for failure. Although the consequence of a single switch failing may be limited to the connectivity of a single rack, there are other factors to consider. Often, in-rack switches are cabled in a left-and-right dual path manner for redundancy (by interconnecting adjacent racks). Given the number of racks that may be required to implement a cloud, this switch and traffic arrangement may experience traffic problems and even more frequent failure than the use of a centralized core switching arrangement would. Consider also the fact that since individual servers will likely have at least one public data port and one hardware platform port, the number of in-rack switches can exceed one.[B] In experience, such a networked infrastructure is not as resilient as you might expect. The number of switches is huge, and this switch sprawl must be managed at the physical and logical level. This drives up operational costs and lowers overall reliability, and it probably will result in occasional switch misconfiguration.

On the other hand, the use of a single core switch for a large number of racks will have very serious consequences if the switch fails to an extent that eclipses the consequences of a single in-rack switch failure. In this regard, consider that carrier-grade core switches are significantly more reliable than the aggregate reliability of a higher number of in-rack switches. Factoring in the cost of acquisition along with the impact of replacing switches upon failure, a core switch may be far more effective than numerous in-rack switches. Carrier-grade switches typically also have failure modes that affect fewer ports at once than in-rack aggregation switches do. Given the higher reliability of a carrier-grade core switch, the ongoing operational and reliability benefits probably outweigh the apparent benefits of a network of switches.

[B]A typical 1RU switch will have 48 data ports. The typical rack will have 42 RU for servers, assuming 46 1RU servers requiring a minimum 46 public data ports on a switch. These servers will also require 46 platform ports somewhere, but since the traffic across those ports is relatively low and the need for reliable links may be less stringent than compared to the public data ports—you might get away with daisy chaining the server platform ports in order to limit the need for the same number of in-rack switches to service platform ports.

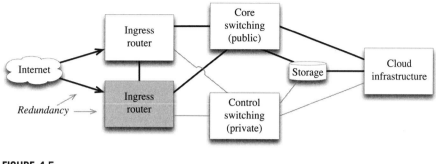

FIGURE 4.5

Redundancy to improve reliability and availability.

Availability and Redundancy

Another network pattern is the use of redundant components, load balancing, and multiple links between critical components to improve reliability and availability. Figure 4.5 depicts the use of redundant Internet drops along with redundant ingress devices. Depending on the need for availability, this pattern can be repeated but at the expense of cost, increased complexity, and higher operational overhead. For instance, a third ingress can be added for greater reliability, but given the use of carrier-grade equipment, the cost benefit is unlikely to warrant it.

The Use of Patterns

A different and more cost-effective approach would be to architect the infrastructure in repeating patterns, whereby the amount of infrastructure drives the need for the addition of another ingress—and the increased bandwidth that comes from it. At that point, the architecture resembles a series of similar blocks where each additional block expands the amount of processing and storage for the cloud. This is depicted in Figure 4.6; but by adding additional blocks of cloud computing infrastructure, we also have the opportunity to leverage identical components to improve the overall reliability of connectivity. It should be noted that the core and control switching infrastructure in both Figures 4.3 and 4.4 could be made redundant for greater reliability as well, but that topic is reserved for later in this chapter when we examine a few example architectures in greater detail.

The Importance of a CMDB

A CMDB is an information repository for managing the components of an IT system. The term comes from ITIL, where it is used to refer to the authorized configuration of components of the IT environment. CMDB implementations can include data from additional sources, such as asset management records.

A CMDB records configuration items (CIs) along with their attributes and relationships. CIs generally store information about the CI and its relationships to other CIs.

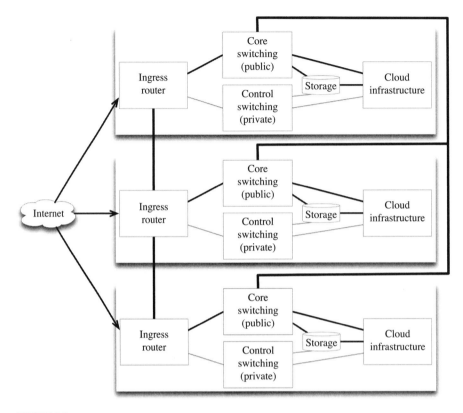

FIGURE 4.6

Regular patterns contribute to reliability and availability.

A CMDB can be used to create and manage an accurate and complete representation of the IT environment it records information about. In that regard, it is critical that the CMDB be maintained if it is to accurately reflect all infrastructure changes.

A CMDB offers tremendous advantages to the operation of a cloud. If cloud management software operates the cloud based in part on information in the CMDB, and if it updates the CMDB with relevant information as it operates the cloud—then automation is enabled to an unprecedented level for functions far beyond provisioning and deprovisioning VMs. One such area is security. The CMDB maintains contextual information about the environment that security systems are reporting on and monitoring.

To date, little work has been done in coordinating security management and monitoring in conjunction with a CMDB, but this area holds great promise for cloud security. In such a pattern, the CMDB—as an accurate model of the system state/configuration—needs to operate closer to real time than how CMDB products are generally used today. For such a cloud use case, the CMDB *reflects* the configuration of the cloud and must be tightly integrated with all the processes that change the state. Verification of the correctness of the state data can indicate process errors or malicious activity. Either case would need to generate alerts to begin resolving the cause of the differences.

The common CMDB activity of discovery would also need to be expanded to continuously verify that the CMDB has a complete and correct perspective of the IT environment. CI attributes would need to be extended as well to support security management and monitoring.

As described above, a CMDB would become a critical component for security and because of the synergy between the operational security realm and the CMDB, security monitoring could transition from alerting and reporting on the detection of security events, issues, and incidents and respond to many common situations with intelligent and contextually valid feedback mechanisms.

Cabling Patterns

Often overlooked in small system builds and many server closets, cabling patterns contribute to a faster and more reliable implementation of infrastructure. The use of the equivalent cable port for the equivalent network connectivity on each machine in a pattern may seem a trivial example, but it is worthwhile to consider the effect that this has on daily operation and during incident response. Likewise, the development of cable color standards does not only make the implementation appear more organized but also reinforces separation of networks when data center personnel perform emergency repairs at 03:00 A.M. when only *Red Bull*, *Monster*, or *Dracula* rule in peak performance.

This becomes far more critical when infrastructure is scaled. A well-designed data center will have a data cable plan that almost explains itself visually. This will reduce common errors, and it will make eventual hardware changes and upgrades faster and more reliable. Following regular cabling patterns also enables periodic physical security audits of infrastructure components. But trivial systems such as color coding will not go far enough to solve real operational problems.

The same holds true for power cables. Many modern data center servers, especially cloud friendly blade servers will have multiple power supplies and multiple power cords. Furthermore, the typical data center will deliver power to racks from at least two separate circuits; thus, it would defeat the purpose to plug both power cords for a dual supply server into the same power circuit. This level of redundancy is intended not only to overcome server power supply failure but also to overcome circuit failure.

Finally, it would be a significant improvement for even a well-designed power and data cable plan if both ends of all cables came with unique factory encodings that are both visually unique and that can be scanned by a hand-held reader. As a cable is assigned to a port or power port, the cable is scanned and the association is uploaded and recorded in the CMDB. Any subsequent inquiry or replacement can either be manually verified by checking both ends of a cable or by CMDB lookup. This use of tags on cables has tremendous benefit to both drive down operational costs and decrease errors that are associated with not being certain where the other end of a given cable terminates.

Resilience and Grace

As true for traditional implementations as it is for cloud computing and cloud services, failure should be expected. The question is How will it be handled? Individual compute resources can exhibit poor performance or failure. If the application is a critical one, then your application logic and strategy must take performance and failure risk into consideration. For cloud architecture, it is important that resource elasticity is gracefully managed for not only adding or shedding a resource but also for when a resource behaves badly or fails. How a system or component fails or responds to failure is becoming an increasingly important area as increasingly more systems are directly involved in operating devices whose failure could have serious and life-threatening consequences. Already today, many mobile apps and mission critical applications are being driven by cloud computing-based services. Where business success depends on an application, it does not matter so much where that application is powered, what matters is that is reliable and that failures are met with appropriately.

The term resilience has to do with the ability to maintain and continue to provide an acceptable level of service when a system is subjected to faults and deviations from normal operation. In this, the cloud model offers great benefit. Individual components can fail with little lasting impact. In fact, components such as disk drives, faulty memory, or even malfunctioning servers can fail and be remotely powered off. These devices can be automatically removed from the pool of available resources and left in a deactivated state until enough failed components warrant sending a cloud engineer to fix or replace them. By its repeated patterns and its scale, a cloud is a very resilient and dependable infrastructure and more fault-tolerant than traditional IT infrastructure. The ease of removing a failed resource from the pool is to the provider's benefit, whereas rapidly allocating and provisioning a new resource for the tenant is their benefit. Also, it is usually trivial for a tenant to have better control of an application architecture that is more resilient to component failures using cloud service offerings (because the virtual data center configuration is easier to specify and control).

Failing in place is a strategy that only works when you have enough resources to allow for it and only when individual resources are not critical to the operation of the cloud. Clearly, there is a difference between a large and expensive ingress router failing compared to one cloud resource such as a server failing.

Another important aspect to resilience has to do with where key infrastructure components are racked. From the standpoint of surviving a power outage or surviving critical equipment fire or water damage, it simply does not make sense to colocate your key redundant components in the same or adjacent racks.

By example, if your security requirements entail the use of multiple syslog or security event archives, a better strategy would be to separate them rather than rack them one above the other!

There are other important aspects to reliability (or in security terms *availability*), but a serious discussion of this topic area is beyond the scope of this book.

Planning for Change

As mentioned earlier in this chapter (General Infrastructure Security Requirements), cloud computing is still a young and evolving field with changes certain to both the models and the underlying technology components. Planning on the future need for change can drive how you design and implement key infrastructure components and how you organize infrastructure. Patterns that you can define should include reserving RUs in infrastructure management or security racks to allow for future expansion if there is any question that your cloud will change its mission in a manner that would require additional support.

Change can also come in the form of dramatic changes to the physical network that implements the cloud. How cable runs to individual systems are initially implemented can make it very difficult to upgrade server or storage hardware that has a greater port density than the current cable runs support. Changing the physical cables in a cable run from a core switch to individual servers can be extraordinarily difficult and at minimum risky from a disruption standpoint. One approach to minimize this is to run Ethernet from core and out-of-band (OOB) switches to terminate in patch panels above server racks and from there run patch cables to server ports. A very good strategy is to consider replacing six Ethernet cable runs from a central switch to an above rack patch panel with a single MRJ21 cable, thereby simplifying the cable plan for the network.

An important plan-for-change strategy is simply to use a Lean/Agile style of planning thought. This is more of a just-in-time way of handling growth and change. No part of the work should be done overly far in advance because it makes too much of a commitment for all the dependent equipment, cabling, networks, and power. Keeping a tight rein on incremental completion with a minimum number of advancing edges allows the next new thing to be as different as needed without ripping up (refactoring) as much of the existing work.

CLOUD SECURITY ARCHITECTURE

The first part of this chapter identified requirements for security and patterns to architect cloud security. Taking that material and composing some of those elements into representative security architectures is our goal for this section.

To some, the security of a cloud computing architecture can be summarized in one phrase: Everything in a cloud is *at scale*. Cloud providers deploy massive amounts of infrastructure to capture economies at scale, tenants and users adopt that infrastructure at scale, and some believe that the threats that occur at the cloud level are threats that may be realized at scale and by everyone in the cloud.

The cloud security space is still evolving, as is the technology used to implement clouds. It appears that the technology that powers the cloud is progressing at a rate that is faster than the technology used to secure clouds. In part, this goes far beyond any particular vendor or software and reflects on the state of systems and security in general.

TIP

Quoted from NIST 800-53[4]:
   Building more secure information systems is a multifaceted undertaking that requires

- Well-defined security requirements and security specifications;
- Well-designed and well-built information technology products;
- Sound systems/security engineering principles and practices to effectively integrate information technology products into information systems;
- State-of-the-art techniques and methods for IT product/information system assessment; and
- Comprehensive system security planning and life cycle management.

Nevertheless, the advantages of clouds are real and as such their security must be addressed. In part, the security of clouds can benefit a great deal from taking a closer look at the relative maturity of cloud computing along with some supporting work done by the Jericho Forum.

Cloud Maturity and How It Relates to Security

In the information security space, in general, the maturity of a particular technology, algorithm, piece of code, or even a process, procedure, or framework can relate, at least in part, to how secure it actually is. Stated simply is the *test of time* tried and true?

One excellent example of this principle in action is the field of cryptology. For a new algorithm to be considered *cryptographically strong*, the maturity of the algorithm is a very important contributing factor. How long an algorithm has been in the field and vetted against attacks inherently contributes to how much value it actually can provide. 3DES is a widely used encryption cipher which is an application of the Data Encryption Standard (DES) cipher algorithm, which was originally developed in the early 1970s. DES was selected as the official Federal Information Processing Standard for the United States in 1976 for governmental usage after a long vetting period. However, through its maturity, weaknesses were discovered and 3DES evolved out of addressing those weaknesses. As a result, it can be said that 3DES has had nearly four decades of testing and evolution.

Another example of this principle in action can be made in the field of software maturity. The more mature a particular piece of software is can also contribute to how secure it actually is. Open source software benefits from this principle immensely. The more widely adopted a particular project is the more peer review it receives. Because open source code is inherently public, peers can scrutinize security very quickly. Threats can be identified, tested, and then corrected in the form of patches. The group as a whole might be able to contribute these patches directly as well. This iterative process inherently makes the project more secure. Therefore, it can be generally said that the longer the project has been around and benefited from this process the better its level of security. The project, after all, through the iterative process it's more secure than when it first started. One caveat to this line of reasoning—the discovery of vulnerabilities can take decades to surface! But, the principle of maturity benefiting security is true—just don't expect each flaw and vulnerability to be vetted by the passage of time.

The same principle that applies to vetting source code for flaws and vulnerabilities also applies to architectures and processes. In the physical world, we benefit from decades of experience with house and commercial building practices. The amount of learning that has been gained from building experts examining the root causes of house fires, structural failures and human injury have collectively lead to the development and continual refinement of building and electric codes.

In the world of software and systems, we also have our *building codes*, but they are not as evolved. ISO 27001, 27002, COBIT, and numerous other compliance efforts are oriented toward making systems more reliable, more secure. Best practices for coding, for building systems, also exist. Nonetheless, large IT systems still fail for reasons that never seem to be so unique. A kind way of putting some failures is to say that the benefits they produced are greatly exceeded by the costs to implement them. Enterprise systems are especially interesting in this regard due to the potential for business crippling costs of failure. At this stage, what might work best to manage the risk of IT failures like these is to adopt an encompassing enterprise risk framework coupled with clear business objectives and a plan to address contingencies. Coupling the architectural approaches of cloud computing as a target for IT, and pursuing this with a unified and coherent plan for the entirety of the business need, and executed in a continual learning process as you build in an agile manner may produce quick results that either work or that can be refined to work more quickly than waiting for the entire waterfall to run dry.

Jericho Forum

It is worth exploring another perspective on security that is articulated by the Jericho Forum (www.opengroup.org/jericho/). This is an Open Group consortium of IT security officers that has been in existence since 2004, originally from a loose affiliation of corporate CISOs in the United Kingdom. One of the issues that Jericho Forum has articulated is deperimeterization. In their view, the corporate perimeter has eroded over the last several years due to various factors. Although the traditional model for corporate network presented the perimeter firewall at the dividing line between the inside (presumed safe) and the outside (presumed dangerous), this boundary has steadily been eroded or bypassed:

- Using a new Internet-based service exposes, a machine located inside a network to be exposed to the service on the Internet.
- Accessing an internal corporate service from outside the network requires passing that traffic through the firewall and terminating it at the service point.
- The internal-trusted environment is continually under assault from mobile computing devices (such as smart phones and laptops) that have been subverted or introduce malware into the corporate network.
- Business servers located external to the company network (that is, in a cloud).

Although organizations in the past have been worried about external threats, the erosion of the perimeter has turned the threats into internal ones. In the view of the Jericho Forum, it is necessary to identify those components that are vital or critical to the operation and ensure that those are adequately secured, whether that is from an external or an internal threat. In a fully deperimeterized environment, every component will have adequate security measures installed on it to ensure that confidentiality, integrity, and availability are assured.

Representative Commercial Cloud Architectures

Although the concept of a cloud has been around for decades in reality, cloud computing in the forms, we know today, are relatively new. For example, below are the dates at which the various types of public and private clouds, SaaS, PaaS, IaaS providers, and technologies associated with them have been in existence!

- **Amazon Web Services (Public Cloud, IaaS)**
  Arguably one of the most mature clouds, launched in July 2002 not really with an IaaS offering, more just pieces of it. It's EC2, or Elastic Compute Cloud, which is classified as an IaaS offering launched officially (non-beta) in October 2008. Many new components of this cloud are still being launched today—see *Amazon VPC*.
- **Amazon Virtual Private Cloud or VPC (Hybrid Cloud Technology)**
  Marries, an Amazon public cloud with an enterprise's private cloud, is still in beta at the time of publishing in 2010.
- **Rackspace Cloud Hosting (Public Cloud, IaaS)**
  Launched publicly in February 2008.
- **GoGrid (Public Cloud, IaaS)**
  Launched in April 2008.
- **Salesforce.com (Public Cloud, SaaS, and PaaS)**
  Although the company was launched March 1999, Salesforce's PaaS, Force.com was launched in January 2008.
- **Google Apps Engine (Public Cloud, PaaS)**
  Its first public beta was launched in April 2008. GovCloud, Google's form of Google Apps that addresses and meets government security mandates was only launched in September 2009.

- **VMware (Private Cloud Technology Provider)**
  Although the company was officially founded in 1998, VMware Server didn't exist publicly until 2001.
- **Microsoft Hyper-V (Private Cloud Technology Provider)**
  Virtualization technology created by Microsoft and deployed in Windows Server 2008, officially launched in June, 2008.

It would be fair to summarize that most modern cloud computing architectures, in their form as they exist today, are generally around 3 years old. This is a far cry from the maturation of modern architectures or common security standards.

NOTE

It's interesting to note that Amazon's *cloud* wasn't even launched originally as a cloud in their official press release[5]:

> *SEATTLE, Jul 16, 2002—Today Amazon.com (Nasdaq: AMZN) launched its first version of "Amazon.com Web Services," a platform for creating innovative Web solutions and services designed specifically for developers and web site owners.*

Representative Cloud Security Architectures

To this point in this chapter we have reviewed cloud security requirements, examined common patterns in cloud computing infrastructure, and reviewed numerous aspects of IT and architecture that relate to security. Next, we will compose some of this into a few examples of cloud security architecture.

Example 1: IaaS, Identity as a Service and DBMS as a Service

Figure 4.7 depicts a public cloud that offers several distinct services:

- Hosted DBMS
- Hosted Identity
- PaaS

Starting at the bottom of Figure 4.7, we see two distinct entry points into the cloud infrastructure. The first, on the left, is referred to as *Access to Control Network*, also referred to as the OOB network. Access to this network must be tightly limited to a subset of the cloud operations and management team. Access via the OOB access router may be limited to coming from whitelisted IP source addresses or from secured jump hosts that are outside the security perimeter. In other words, the OOB routers may simply shun (or drop) all connection attempts that are not from IP addresses that are known to be associated with legitimate operations personnel. In addition, such access must be authenticated for identity, which in the case of administrative level, operations and security personnel really needs to be fairly robust. Two-factor authentication (token card, plus pin) is necessary for several reasons that together increase the assurance that authentication is secure. This is our first in-practice example of defense-in-depth.

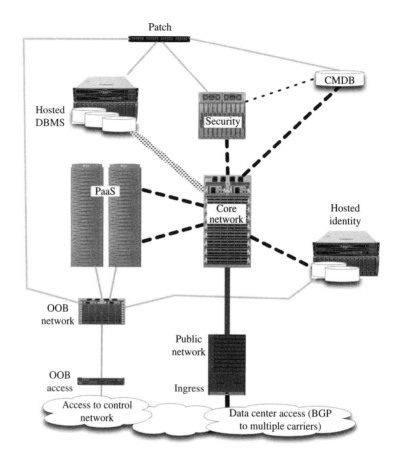

FIGURE 4.7

A hypothetical public DBMS, PaaS, and identity as a service.

The second entry into the cloud infrastructure is the ingress, which is composed of two (redundant) industrial-grade routers. This implements the entrance to the public side of the cloud infrastructure.

Figure 4.7 also depicts three primary internal networks:

- **OOB** This network offers access to the management side of the cloud infrastructure and is physically separated from the core network.
- **Core** This network is the one that all user traffic transects.
- Also shown is a network link between the DMBS and the core switch, but this (as for any link) can be implemented as an aggregated set of links for bandwidth and reliability.

Figure 4.7 also depicts the hosted DBMS which would be expressed as a service of some sort, depending on the CSP APIs. End users operating from within a remote enterprise might access this service remotely or locally via leased services in the PaaS that is depicted below the DMBS.

Likewise, a hosted identity service is depicted, which would be accessed remotely or locally via leased services in the PaaS. Also depicted are a CMDB and security services, which were previously discussed and which we will go into greater detail with the next example.

Example 2: A Storage and Compute-rich Cloud for IaaS

The second security architecture diagram we will look at is Figure 4.8, which depicts a fairly complex implementation of a hypothetical public cloud. This infrastructure has a generous amount of storage and computing resources, and it enjoys a very beefy network hardware suite for public ingress, management entry, and internal switching. It follows several patterns for high availability, and it has a dedicated pair of security stacks.

Network Entry

As in the previous architecture (Figure 4.7), in second architecture (Figure 4.8), we see two distinct entry points into the cloud infrastructure: An OOB and a public access point. In Figure 4.8, we have a redundant pair of OOB access routers

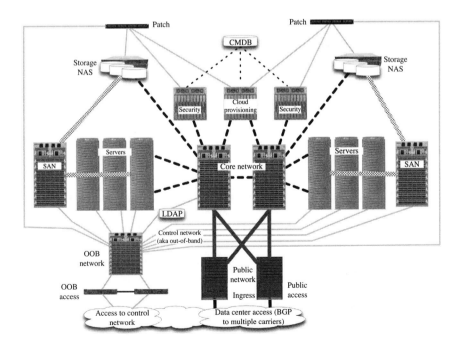

FIGURE 4.8

A hypothetical public cloud architecture.

(with sophisticated firewall capabilities). And, similar to the first architecture diagram earlier (Figure 4.7), the second entry into the cloud infrastructure is the ingress, which in this case is composed of two (redundant) industrial-grade routers. These will typically have several layers of security functionality in them, including traffic inspection, black listing capabilities, and so on. (Figure 4.8 also shows two patch panels that serve the purpose of simplifying the depiction of the OOB connectivity in the drawing.)

Where the public cloud entry is likely to be a pair of substantial and expensive carrier-grade network routers, the OOB access devices will not need to be as substantial due to several reasons. First, they can be configured to shun most traffic. Second, they will only allow a tightly constrained set of protocols (SSH for instance). Third, the amount of traffic and concurrent sessions will be very light compared to the public network. It is certainly possible to use the ingress routers to serve as the network entry for OOB traffic, as long as that traffic is immediately routed to a separate network.

Also, the OOB access won't be the primary method used to access and manage the infrastructure components. It provides the mechanisms to remotely bootstrap and initially configure some of the components, and it serves as the last-ditch mechanism to deal with disasters. Most of the normal operation and configuration of the infrastructure is done within normally secured partitions of the core network.

Separate Networks

The remainder of Figure 4.8 depicts three separate networks: The OOB, the public network, and a storage area network (SAN). As in Figure 4.7, the OOB offers access to the management side of the cloud infrastructure and is completely separated from the other two networks. However, things can be a bit more complicated. Depending on need, the OOB entry point may afford access to additional networks for administrative purposes, but this will be a function of your specific needs and your security approach as specified in your security policy. One approach is to have the management servers live on the OOB, and thereby mixing management traffic with platform service traffic. Clearly, separate networks are better from a security perspective, but they incur a cost in terms of entailing extra steps by operations when cloud personnel manage the infrastructure.

Switches

Figure 4.8 depicts three switches, two in the center serve as the core network and one on the left as the OOB network. The core switches are most efficient and minimize switch sprawl when core switches direct connect to each device, typically via Gb or faster Ethernet. Switch port density will, thus, be a critical component as to determine how many servers can be switched by a single switch. Extending this number can be achieved by various means, but doing so by repeating the pattern of n servers per core switch is very effective in practice. This drives toward a number of efficiencies, including minimizing switch configuration and management overhead. Large switches do not tend to fail at the chassis level as frequently as they do at the interface card level (a subset of the overall ports on the entire switch). In fact, large switches tend to fail less frequently than do smaller switches. So, this pair of characteristics lends itself to lights-out-operation in a large cloud. Passive backplanes in these large switches make the individual line cards fail independently (assuming redundant power). The line cards are often built as parallel chunks of switching circuitry with few shared components and where each chunk handles only a handful of ports. The failures seen in practice generally affect only one port or a small group of ports, whereas the rest of the switch continues to run unaffected.

The OOB switch is generally going to be a smaller capacity device where port aggregation via smaller switches or daisy chaining OOB service ports on platforms is a completely viable strategy given a number of factors including the lesser amount of traffic and the nature of that traffic (delays are far more tolerable than with the core network).

The OOB switch gives access to operations to control the platforms and the network devices in the infrastructure by connecting to the component management ports, service processors, and consoles. Not depicted, are several other networks that can further isolate specific traffic, such as security management or network management, from the remainder of the environment. The key is that these would not route among themselves.

Compute Servers and Storage

Figure 4.8 also depicts a pair of SAN switches along with a pair of SANs. By keeping the storage traffic OOB from the public or core data network, we can improve performance and gain advantages for security as well. Note that the computing servers and SAN are connected to three networks in a manner that does not bridge or route across these. In contrast, integrating SAN functionality into the core network can drastically reduce network costs but requires more careful handling of the storage service security and potential performance conflicts.

Also evident in Figure 4.8 are the core servers, which together with storage are largely the point of the cloud. There are numerous strategies for servers, from the standpoint for high end gear that offers performance and an upgrade path; blade servers seem to have great appeal. A point of some discussion will likely be the presence of internal disk drives on servers, but it and other hardware topics are best left for other books as the technology changes quite quickly and the trade-offs are complex. However, from the cost of ongoing operations and eventual hardware refresh, it makes sense to consider the pros and cons of different server strategies before building your *Cloud 1.0*; least you discover, your operational costs are significantly higher than those of others and you have no easy path out. Of all the infrastructure components, it is likely that your servers and storage will warrant more complete upgrades faster than other components.

CMDB and Cloud Control/Provisioning

As stated earlier in this chapter, The Importance of a CMDB, as an information repository, is critical for managing the components of an IT system. A CMDB stores key information not only for the operation of the cloud but also for managing security of the cloud.

Provisioning and cloud control software is a rapidly evolving set of capabilities that will likely continue to evolve and drive supporting changes into the very OSes and VM frameworks that are used in cloud infrastructure. It is likely that these changes will bring greater integration of security across these various levels from hardware via service consumption.

Security Servers

Figure 4.8 depicts a pair of blade chassis that are fully loaded with blades dedicated to security. The range of activities performed by these security devices will be broad and critical to the health and continued operation of the cloud. From auditing, monitoring, expressing a virtual security operations center (SOC), and security scanning, the need for computing power and bandwidth are as important as the reliability of these functions.

Chapter 6 will cover cloud security monitoring in great depth, but by way of introduction, Figure 4.9 depicts the various typical security functions that a cloud security stack might have.

Note that the security stack has a dedicated security network and that individual security functions are expressed as a combination of dedicated physical blades (syslog archive) and virtual machines. The list of functions includes:

- **Jumphost & VPN** This is a security team-only set of mechanisms, to gain access to the security network. A security engineer would enter the cloud via the core or OOB routers, which would direct the connection to the security jumphost or VPN, depending on source address.
- **Virtual SOC** This would be a series of user interfaces to monitor consoles and other security consoles for scanning, reporting, and analysis. Since the cloud is probably being operated in a lights out and largely remote manner, these security interfaces should be accessible in that manner as well. Some information may be expressed via a broader consumption dashboard that could depict outages or ongoing incidents to allow collaboration between security and other teams.
- **Collection & Analysis** This is a broad set of capabilities that starts with the collection of syslog and other security information from computing SAN and other systems and is routed via the core and OOB networks to the syslog archive. From there it is relayed to the analysis, alerting, and IDS components.
- **Directed Network Monitoring** There are further forms of monitoring that in part involve inspection of network traffic and in part involve the periodic vulnerability scanning of systems in the environment.

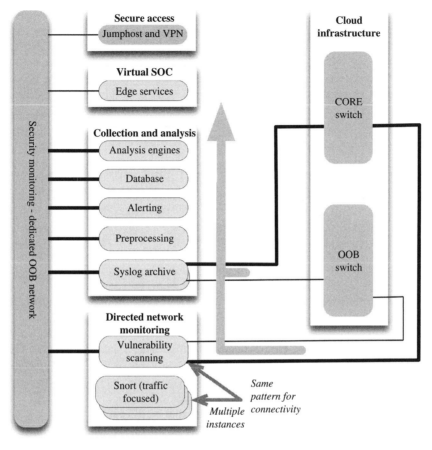

FIGURE 4.9

Overview of cloud security monitoring architecture.

PLANNING KEY STRATEGIES FOR SECURE OPERATION

The process of architecting a cloud can benefit from planning for the activities of operating the cloud. Understanding eventual operational processes and constraints can lead to better architecture and to a cloud that is more effectively operated and more secure. This section explores several areas that can offer key strategies that will pay off later in the cloud life cycle.

Classifying Data and Systems

Knowing what you have and having a formal structure for it is a great advantage when planning for how to protect it. To begin, one can identify categories of information that can be processed with lesser security concern and fewer controls than other kinds of data. That sort of information classification would lend itself to a public cloud, to hybrid cloud processing, or to a community cloud.

Various types of data bring with them the need for higher security concern, regulatory handling requirements, and even national security level processing requirements (you know who you are). National security information, be it Federal, military, or intelligence data will generally fall under the following hierarchical classification levels: Unclassified, Sensitive But Unclassified, Confidential, Secret, and Top Secret. These levels are hierarchical in terms of entailing increasing levels of security and additional handling requirements. Users are vetted before they can obtain a clearance to access data at a given classification level, and then access is generally granted on a need-to-know basis. Additional subcategories of classification can be as sedimented within a classification level and entail the need to maintain separation even from users who are cleared at the same, say Top Secret level but who have not been read into the category in question. The national security information classification scheme is very mature and quite effective in managing control over and access to classified information. However, it also tends toward overclassifying information based on the consequences of data exposure.

In the commercial world, different categories generally apply, but these tend not to be hierarchical.

If data falls under the need for PCI or other regulatory requirements, then it could still be processed in a public cloud, but the cloud provider would need to be compliant with the regulatory requirements…It is most likely that as time progresses, more cloud providers will architect for higher security and will invest in the compliance testing necessary to support managing and processing data for customers whose regulatory compliance needs could not formerly be met by the public cloud model. In a sense, the solution is more of a community cloud than a public cloud.

Define Valid Roles for Cloud Personnel and Customers

This section discusses two broad kinds of *roles*. Some define authorization classes for operational segregation, whereas the other roles define authority for policy, design, and standards. There will be several roles for internally infrastructure-focused personnel, system-focused personnel, security-focused personnel, management-focused personnel, externally service consumer-focused personnel as well as end user roles. Understanding these various roles is critical for policy, operations, and developing an effective and well-run cloud. The following list is derived from the Open Security Architecture 6, and serves as an example for such roles[6]:

- **End Users** Will require security awareness training and *access agreements*. To support users, need: Access management, access enforcement, user identification and authentication, device identification and authorization, cryptographic keys …
- **Architect** Information flow enforcement, acquisitions, information system documentation …

- **Business Manager** Responsible for risk assessment, risk assessment updates, allocation of resources ...
- **IT Manager** Access control policies and procedures, supervision and review of access controls, security awareness and training policy, among many similar functions.
- **Other** Other roles include Independent Auditors, Developers, Security Administrators, Server Administartors, and Network Administrators.

SUMMARY

In this chapter, we presented a number of security requirements for cloud computing architecture. We took those requirements and for several times, we identified security patterns and architectural elements that make for better security. We then looked at a few representative cloud security architectures and discussed several important aspects of those. We ended by examining several key strategies that if considered during design can present considerable operational benefits.

In the next chapter, we will examine the broad topic of data security in the cloud. As we will see, sensitive data and control data should be encrypted for confidentiality. Network traffic to and from access points in the cloud should be encrypted for confidentiality, integrity, and ongoing availability (protection against compromise). Information and data encryption should be used for data at rest to protect confidentiality and integrity. Whether encryption of data is performed at the granularity data elements, files, directories, or volumes can be complicated by many factors including performance and functionality.

Endnotes

1. Mell P, Grance T. The NIST Definition of Cloud Computing Version 15; 2009, National Institute of Standards and Technology, Information Technology Laboratory.
2. Swanson M, Hash J, Bowen P. NIST Special Publication 800-18 "Guide for Developing Security Plans for Federal Information Systems," US Department of Commerce; 2006.
3. Winkler J, O'Shea C, Stokrp M. Information Warfare and Dynamic Information Defense, 1996, Proceedings: 1996 Command and Control Symposium, Naval Postgraduate School, Monterey CA.
4. Ross R, et al. NIST Special Publication 800-53 Revision 2, Recommended Security Controls for Federal Information Systems, Computer Security Division Information, Technology Laboratory, National Institute of Standards and Technology Gaithersburg, MD 20899-8930; 2007.
5. Amazon Web Services. http://findarticles.com/p/articles/mi_m0EIN/is_2002_July_16/ai_89075779/ [accessed 22.03.11].
6. Open Security Architecture, http://www.opensecurityarchitecture.org/ [accessed 22.03.11].

Securing the Cloud: Data Security

INFORMATION IN THIS CHAPTER

- Overview of Data Security in Cloud Computing
- Data Encryption: Applications and Limits
- Cloud Data Security: Sensitive Data Categorization
- Cloud Data Storage
- Cloud Lock-in (the Roach Motel Syndrome)

This chapter examines data security in cloud computing along with data protection methods and approaches. Cloud data security involves far more than simply data encryption. As stated in Chapter 4 (Securing the Cloud: Architecture), requirements for data security vary depending on the three service models (SaaS, PaaS, and IaaS), the four deployment models (private through public), as well as on your tolerance for risk (see Chapter 3, Security Concerns, Risk Issues, and Legal Aspects). Meeting the requirements for cloud data security entails applying existing security techniques and following sound security practices. To be effective, cloud data security depends on more than simply applying appropriate countermeasures. Taken collectively, countermeasures must comprise a resilient mosaic that protects data at rest as well as data in motion.

While the use of encryption is a key component for cloud security, even the most robust encryption is pointless if the keys are exposed or if encryption endpoints are insecure. Customer or tenant control over these endpoints will vary depending on the service model and the deployment model.

OVERVIEW OF DATA SECURITY IN CLOUD COMPUTING

It is understandable that prospective cloud adopters would have security concerns around storing and processing sensitive data in a public or hybrid or even in a community cloud. Compared to a private data center, these concerns usually center on two areas:

- Decreased control by the owning organization when data is no longer managed within an organization's premises

- Concern by the owning organization that multitenancy clouds inherently pose risks to sensitive data

In both cases, the potential risk of data exposure is real but not fundamentally new. This is not to say that cloud computing does not bring unique challenges to data security.

Control over Data and Public Cloud Economics

In contrast to use of a public cloud, maintaining organizational physical control over stored data or data as it traverses internal networks and is processed by on-premises computers does offer potential advantages for security. But the fact is that while many organizations may enforce strict on-premises-only data policies, few organizations actually follow through and implement the broad controls and the disciplined practices that are necessary to achieve full and effective control. So, additional risks may be present when data doesn't physically exist within the confines of an organization's controlled facility—this is not necessarily the security issue that it may appear to be. To begin, achieving the potential advantages with on-premises data requires that your security strategy and implementation deliver on the promise of better security.

The basic problem is that most organizations are neither qualified to be in the information security business nor are they in that business—they are simply using computers and networks to get their work done! Although secure computing is a desired quality, information security expertise is not a core-competency for most computer users nor is it common in most organizations. Returning to the point:

- Moving data off premises does not necessarily pose new risks, and it may in fact improve your security.
- Entrusting your data to an external custodian may result in better security and may well be more cost effective.

Two examples that underscore this are the commercial service offerings to either store highly sensitive data for disaster recovery or assure the destruction of magnetic media. In both cases, many highly paranoid organizations tightly control how they use these services—but the point is that they use external services, and when they do so, they entrust their data to external custodians.

It is important to state that some kinds of data are simply too sensitive and that the consequence of data exposure is too great for some customers to seriously consider using a public cloud for processing. This applies to any information category that entails national security information or information that is subject to regulatory controls, which cannot yet be met by public target cloud offerings. Likewise, it is unlikely that a well-governed organization would release highly sensitive future product plans to any environment where the organization would be uncertain that the information custodian (the CSP) did not enforce the information-owning organization's interests as well as the organization itself would.

> **TIP**
>
> Regardless of whether you are backing up data for a cloud or in a cloud, you should at a minimum retain two copies of a backup. At least one of those copies should be located where it is not subject to destruction at the same time that your other copy is located. At minimum, keep it in another room, or better yet store it off-site.
>
> By example, when backing up a personal computer, a best practice is to have two physically separate backup devices to which you alternate backups to. Affix a label to these two devices, for instance: *Laptop Backup A* and *Laptop Backup B*. Over time, as you make each backup, scratch out the previous date on that label and write the current date on it. In this manner, you will always have two backups, one older than the other.
>
> Backup can take several forms, most simply explained you can either perform a full backup of a file system or source disk, you can backup selected directories, or you can restrict your backups to only those files that changed since the last backup. The utility of these varies according to your needs and the time you have to perform a backup. A full disk backup takes longest, but such a backup can also be made to allow booting from it. A full disk backup will simplify recovery from a catastrophic disk failure, whereas a backup of selected directories will both take the least amount of time to create and offer rapid access to a backup for an inadvertently deleted file.
>
> But even a backup can fail when you need it the most, so an even better practice would be to use a cloud-based backup service in addition to your on-site backups. The cost and ease of using such cloud services makes their use very practical if you have reliable network connectivity. Many of these services support encryption of your data before it is sent to the cloud backup service, greatly reducing concern over using such a facility for any but your most sensitive personal information.

In these examples, it is not the case that security needs for these categories can't be met in a public cloud, rather the cost of providing such security assurance is incompatible with the cost model of a public cloud. If a CSP is to meet these needs that would demand additional controls, procedures, and practices that would make the cloud offering noncompetitive for most users. Consequently, where such data security needs prevail, other delivery models (community or private cloud) may be more appropriate. This is depicted in Figure 5.1. Note that this situation is a function of generally available and anticipated offerings in the public cloud space. Quite likely, this will change as security becomes more of a competitive discriminator in cloud computing. One can easily imagine future high-assurance public clouds that charge more for their service than lower-assurance public clouds do today. We might also expect that some higher-assurance clouds would limit access by selective screening of customers based on entry requirements or regulation. Limiting access to such a cloud would reduce risk—not eliminate it—by limiting access if screening is effective.

Organizational Responsibility: Ownership and Custodianship

While an organization has responsibility for ensuring that their data is properly protected as discussed above, it is often the case that when data resides within premises, appropriate data assurance is not practiced or even understood as a set

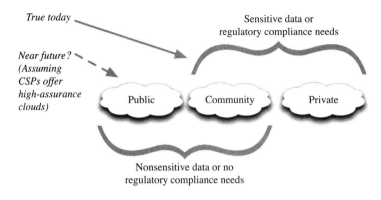

FIGURE 5.1

Meeting security needs: public, community, and private clouds.

of actionable requirements. When data is stored with a CSP, the CSP assumes at least partial responsibility (PaaS) if not full responsibility (SaaS) in the role of data custodian. But even with divided responsibilities for data ownership and data custodianship, the data owner does not give up the need for diligence for ensuring that data is properly protected by the custodian.

By the nature of the service offerings, and as depicted in Figure 5.2, a data owning organization can benefit from their CSP having control and responsibility for customer data in the SaaS model. The data owning organization is progressively responsible beginning with PaaS and expanding with IaaS. But appropriate data assurance can entail significant security competence for the owning organization.

Ultimately, risks to data security in clouds are presented to two states of data: data that is at rest (or stored in the cloud) and data that is in motion (or moving into or out of the cloud). Once again, the security triad (confidentiality, integrity, and availability) along with risk tolerance drives the nature of data protection mechanisms, procedures, and processes. The key issue is the exposure that data is subject to in these states.

Data at Rest

Data at rest refers to any data in computer storage, including files on an employee's computer, corporate files on a server, or copies of these files on off-site tape backup. Protecting data at rest in a cloud is not radically different than protecting it outside a cloud. Generally speaking, the same principles apply. As discussed in the previous section, there is the potential for added risk as the data owning enterprise does not physically control the data. But as also noted in that discussion, the trick to achieving actual security advantage with on-premises data is following through with effective security.

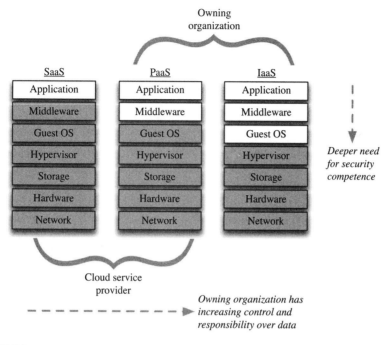

FIGURE 5.2

Owning organization has increasing control and responsibility over data.

Referring back to Figure 5.1, the less control the data owning organization has—decreasing from private cloud to public cloud—the more concern and the greater the need for assurance that the CSPs security mechanisms and practices are effective for the level of data sensitivity and data value. (But in Figure 5.2, we saw that the owning organization's responsibility for security runs deeper into the stack for the owning organization as they move from SaaS to PaaS and again to IaaS.)

If you are going to use an external cloud provider to store data, a prime requirement is that risk exposure is acceptable. (Refer to Chapter 1, Cloud Computing and Security: An Introduction.) Risk exposure varies in part as a function of service delivery as it does for deployment.

A secondary requirement is to verify that the provider will act as a true custodian of your data. A data owning organization has several opportunities in proactively ensuring data assurance by a CSP. To begin with, selecting a CSP should be based on verifiable attestation that the CSP follows industry best practices and implements security that is appropriate for the kinds of data they are entrusted with. Such certifications will vary according to the nature of the information and whether regulatory compliance is necessary. Understandably, one should expect to pay more for services that involve such certifications (This is discussed further in chapter 8,

Vendor Claims and Independent Verification.) One likely trend here is that higher assurance cloud services may come with indemnification as a means of insurance or monetary backing of assurance for a declared level of security. Whatever the future may hold, we can expect that practices in this space will evolve.

Data in Motion

Data in motion refers to data as it is moved from a stored state as a file or database entry to another form in the same or to a different location. Any time you upload data to be stored in the cloud, the time at which the data is being uploaded data is considered to be *data in transit*. Data in motion can also apply to data that is in transition and not necessarily permanently stored. Your username and password for accessing a Web site or authenticating yourself to the cloud would be considered sensitive pieces of data in motion that are not actually stored in unencrypted form.

Because data in motion only exists as it is in transition between points—such as in memory (RAM) or between end points—securing this data focuses on preventing the data from being tampered with as well as making sure that it remains confidential. One risk has to do with a third party observing the data while it was in motion. But funny things happen when data is transmitted between distant end points, to begin with packets may be cached on intermediate systems, or temporary files may be created at either end point. There is no better protection strategy for data in motion than encryption.

Common Risks with Cloud Data Security

Several risks to cloud computing data security are discussed in this section. None of these are unique to the cloud model, but they do pose risk and must be considered when addressing data security. They include phishing, CSP privileged access, and the source or origin of data itself.

Phishing

One indirect risk to data in motion in a cloud is phishing. Although it is generally considered unfeasible to break public key infrastructure (PKI) today (and therefore break the authentication and encryption), it is possible to trick end users into providing their credentials for access to clouds. Although phishing is not new to the security world, it represents an additional threat to cloud security. Listed below are some protection measures that some cloud providers have implemented to help address cloud-targeted phishing related attacks:

- **Salesforce.com Login Filtering** Salesforce has a feature to restrict access to a particular instance of their customer relationship management application. For example, a subscriber can tell Salesforce not to accept logins, even if valid credentials are provided, unless the login is coming from a whitelisted IP address range. This can be very effective in preventing phishing attacks by preventing an attacker login unless he is coming from a known IP address range.

- **Google Apps/Docs/Services Logged In Sessions & Password Rechecking**
  Many Google services randomly prompt users for their passwords, especially
  in response when a suspicious event was observed. Furthermore, many
  Google's services display the IP address from the previous login session
  along with automatic notification of suspicious events, such as login from
  China shortly after an IP address from the United States did for the same
  account.
- **Amazon Web Services Authentication** Amazon takes authentication to cloud
  resources seriously. When a subscriber uses EC2 to provision a new cloud-
  hosted virtual server, by default, Amazon creates cryptographically strong PKI
  keys and requires those keys to be used for authentication to that resource. If
  you provision a new LINUX VM and want to SSH to it, you have to use SSH
  with key-based authentication and not a static password.

But these methods are not always fool proof—with phishing, the best protection is employee/subscriber training and awareness to recognize fraudulent login/
capturing events. Some questions that you might ask your CSP related to protection from phishing-related attacks are:

- **Referring URL Monitoring** Does the CSP actively monitor the referring
  URLs for authenticated sessions? A wide-spread phishing attack targeting
  multiple customers can come from a bogus or fraudulent URL.
- **Behavioral Policies** Does the CSP employ policies and procedures that
  mandate that a consistent brand is in place (often phishing attacks take
  advantages of branding weaknesses to deceive users)? Does their security
  policy prohibit weak security activities that could be exploited? An example
  would be if they prohibit the sending of e-mails with links that users can click
  on that automatically interact with their data. Another example would be
  whether they allow password resets to occur without actively proving user
  identity via a previously confirmed factor of authentication (that is, initiate a
  password request on the Web and they confirm the identity of the user based
  on an out-of-band SMS text message to their cell phone).

Phishing is a threat largely because most cloud services currently rely on simple username and password authentication. If an attacker succeeds in obtaining
credentials, there is not much preventing them from gaining access.

Provider Personnel with Privileged Access

Another risk to cloud data security has to do with a number of potential vectors
for inappropriate access to customer sensitive data by cloud personnel. Plainly stated, outsourced services—be they cloud-based or not—can bypass the typical controls that IT organizations typically enforce via physical and logical controls. This
risk is a function of two primary factors: first, it largely has to do with the potential for exposure with unencrypted data and second, it has to do with privileged
cloud provider personnel access to that data. Evaluating this risk largely entails

CSP practices and assurances that CSP personnel with privileged access will not access customer data.

Data Origin and Lineage

The origin, integrity, lineage, and provenance of data can be a primary concern in cloud computing. Proving the origin of information or data has importance in many areas, including patents or proving ownership of valuable data sets that are based on independent analysis of commonly available information sources. For compliance purposes, it may be necessary to have exact records as to what data was placed in a public cloud, when it occurred, what VMs and storage it resided on, and where it was processed. In fact, it may be equally important to be able to prove that certain datasets were not transferred to a cloud, for instance, when there are sensitivity or EU-privacy concerns about what national borders such data may have crossed.

While reporting on data lineage and provenance may be very important for regulatory purposes, it may be very difficult to do so with a public cloud. This is largely due to the degree of abstraction that exists between actual physical resources—such as disk drives and servers—and the virtualized resources that a public cloud user has access to. Visibility into a provider's operations in terms of technical mechanisms can be impossible to obtain, for understandable reasons.

Where such requirements exist that the origin and custody of data or information must be maintained in order to prevent tampering, to preclude exposure outside a jurisdictional realm, or to assure continuing integrity of data, it may be completely inappropriate to use a public cloud or even a low-assurance private cloud. One can imagine that if such requirements become increasingly common, cloud-based services will arise to profit from the opportunity. In the absence of a public service and where a private cloud is cost prohibitive, alternative approaches should be considered—easiest among them the use of a hybrid or community cloud.

DATA ENCRYPTION: APPLICATIONS AND LIMITS

In a recent article,[1] Bruce Schneier discussed how the information age practice of encrypting data at rest deviates from the historical use of cryptography for protecting data while it is communicated or in transit. One of Schneier's key points is that for data in motion, encryption keys can be ephemeral, whereas for data at rest, keys must be retained for as long as the stored data is kept encrypted. As Schneier points out, this does not reduce the number of things that must be stored secretly; it just makes those things smaller (the size of a key is far smaller than a typical data file). As Schneier states: "This whole model falls apart on the Internet. Much of the data stored on the Internet is only peripherally intended for use by people; it's primarily intended for use by other computers. And therein lies the problem. Keys can no longer be stored in people's brains. They need to be stored on the same computer, or at least the network, that the data resides on. And that is much riskier."[2] In meeting this challenge, there has been a recent rise in the number of security appliances that are intended to address this and related security implementation issues for data security in clouds.

WARNING

When you need to use cryptography in your cloud implementation, remember:

- Developing cryptographic algorithms is a specialized and difficult challenge.
- Correctly implementing cryptography in software is nearly as difficult.
- Many products use cryptography in deeply flawed ways.
- A single flaw in cryptography undermines security, much as a weak link compromises the integrity of the entire chain.
- Many commercial and free cryptographic products have been shown to be insecure. There is a long history of products that do not work as claimed, products that are flawed, and products that use algorithms that have not been subjected to the test of time or the scrutiny of other cryptographers. Based on past experiences, it is wise to be skeptical about claims regarding a new product with a revolutionary or patent-pending cryptographic algorithm or some secret technique. The road to better cryptography is littered with products that failed to meet some or all advertised claims.
- Especially to be avoided are products that use *secret* cryptographic algorithms. Pick a cryptographic solution that is based on a recognized algorithm that has withstood the test of time and whose implementation has been tested by a recognized testing organization.
- Pick a known product that uses a thoroughly vetted algorithm and obtain it through secure means—don't download cryptographic or security software from Internet-based servers without the means to verify the content.

Overview of Cryptographic Techniques

Introduced in Chapter 1 (Cloud Computing and Security: An Introduction), cryptography is a complex and esoteric field. In modern times, cryptography has expanded from protecting the confidentiality of private communications to including techniques for assuring content integrity, identity authentication, and digital signatures along with a range of secure computing techniques. Given that range of functional utility, cryptography has been recognized as being a critical enabling technology for security in cloud computing. Focusing on data security, cryptography has great value for cloud computing.

To effect cryptographic data confidentiality, plaintext is converted into cyphertext by numerous means, but the ones of practical value are all based on mathematical functions that must meet several requirements, including:

- The algorithm and implementation must be computationally efficient in converting plaintext to cyphertext, as well as in decryption.
- The algorithm must be open to broad analysis by a community of cryptographers and others.
- The resulting output must withstand the use of brute force attacks even by vast numbers of computers (such as in a computing grid or cloud).

In operation, plaintext is encrypted into cyphertext using an encryption key, and the resulting cyphertext is later decrypted using a decryption key. In Symmetric cryptography, these keys are the same (Figure 5.3). Symmetric cryptography has broad applicability, but when it is used in communication between parties, the complexity of key management can become untenable since each pair of communicators should share a unique secret key. It is also very difficult to establish a secret key between communicating parties when a secure channel does not already exist for them to securely exchange a shared secret key.

By contrast, with asymmetric cryptography (also known as in public–private key cryptography), the encrypt key (public key) is different but mathematically related to the decrypt or private key (Figure 5.4). The primary advantage of asymmetric cryptography is that only the private key must be kept secret—the public key can be published and need not be secret. Although public–private key pairs are related, it is infeasible to computationally derive a private key from a public key.

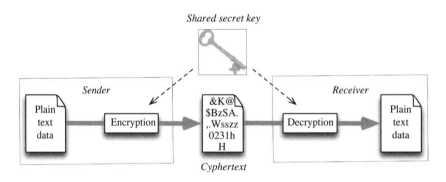

FIGURE 5.3

Symmetric encryption.

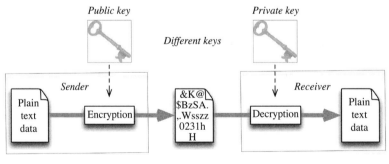

FIGURE 5.4

Asymmetric encryption.

This use of public–private keys is a great enabler for confidentiality in cloud computing, and not just for encryption of content. A private key can be used to authenticate a user or computational component, and it can also be used to initiate the negotiation of a secure channel or connection between communicating parties.

Going one level deeper in our background treatment of cryptography, for the purpose of this book, there are four basic uses of cryptography:

- **Block Ciphers** These take as input a key along with a block of plaintext and output a block of cyphertext. Because messages are generally larger than a defined block, this method requires some method to associate or knit together successive cyphertext blocks.
- **Stream Ciphers** These operate against an arbitrarily long stream of input data, which is converted to an equivalent output stream of cyphertext.
- **Cryptographic Hash Functions** Hash functions take an arbitrarily long input message and output a short, fixed length hash. A hash can serve various purposes, including as a digital signature or as a means to verify the integrity of the message.
- **Authentication** Cryptography is also widely used within authentication and identity management systems.

Although cryptography is a cornerstone of security, many an adopter has insecurely used it or worse attempted to implement cryptography to either save money or cut corners. The field of cryptography is well beyond the scope of this book, so the reader is encouraged to refer to widely available texts on cryptography in order to develop a better understanding of cryptography, its implementation, and secure application.

TOOLS

Sometimes you need to transfer files via secure physical media. When you do so, it is best to have the data secured on the media. To do this, you would typically create an encrypted image first and then copy it to the physical transfer media. However, you can also use encrypting media such as hardware encrypting USB flash drives. Two of the hallmarks of such devices are automated and integral encryption/decryption and hardware-based tamper resistance. They are very good as a backup for personal or sensitive data that you do not want to include in an unencrypted full disk backup. But these devices are excellent for transferring sensitive data in a highly protected manner when the transfer has to be physical.

Since technology changes rapidly and vendors come and go, search for *tamper resistant encrypting USB drive*. Some of these products use very strong cryptography, and some have additional features.

Common Mistakes or Errors with Data Encryption

Cryptography has become pervasive and broadly accessible for even the average computer users to secure their digital files on local or remote storage, as well as for communication. But as commonly available as cryptography is, it is too often either not used when it should be or it is implemented or used in insecure or ineffective ways. The most obvious example of the ineffective use of cryptography might well be using cryptography to achieve secure communications and authentication with an Internet service, only to do so from a PC that is hopelessly out-of-date in security patches or that harbors spyware and is otherwise compromised. In such a case, the dedicated use of strong cryptography from this platform amounts to affixing a bank vault door on a cardboard box.

Given the rigor and thought invested by cryptographers when creating and verifying a cryptographic algorithm or implementation, one marvels at the number of errors and failures that have been reported over the years. What are the causes behind these? The most common mistakes or errors include:

- Failing to use cryptography when cryptographic security is a viable option. Most likely, all payloads should be encrypted by default.
- Failing to use cryptographically secured protocols when you have a choice. Using FTP, telnet, or HTTP rather than a secured version of these plaintext protocols is simply negligent. Network packet sniffing is a pastime on many machines that take part in sending packets back and forth between your laptop and a cloud-based service. Although these protocols should have been retired long ago, they are still common and being available they are used. No cloud implementation should allow these, and they should probably all be blocked as services.
- Believing that you are a cryptographer, or inventing your own algorithm (when you shouldn't).
- Thinking you can implement an existing cryptographic algorithm (when you shouldn't). Instead of reinventing the wheel, use a proven implementation.
- Embedding a password or plaintext secret key in a binary, configuration, or *secret* file (such as a dotted hidden file in UNIX). Although this may seem to enable automation of functions or scripting, it often leads to exposure of secret keys or the inability to change such keys. In the case of storing secret keys in binaries, this exposes keys in unanticipated ways including in swap and crash (core) files. (It's 2 AM, do you know where your keys are?) However, bootstrapping encryption between such systems is often necessary to securely identify a system that interoperates in a trust relationship with other systems.
- Storing keys with data. This error is so profoundly egregious, one would expect not to need mentioning it except (sadly) there are reports that it happens time and time again.
- The bus test. If critical keys for the organization are kept by only one or a few individuals, how will your organization recover if these individuals suffer a disaster such as being hit by a bus?
- Sending sensitive data in unencrypted e-mail. Sending passwords, PINs, or other account data in unencrypted e-mail exposes that data in multiple places.

CLOUD DATA SECURITY: SENSITIVE DATA CATEGORIZATION

When it comes to cloud data protection methods, no particularly new technique is required. Protecting data in the cloud can be similar to protecting data within a traditional data center. Authentication and identity, access control, encryption, secure deletion, integrity checking, and data masking are all data protection methods that have applicability in cloud computing. This section will briefly review these methods and will note anything that is particularly unique to when these are deployed in a cloud.

> **NOTE**
>
> A centralized identity system must meet many criteria and must have high availability and integrity. The essential use cases for identity management are:
>
> - **Login** A user logs in to a system, an application, or other controlled access context.
> - **Logout** A user logs out of a system, an application, or other controlled access context.
> - **Single Sign On** A user logs in to one system, application, and so on and is thereby granted access to other related systems.
> - **Password and Identity Information Synchronization** When a password or other user identity information is changed, it is synchronized throughout the identity realm.
> - **Add/Delete User** Identity information is added or deleted for a user throughout the identity realm.
> - **Authentication** The identity system verifies a user's identity.
> - **Authorization** The identity system verifies that the authenticated subject has specific permissions to perform an operation or access a specific resource.
> - **Audit and Reporting** The logging of security relevant events related to any identity operation.

Authentication and Identity

Maintaining confidentiality, integrity, and availability for data security is a function of the correct application and configuration of familiar network, system, and application security mechanisms at various levels in the cloud infrastructure. Among these mechanisms are a broad range of components that implement authentication and access control. Authentication of users and even of communicating systems is performed by various means, but underlying each of these is cryptography. Authentication of users takes several forms, but all are based on a combination of *authentication factors*: something an individual knows (such as a password), something they possess (such as a security token), or some measurable quality that is intrinsic to them (such as a fingerprint). Single factor authentication is based on only one authentication factor. Stronger authentication requires additional factors; for instance, two factor authentication is based on two authentication factors (such as a pin and a fingerprint).

Authentication is usually predicated on an underlying identity infrastructure. The most basic scheme is where account information for one or a small number of users is kept in flat files that are used to verify identity and passwords, but this scheme does not scale to more than a very few systems. A full discussion of identity and access controls is beyond the scope of this book, but the key to effective access controls is the centralization of identity.

One problem with using traditional identity approaches in a cloud environment is faced when the enterprise uses multiple CSPs. In such a use case, synchronizing identity information with the enterprise is not scalable. Another set of problems arises with traditional identity approaches when migrating infrastructure toward a cloud-based solution. Infrastructure tends to employ domain-centric identity approaches that do not allow for looser alignment such as with partnership. For these reasons, federated identity management (FIM) is an effective foundation for identity in cloud computing. However, federated identity uses a claim-based token model, which entails a departure for traditional schemes. However, traditional identity needs can still be supported by a federated token model. For a lengthy discussion on identity in cloud computing, the reader is referred to the April 2010 *Domain 12: Guidance for Identity & Access Management V2.1* that was prepared by the Cloud Security Alliance.[A]

Access Control Techniques

Access control mechanisms are a key means by which we maintain a complex IT environment that reliably supports separation and integrity of different levels or categories of information belonging to multiple parties. But access controls do not stand on their own; they are supported by many other security capabilities. In addition, as we will discuss in Chapter 7 (*Security Criteria: Building an Internal Cloud*), access control is dependent on an identity management capability that meets the needs for the implementation.

When we discuss access controls, we refer to:

- *Subjects* which are people or processes acting on their behalf
- *Objects* such as files or other resources (a directory, device, or service of some sort)

Access controls are generally described as either discretionary or non-discretionary, and the most common access control models are:

- **Discretionary Access Control (DAC)** In a system, every object has an owner. With DAC, access control is determined by the owner of the object who decides who will have access and what privileges they will have. Permission management in DAC can be very difficult to maintain; furthermore, DAC does not scale well beyond small sets of users.
- **Role Based Access Control (RBAC)** Access policy is determined by the system. Where with MAC access is based on subject trust or *clearance*, with

---

[A]www.cloudsecurityalliance.org/guidance/csaguide-dom12.pdf

RBAC access is based on the role of the subject. A subject can access an object or execute a function only if their set of permissions—or role—allows it.

- **Mandatory Access Control (MAC)** Access policy is determined by the system and is implemented by sensitivity labels, which are assigned to each subject and object. A subject's label specifies its level of trust, and an object's label specifies the level of trust that is required to access it. If a subject is to gain access to an object, the subject label must dominate—be at least as high as—the object label.

Finally, although these three access models vary in fundamental ways, they are not inherently incompatible and can be combined in different ways. As implemented, DAC generally includes a set of ownership representations (in UNIX: User, Group and Other), a set of permissions (again, in UNIX: Read, Write, Execute), and an access control list (ACL), which would list individuals and their access modes to the object, groups, and others. Although this use of DAC may be easy to setup for a resource, as soon as there is any turnover in personnel or when the

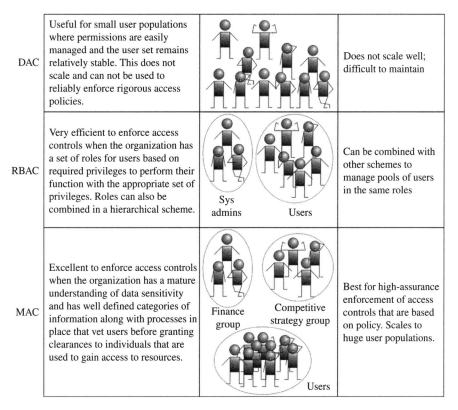

DAC	Useful for small user populations where permissions are easily managed and the user set remains relatively stable. This does not scale and can not be used to reliably enforce rigorous access policies.	Does not scale well; difficult to maintain
RBAC	Very efficient to enforce access controls when the organization has a set of roles for users based on required privileges to perform their function with the appropriate set of privileges. Roles can also be combined in a hierarchical scheme.	Can be combined with other schemes to manage pools of users in the same roles
MAC	Excellent to enforce access controls when the organization has a mature understanding of data sensitivity and has well defined categories of information along with processes in place that vet users before granting clearances to individuals that are used to gain access to resources.	Best for high-assurance enforcement of access controls that are based on policy. Scales to huge user populations.

FIGURE 5.5

MAC scales better for data security than other schemes do.

list of individuals grows, the scheme becomes unwieldy. By contrast, MAC-based enforcement scales to global user populations. Figure 5.5 depicts this point by contrasting MAC with discretionary access controls (DAC) and role-based access controls (RBAC).

Data Categorization and the Use of Data Labels

Putting in place effective and appropriate controls for information systems requires an understanding of the nature of the information. In this regard, sensitive or otherwise valuable data should be categorized to support data security. By identifying data according to sensitivity, one can implement various strategies to better protect such data. Unfortunately, understanding what other cloud data may require protection may not always be clear. Data that a user chooses to store in the cloud may not require protection if it is not sensitive or if it can easily be recovered. But generally, protecting data is a universal requirement regardless of its value, if for no other reason than failing to do so leads to all manner of complexity, consequence, and mischief.

In identifying and categorizing data, what we face is a multifaceted problem. Besides identifying classes of information that are sensitive or otherwise have value and labeling such information according to its characteristics, we need to protect such data, usually by means such as file permissions, encryption, or more sophisticated container approaches. We also need identity-based access controls to support organizational access policies. Procedures are also necessary for security across phases of the data life cycle, for instance, to limit exposure of such data when we create copies or backups. Also, we need mechanisms to detect when the valuable resource is accessed in ways that warrant concern.

Data or information labeling is one information security technique that has been used to great success for classified information such as the hierarchical categories of Unclassified, Confidential, Secret, Top Secret, and Compartmented. Labeling also supports non-classified and non-hierarchical categories such as Finance, Business Strategy, and Human Resources. The objective of information identification and categorization is to put in place an information-centric framework for controls and data handling.

SELinux and Trusted Solaris are two example operating systems that support information categorization and access enforcement for U.S. Department of Defense style mandatory access controls (MAC). Briefly, this amounts to sophisticated access enforcement by the OS and network controls. At the heart of MAC-based security are two concepts. First, every file, discrete piece of data or network connection is marked to bound its security level with a label that the OS uses to enforce access. Second, every subject (user or process acting on behalf of a user) has a set of permissions including clearances and roles. The OS mediates all operations that subjects perform against data enforcing complex logical security operations. Although this may sound complex, and while such enforcement technology must be implemented with correctness and completeness, the concept is quite simple and the benefits enable a simplification of what otherwise would be highly complex and prone to error alternative implementations.

The Ostrich Approach (or How I Learned to Hide My Head in the Sand)

In contrast to identifying sensitive data, there are many consequences when you uniformly treat all data as being equal in sensitivity or value. Without any data sensitivity oriented controls, a relatively small percentage of sensitive data is mixed in with far more nonsensitive data and is accessible to anyone with overall access. Failing to identify sensitive data complicates incident resolution and can be problematic when compromised data includes data subject to regulatory controls.

There is one misguided school of thought about this, and it can be described as the notion of hiding valuables in plain sight and hoping for the best. This is a strategy that is doomed even at the level of an individual computer used by multiple parties. By example, one might think that credit card data can be discretely squirreled away in a file and almost impossible to locate via a search if the file system has enough files. However, such data follows defined regular patterns both in terms of the number of digits and key digits of the number. Searching for well-known strings is trivial with a computer, and because of this, several pieces of spyware do exactly that by first identifying strings such as a credit card number or a social security number and then extracting enough characters around these prizes to obtain expiration date, associated names, and along with other personal data.

Over Use of Classification

A second problem with sensitive information is a common inclination to classify or label everything as sensitive or for instance *Secret*. But over classification can lead to a reduction in care in handling actually sensitive data. What we need is a balance in managing sensitive information and sound strategies for protecting the data.

Application of Encryption for Data at Rest

Encryption is a key component to protect data at rest in the cloud. Employing appropriate strength encryption is important: Strong encryption is preferable when data at rest has continuing value for an extended time period. If such long-term value encrypted data is obtained by a third party and if they have an extensive period of time to break or *crack* the encryption, then the reward can be well worth the effort.

There are multiple ways of encrypting data at rest. Following is an outline of various forms of encryption that serve as protection methods for securing data at rest in the cloud.

- **Full Disk** Encryption of data at the disk level—the operating system, the applications in it, and the data the applications use are all encrypted simply by existing on a disk that is encrypted. This is a brute-force approach to encrypt data since everything is encrypted, but this also entails performance and reliability concerns. If encryption is not done at the drive hardware level, then it can be very taxing on a system in terms of performance. Another consideration is that even minor disk corruption can be fatal as the OS, applications, and data.

- **Directory Level (or Filesystem)** In this use of encryption, entire data directories are encrypted or decrypted as a *container*. Access to files requires use of encryption keys. This approach can also be used to segregate data of identical sensitivity or categorization into directories that are individually encrypted with different keys.

- **File Level** Rather than encrypting an entire hard drive or even a directory, it can be more efficient to encrypt individual files.

- **Application Level** The application manages encryption and decryption of application-managed data.

Critical to implementing any of these forms of encryption is the need to manage the keys that are used to encrypt and decrypt data. In addition, identifying recovery methods for when encryption keys are lost needs to be considered. When a key is lost or not available, it is important to know what options are available to recover the data for instance, do backups exist?

Also, consider the potential for side channel attacks with encryption. Simply defined, side channel attacks are attacks that target the operating nature (or environment) where the encryption is occurring in contrast to exploiting the encryption mechanisms themselves. In the context of cloud security, side channels may potentially exist by virtue of operating within the same physical infrastructure and using shared resources with other subscribers. The site sidechannelattacks.com has an extensive list of different types of side channel attacks.[B]

Application of Encryption for Data in Motion

The two goals of securing data in motion are preventing data from being tampered with (integrity) and ensuring that data remains confidential while it is in motion. Other than the sender and the receiver, no other party observing the data should be able to either make sense of the data or alter it. The most common way to protect data in motion is to utilize encryption combined with authentication to create a conduit in which to safely pass data to or from the cloud.

Encryption is used to assure that if there was a breach of communication integrity between the two parties that the data remains confidential. Authentication is used to assure that the parties communicating data are who they say they are. Common means of authentication themselves employ cryptography in various ways. Transferring data via programmatic means, via manual file transfer, or via a browser using HTTPS, TLS, or SSL are the typical security protocols used for this purpose. A PKI is used to authenticate the transaction (trusted root CAs), and encryption algorithms are used to protect the payload.

[B]This site was created as a research tool for the Reliable Computing Laboratory at Boston University. For more information, see http://sidechannelattacks.com.

Impediments to Encryption in the Cloud

In one example, a Software-as-a-Service public cloud, because of its very nature, might not allow subscribers to encrypt their data. This may be due to functional limitations with the actual service itself. In the example of currently available social networks including Facebook, MySpace, and Linkedin, it is simply not possible to use encryption to ensure the confidentiality of your personal information. Nor would the cloud provider have any motivation to agree to allow this kind of data to be encrypted since many SaaS operators might not be able to provide revenue-generating services if they have an obscured view to the data they are interacting with. For instance, if Facebook was unable to intelligently interpret what kind of activities were occurring in their cloud, then how could they target you with advertisements that are most effective if they relate to your posted activities? If your data was encrypted, then that aspect of the provider's business model would be broken.

This same fact holds true to other kinds of clouds as well. IaaS providers might not be capable of encrypting at the operating system level because it would hinder their ability to monitor and therefore manage these instances.

EPIC FAIL

The Facebook service is a tangible example that can be used when illustrating many cloud security issues. Facebook suffered a breach of data privacy due to its comingling of data—which is an absolute necessity for how their service simply works. As a result, the security of the data relies on the application that is used to access it. The application in this case is the Facebook.com Web application. When the application used to access the comingled data has a bug or other serious security vulnerability, the data is obviously then also at risk. This vulnerability, when exploited, exposed all data that users uploaded, such as photographs, private contact information, and personal details as well as real-time data such as instant messaging conversations. This data was exposed to other Facebook users and exploiting it was a trivial matter. Facebook's CEO himself, Mark Zuckerberg, was a victim of this data leakage. No matter how security conscious Facebook subscribers were, they were exposed simply because their data was in the Facebook service.

Deletion of Data

When it is time to delete sensitive or valuable data in a cloud, it is important to understand how that data is deleted. The U.S. Department of Defense has an excellent and well accepted definition illustrating the two key aspects of data deletion, as stated in *DoD 5220.22-M, National Industrial Security Program Operating Manual*[3]:

a. Clearing. Clearing is the process of eradicating the data on media before reusing the media in an environment that provides an acceptable level of protection for the data that was on the media before clearing. All internal memory, buffer, or other reusable memory shall be cleared to effectively deny access to previously stored information.

b. Sanitization. Sanitization is the process of removing the data from media before reusing the media in an environment that does not provide an acceptable level of protection for the data that was in the media before sanitizing. IS resources shall be sanitized before they are released from classified information controls or released for use at a lower classification level.

More often than not, data that is stored in a public cloud is not sanitized to DoD levels. The consequence is that if disks are decommissioned, then data is at risk of being exposed. This is the case because under various circumstances, even data that has been erased can be restored. Since computer data is stored in essentially magnetic form (disk and tape) or as electrical charges (memory and solid state disk), it is demonstrably possible to either electronically access remnants of such deleted data using esoteric means or by gaining physical access to the media and using very advanced techniques to identify magnetic or electrical charge remnants and recreate the data they still represent. Even more simply, when a file is deleted, the file blocks that comprised it are released to the file system for reuse. The question is: Does the file system in question clear these blocks when the file blocks are released or does the file system clear these blocks when they are subsequently allocated to the next file and possibly a different user? Different file systems implement deletion and clearing differently.

Deleted data can also be accessed well after it's been deleted simply because it also exists in archives or data backup volumes. If a subscriber deletes a portion of the data and the cloud provider backs up that data every night to tape and archives tapes for 6 months, that data is existing well past the point that the subscriber deleted it and the subscriber cannot do anything to influence this. Acknowledging this in the Information Security Policy when adopting a cloud is paramount to its integrity.

Data Masking

Data masking is a technique that is intended to remove all identifiable and distinguishing characteristics from data in order to render it anonymous and yet still be operable. This technique is aimed at reducing the risk of exposing sensitive information. Data masking has also been known by such names as data obfuscation, de-identification, or depersonalization. These techniques are intended to preserve the privacy of records by changing the data so that actual values cannot be determined or re-engineered. A common data masking technique involves substitution of actual data values with keys to an external lookup table that holds the actual data values. In operation, such resulting masked data values can be processed with lesser controls than if the original data was still unmasked.

But data masking must be performed carefully, or the resulting masked data can still reveal sensitive data. By example, if you mask salary data in an HR database by tokenizing what originally were employee names with name look up keys, the highest salary will probably be the CEOs. By using simple analysis techniques and methodically cross-referencing partially masked records with other employee information, more may be inferred by a process of elimination than should be.

Regardless of the masking method that is used, it is important that structures and relationships that are formed between database rows, columns, and tables are correctly maintained with each masking operation. By example, if a key to an employee table is EMP_NUMBER, changes to EMP_NUMBER must be made with identical changes in all other tables.

Correctly implemented, data masking demonstrates due diligence regarding compliance with data privacy requirements, and it can also be an effective strategy for reducing the risk of data exposure and a good strategy for countries whose privacy requirements preclude the use of cloud computing off-EU territory for privacy information.

CLOUD DATA STORAGE

Among other advances, cloud computing has brought advantages in the form of on-line storage. In this section, we are referring to Storage-as-a-Service. The range of service offerings in this space is remarkable, and they are continuing to grow. Data security for such a cloud service encompasses several aspects including secure channels, access controls, and encryption. And, when we consider the security of data in a cloud, we must consider the security triad: confidentiality, integrity, and availability.

In the cloud storage model, data is stored on multiple virtualized servers. Physically the resources will span multiple servers and can even span storage sites. Among the additional benefits of such generally low-cost services are the storage maintenance tasks (such as backup, replication, and disaster recovery), which the CSP performs. The most notable provider in this space is Amazon with its S3 (Simple Storage Service). Amazon launched S3 in March of 2006.

A common aspect of many cloud-based storage offerings is the reliability and availability of the service. Figure 5.6 depicts an abstracted view of how many individual disks in many aggregated storage devices are composed into a virtualized unit of storage. Replication of data is performed at a low level by such mechanisms as RAID or by a file system. One such file system is ZFS, which was designed by Sun Microsystems as both a file system and a volume manager. ZFS supports high storage capacities and performs numerous security relevant functions including copy-on-write cloning and continuous integrity checking along with automatic repair.

One of the more recent trends in online cloud-based storage is the cloud storage gateway. Several vendors offer such solutions that are generally implemented as an appliance that resides onsite at the customer premises. These appliances can provide multiple features, including:

- Translation of client-used APIs and protocols (such as REST or SOAP) to those that are used by cloud-based storage services (such as NFS, iSCSI, or Fibre Channel). The goal is to enable integration with existing applications over standard network protocols.

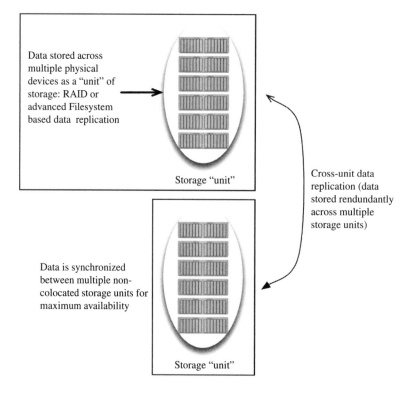

Data stored across multiple physical devices as a "unit" of storage: RAID or advanced Filesystem based data replication

Storage "unit"

Cross-unit data replication (data stored rendundantly across multiple storage units)

Data is synchronized between multiple non-colocated storage units for maximum availability

Storage "unit"

FIGURE 5.6

Cloud storage: replication and availability.

- Backup and recovery capabilities that work with in-cloud storage.
- Onsite encryption of data that keeps keys local to the onsite appliance.

The vendors and products in this space include Gladnet, Nasuni Cloud Storage Gateway, StorSimple, and Emulex. The product and solutions that are available are seeing rapid changes and new functionality. Figure 5.7 depicts a typical cloud storage gateway application as it is used to augment local storage by acting as an onsite secondary copy and as an intermediary to the CSP storage service.

CLOUD LOCK-IN (THE ROACH MOTEL SYNDROME)

A number of questions about adopting public clouds have to do with what might happen when an external cloud becomes business-critical for the organization. One of these questions involves concern over cloud lock-in. As George Harrison wrote in the song *Stuck Inside a Cloud*: "Talking to myself, Crying out loud,

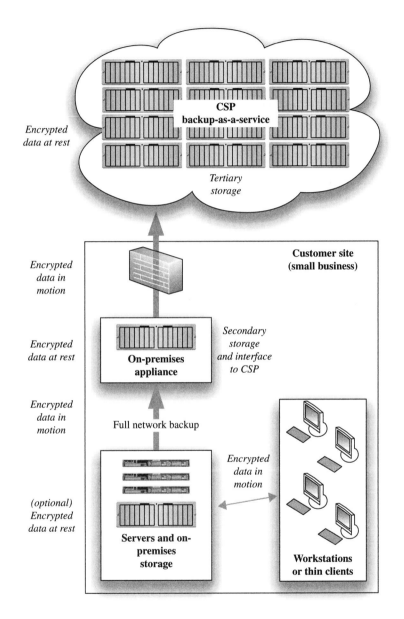

FIGURE 5.7

Cloud storage gateway appliance.

Only I can hear me, I'm stuck inside a cloud."[C,4] The concern here is that once you become dependent on the services of a cloud provider, you may find it extremely difficult to switch providers due to any number of technical reasons.

In one lock-in example, a company may subscribe to a specific public CSP service as their customer relationship management tool. This service may consequently end up being used to house all of the company's data relating to their customers. The company may invest significant effort in customizing rules or reporting routines in their use of this service. The service may also become the primary reporting engine that provides management insight to the health of the business. If the service entails proprietary formats or APIs, then the service subscriber may very well not own anything other than the data. If the company decides to discontinue the service, then the organization may retain no value for any effort they performed in tailoring the service for their needs. If the data formats are proprietary, the company could conceivably face serious challenges when migrating their data to a replacement system or service.

Metadata

Further questions in this lock-in scenario might include what happens to a customer's data when they terminate their service? Who else might be able to access it? This is further complicated by the fact that if the organization used the cloud service over a considerable length of time, then it is almost guaranteed that there is a tremendous amount of data that was developed by simply using the cloud—sometimes referred to as cloud metadata. Metadata is simply data about data, or more precisely, it is high-level information about such things as to where the data came from, who performed what operations against it, and when changes were made. But cloud metadata that is developed may include other very valuable information that records associative context based on users and their relationship with content. In a SaaS solution, this kind of information may be developed over time by the CSP's software.

Back to the question of what happens to the metadata if the subscriber decides to discontinue use of the service. While planning their use of a cloud based service, customers may overlook such questions as what will happen if they become so reliant on the service that it becomes impossible for them to replace it. This can have important bearing on the customer's very business—enterprises adopting a cloud might not have any intention of ever leaving it, but there can be extenuating circumstances where their departure from the cloud might be required. For instance, what if the cloud provider goes out of business or if their business model changes? By example, Facebook has undergone a significant change from a private-based business model to a more open model.

[C]*Stuck inside a cloud* was the seventh track on George Harrison's posthumous album *Brainwashed*. Fans will note that seven was Harrison's favorite number, and the seventh track was supposedly his favorite for all his albums. (Oddly enough, Googling *seven and information security* will return a number of interesting results that have nothing to do with either George Harrison or cloud computing.)

Avoiding Cloud Lock-in (the Roach Motel Syndrome)

Fortunately, many of the large public cloud services organizations that exist today provide the ability to export not only data but also metadata generated by its subscribers. Any enterprise should seriously consider this as a vital feature to have before adopting any cloud service that could become critical to their business. It could be unrealistic to assume that you will always maintain a service with a particular cloud provider. If there is no mechanism to retrieve your data, then the resulting situation can present a dilemma of costly proportions.

The presence of such a mass export feature isn't the only such requirement. How accessible and usable the data is after it has been exported is also important. If the data is exported in a proprietary file format, then that format might not be able to be intelligibly parsed. If it is exported in a plaintext format, it will have to be imported into the new system (or provider) in some intelligible way as well. As a result, one needs a real understanding of such challenges if you choose to leave a cloud.

Below are some examples of the cloud providers leading the industry in helping to avoid these lock-in concerns:

- Salesforce.com offers its subscribers the ability to generate a complete export of all data within a subscribers instance on an on-demand basis. While some subscription levels include this export feature as a part of the package and others at an additional fee, it is available as an option. The exported data is available in a ZIP file containing plaintext CSV files, which have the raw data for each Salesforce object. This can also be setup in an automated task as well always archiving the data. If you are a subscriber, this feature is accessible under their Web Interface under **Setup | Data Management | Data Export | Schedule Export**. Also worth mentioning is that at the time of publishing, there are several other alternatives to Salesforce that are able to intelligibly and automatically parse this data, proving that it is indeed useful and not just satisfying a feature checkbox.

Google has gone so far as creating what they call the Data Liberation Front. An example of this effort in action can be seen in Google Docs. Google Docs can act as a repository for all of users (or organizations) word processing documents, spreadsheets, and more, and as such this naturally should be very portable. Google responded and added a feature that easily allows the exporting of all Google hosted documents in a few clicks. They even went so far as allowing the documented to be exported in multiple different formats as well including Microsoft and Open Office formats. It's worth quoting Google's description of this group and their mission statement for this organized effort is a rarity in the cloud space[5]:

> *The Data Liberation Front is an engineering team at Google whose singular goal is to make it easier for users to move their data in and out of Google products. We do this because we believe that you should be able to export any data that you create in (or import into) a product. We help and consult other*

engineering teams within Google on how to "liberate" their products. This is our mission statement:

Users should be able to control the data they store in any of Google's products. Our team's goal is to make it easier to move data in and out.

- Another example of a public cloud provider helping to lead the way of addressing the lock-in problem is Amazon's Web Services and more specifically their Elastic Compute (EC2) service. The same is also true for their surrounding cloud services for data storage, database computing, and several other services. Their approach to the problem is to offer an import/ export feature that accommodates amounts of data that are not feasible to transfer via a file download on the Internet. Subscribers can prepare a portable hard drive and submit a job to Amazon to perform a data import or export. At that point, the subscribers can physically mail their portable hard drive to an Amazon provided address, and the data migration occurs.

It's also worth mentioning that there are companies being formed solely to address the lock-in issues of other public cloud providers. Backupify (www. backupify.com) is a perfect example of this. Their primary product or service is offering the ability for its subscribers to automatically back up and archive all of the data relating to their cloud services. Today their product has a more consumer focus, supporting the automated backup and archival of data from Facebook, Flickr, Twitter, and Google Docs, but it is only a matter of time for similar companies targeting enterprise cloud services to start addressing the lock in issues for enterprise clouds as well.

SUMMARY

The security concerns around storing data in the cloud are not inherently unique compared to data that is stored within the premises of an organization. That is not to say that the risks to data are the same in these very different environments. Ultimately, the concerns can be broken down and addressed in three key areas:

- Identify what data and applications you will store in a non-private and non-high-assurance cloud. Knowing what data will exist within a cloud is half the battle. The answer isn't going to be obvious either as additional questions around data provenance will arise in many environments. Also, data that is created or modified by using a cloud will be just as important as the original data itself. Metadata should also be identified and protected. Understanding where it is physically stored and what laws govern it is also important when such data falls under regulatory or legal coverage.
- Avoiding cloud data *Lock-in*—Make sure you are aware of the options that are available in case you need to move to another cloud provider. If your data

stored in a proprietary CSP format or if it cannot be easily be exported or modified for a new environment, you may be subject to lock-in.

- Understand the data protection options you have available and implement a sound strategy for protecting your sensitive or valuable data—Just as when protecting data that is in a traditional IT environment, encryption and authentication are key factors to employ for data that is stored in the cloud. If encryption is being used, understand what kind of encryption and what provisions are in place for key. Understanding how data is deleted and how long it is retained in CSP backups.

Finally, be selective in choosing a CSP. The biggest risks to your data may well reside with the CSP personnel accessing your data or mishandling your data in its various forms. Chapter 6, Securing the Cloud: Key Strategies and Best Practices, will go into some further depth on best practices around cloud security. Later, Chapter 8 (Security Criteria: Selecting an External Cloud Provider) and Chapter 9 (Evaluating Cloud Security: An Information Security Framework) will present criteria and methods for making informed decisions as to how to select an external CSP or how to evaluate the security of an external or internal cloud. Throughout those chapters, data security is a primary focus and concern.

Endnotes

1. Schneier B. http://www.schneier.com/blog/archives/2010/06/data_at_rest_vs.html; 2010 [accessed 7.10.10].
2. Ibid.
3. DoD 5220.22-M. National Industrial Security Program Operating Manual, United States Department of Defense; 2006.
4. Harrison G. Stuck Inside a Cloud, Brainwashed 2002 Parlophone, Dark Horse, Capitol Records (Published posthumously); 2002.
5. http://www.dataliberation.org/ [accessed 22.03.11].

Securing the Cloud: Key Strategies and Best Practices

6

INFORMATION IN THIS CHAPTER

- Overall Strategy: Effectively Managing Risk
- Overview of Security Controls
- The Limits of Security Controls
- Best Practices
- Security Monitoring

The intent of this chapter is to build on material that was introduced throughout earlier chapters and make it actionable so that it can be applied in practice. In practical terms, security engineers and administrators, along with cloud designers, seek to prevent, detect, and respond to security vulnerabilities and threats in an effective manner:

- With prevention, we strive to implement security controls that provide protection from threats. For numerous reasons, prevention can't be completely effective.
- A sound security strategy must include detection to identify threats or compromises. Timeliness and effectiveness of detection is critical, if effective responses are to be activated.
- With response activities we seek to address threats as they are detected or afterward with remediation, recovery, and forensics.
- Maintaining effective security is an ongoing process in which security controls, procedures, and supporting activities are kept relevant as systems evolve and risks change.

Therefore, one key strategy for cloud security is to implement effective security monitoring and vulnerability detection. This chapter goes into significant depth in describing a forward-looking approach to security monitoring for a cloud implementation. In addition, this chapter presents best practices and key strategies for implementing, maintaining, and assuring cloud security. Some of these are targeted at a CSP, whereas others are relevant to subscribers. These strategies are defined to support the three principal cloud security objectives: Assuring the confidentiality, integrity, and availability of information resources.

153

OVERALL STRATEGY: EFFECTIVELY MANAGING RISK

Addressing security risks can be done in various ways, but without a sound process and a considered strategy such efforts often prove ineffective. Appropriate approaches in different realms (for instance finance and healthcare) can vary significantly. Consequently, suitable security controls will also vary. Whether building a cloud infrastructure or adopting a public cloud service, leveraging the right process and strategy for managing your risks will have recurring benefits in better security, in lower ongoing operational costs and quite likely in your reputation for taking security seriously enough to plan ahead.

However, throwing every available security control at a cloud service without first establishing requirements or defining a governing policy is not practicing effective security—and it may result in neutering end-user functionality. In contrast, implementing only marginal security is asking for trouble, and trouble will most likely come in the form of much higher remediation costs along with excessive damages. Likewise, simply accepting CSPs security claims in the absence of certifications amounts to blind trust. Effective security is the desired result where security requirements were well considered, when countermeasures and controls were planned and selected to be cost effective within the context of the life cycle of a system and all its supporting activities.

One complicating factor in the appropriate security controls equation is that although organizational budgets roll up to a single level, individual cost quickly lose their relationships to other items. By example, the prevention investment cost to avoid incidents is not tied to higher maintenance and recovery costs that result from insufficient prevention. The point being that the best way to ensure overall cost reduction is to invest in prevention up front. Otherwise, you should expect a constant diet of unexpected incident handling and exploit recovery costs.

It should also be recognized that risk management does involve business decisions about the costs on either side of the equation. On the one side, you have the costs involved in the consequences of a security breach or being subject to an exploit. On the other side, you have various costs associated with implementing security counter measures. There comes a point for any system where additional preventative actions incur costs that bring fewer and fewer returns—as economists say *diminishing returns*. Very different actors, engineers, and security personnel on one side and business people on the other side populate both sides of that equation. Pragmatic security engineers need to be sensitive to business realities and to the difficulty in conveying the need for implementing controls that may appear to be duplicative to business types.

Risk Management: Stages and Activities

Effectively managing security risk involves multiple activities that extend over time. These activities can be grouped into four stages:

1. **Plan** This stage is a prerequisite to properly match security controls to address risks in an effective manner.

2. **Implement** This involves placing and configuring security controls.
3. **Evaluate** Assessing the efficacy of security controls and periodically reviewing their adequacy.
4. **Maintain** In this stage the system and security controls are in operation. Periodically, it will become necessary to perform configuration changes and updates. To improve or even to maintain security, any security-relevant modifications must follow the initial stages (plan, implement, and evaluate).

Each stage includes discrete steps, these include activities such as: developing a comprehensive security policy, classifying data and systems, and performing a risk assessment. (Risk management was discussed earlier in Chapter 1; security standards and policies were covered in Chapters 4 and 5 included a discussion on sensitive data categorization.) The following characterizations are derived from previous work that is documented in many domains, including recently by NIST[A] (notably 800-53) and International Organization for Standardization (ISO)[B]:

- **Information Resource Categorization** The goal of this step is to establish the criticality and sensitivity of information resources. This understanding will drive subsequent steps.
- **Select Security Controls** Security controls must be appropriate to the information systems and the risks they are subject to. This step should include thorough documentation of the controls along with clear rationale for their selection.
- **Risk Assessment** Determine whether the controls are sufficient and appropriate and if they will provide adequate protection against anticipated threats along with a plan for risk mitigation. If necessary, augment or revisit the set of security controls.
- **Implement Security Controls** This involves architecture, engineering, and expertise in the placement and configuration of security controls.
- **Assess Security Controls** This step seeks to determine the effectiveness of implemented controls and involves verifying that controls are correctly implemented and operating as intended.
- **Periodic Review and Update** Security measures must be reviewed on a periodic basis to determine their continuing efficacy in light of mission and operational changes.

Figure 6.1 depicts these discrete steps and an example framework for managing security risks.

This framework for managing security risks is adapted from well-known practices in the security industry (including 27001, NIST guidance, and CoBIT), and it has been applied in building several large grid computing and cloud computing implementations.

[A]NIST Special Publication 800-53 Revision 3, Recommended Security Controls for Federal Information Systems and Organizations. August 2009.
[B]See http://www.iso.org/iso/home.html for information on the ISO2700x series.

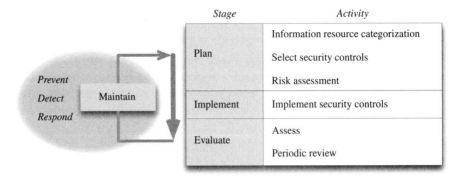

FIGURE 6.1

Framework for managing security risks.

As stated above, cost savings in operations will largely stem from the planning and implementation phases. Periodic assessment and review are critical to verifying that the overall strategy and its implementation are appropriate and have not become undermined by newly exposed vulnerabilities or classes of exploits. In the next section we will begin to examine specific security controls that are used to implement a security strategy.

OVERVIEW OF SECURITY CONTROLS

What *are* security controls? In essence, security controls are countermeasures or safeguards to prevent, avoid, counteract, detect, or otherwise respond to security risks. They can be technical mechanisms, manual practices, or procedures. In this section we will investigate this question further by examining several different approaches in organizing and characterizing security countermeasures.

The categorization of security controls varies and there are various schemes that are used in different realms (government, health care, accounting, and so on). In this section we will present a few representative categorizations and then we will survey several critical classes and specific security controls. Later in the book—in Chapter 9 (Evaluating Cloud Security: An Information Security Framework) we will build further on this topic and present a framework that identifies classes of security controls for the purpose of assessing—or planning—cloud security.

Cloud Security Controls Must Meet Your Needs

NIST Special Publication 800-53 states that in order for Federal Agencies to comply with federal standards: "organizations must first determine the security category of their information system in accordance with FIPS 199, Standards for

Security Categorization of Federal Information and Information Systems, derive the information system impact level from the security category in accordance with FIPS 200, and then apply the appropriately tailored set of baseline security controls in NIST Special Publication 800-53, Security Controls for Federal Information Systems and Organizations."[1] For many reasons, this is sound advice. First, systems manage or process various categories of information, some of these—for instance, financial or healthcare—entail special concerns due to the kind or sensitivity of information. Secondly, why reinvent the *entire* wheel? The security controls that NIST identifies for low, moderate, or high systems are not fundamentally different in terms of technology or process from what will be required by a system that serves finance or other nongovernment needs.

NIST Definitions for Security Controls

NIST Special Publication 800-53 Revision 3, *Recommended Security Controls for Federal Information Systems and Organizations* was the result of an extensive review of security controls that were used in different sectors including the financial, defense, healthcare, intelligence, and other realms. The result of that effort led to a comprehensive set of controls that meet the needs of a broad and deep range of security requirements. Although this is targeted at U.S. federal agencies, this document is very well developed and is expected to serve many CSPs, cloud developers, and adopters.

The NIST-defined controls are divided into several broad classes: Technical, Operational, and Management. Security controls are further organized into 18 families that fall into these 3 classes. This is depicted in Figure 6.2.

For each of these categories, NIST identified a series of security controls. Each of these has a unique identifier—for instance, AU-5 *RESPONSE TO AUDIT PROCESSING FAILURES*, is the fifth security control in the Audit and Accountability family and the Technical class. Each control is well defined and is of the following form:

- **Control Identifier** (such as *AU-5*)
- **Control Statement** Describes specific activities or actions that must be carried out
- **Supplemental Guidance** This provides additional information, which should be applied as appropriate.
- **Control Enhancements** These statements are provided to build additional control functionality and/or increase the strength of controls.
- **References** Identifies applicable federal laws, standards, and so on that are relevant to the control or control enhancement.
- **Priority and Baseline Allocation** This allows for the sequencing of specific controls in a prioritized manner.

By example, Figure 6.3 depicts NIST Control AC-14 *PERMITTED ACTIONS WITHOUT IDENTIFICATION OR AUTHENTICATION*. Note the Priority and Baseline Allocation section. This identifies the priority of AC-14 as *P1*, which indicates

ID	Family	Class
AC	Access control	Technical
AT	Awareness and training	Operational
AU	Audit and accountability	Technical
CA	Security assessment and authorization	Management
CM	Configuration management	Operational
CP	Contingency planning	Operational
IA	Identification and authentication	Technical
IR	Incident response	Operational
MA	Maintenance	Operational
MP	Media protection	Operational
PE	Physical and environmental protection	Operational
PL	Planning	Management
PS	Personnel security	Operational
RA	Risk assessment	Management
SA	System and services acquisition	Management
SC	System and communications protection	Technical
SI	System and information integrity	Operational
PM	Program management	Management

FIGURE 6.2

NIST's security control classes, families, and identifiers.[2]

that it should be implemented with priority over a P2 (which should be implemented with priority over a P3).

In addition, note that there are three additional codes *LOW*, *MOD*, and *HIGH*. These refer to *low-impact*, *moderate-impact*, or *high-impact* information and information systems that the security controls apply to. This scheme for describing information systems will be discussed in greater depth in the next section Unclassified Models.

Unclassified Models

Not all security needs are identical, in other words the same controls do not necessarily apply to systems with different security requirements. By example, in the U.S. federal government, nonclassified systems are characterized according to low-impact, moderate-impact, or high-impact information systems. In a low-impact system, failure in confidentiality, integrity, or availability is less critical than for a medium-impact system and for a high-impact system *loss of confidentiality, integrity, or availability could be expected to have a serious adverse effect on organizational operations, organizational assets, or individuals.*[3]

AC-14 **Permitted actions without identification or authentication**

Control: The organization:

a. Identifies specific user actions that can be performed on the information system without identification or authentication; and

b. Documents and provides supporting rationale in the security plan for the information system, user actions not requiring identification and authentication.

Supplemental guidance: This control is intended for those specific instances where an organization determines that no identification and authentication is required; it is not, however, mandating that such instances exist in given information system. The organization may allow a limited number of user actions without identification and authentication (e.g., when individuals access public websites or other publicly accessible federal information systems such as http://www.usa.gov). Organizations also identify any actions that normally require identification or authentication but may under certain circumstances (e.g., emergencies), allow identification or authentication mechanisms to be bypassed. Such bypass may be, for example, via a software-readable physical switch that commands bypass of the login functionality and is protected from accidental or unmonitored use. This control does not apply to situations where identification and authentication have already occurred and are not being repeated, but rather to situations where identification and/or authentication have not yet occurred. Related control: CP-2, IA-2.

Control enhancements:

(1) The organization permits actions to be performed without identification and authentication only to the extent necessary to accomplish mission/business objectives.

References: None.

Priority and baseline allocation:

P1	**LOW** AC-14	**MOD** AC-14 (1)	**HIGH** AC-14 (1)

FIGURE 6.3

NIST representative security control AC-14.[2]

It might be argued that the emphasis on security controls in this unclassified realm is not as much on confidentiality as it is on integrity and availability. One might argue the same for retail banking systems—correctly maintaining financial balances (integrity) trumps confidentiality and availability. It's not that customer confidentiality isn't important, just that integrity and availability may be more so— an assessment that is based on where the emphasis seems to be for such systems. On the other hand, an e-mail CSP will state that C.I.A. are all important, whereas one might suppose that availability is the constant nag and confidentiality the occasional headache. Although this argument is admittedly problematic, the point in these examples is that the emphasis on security controls will be put on those areas where the business puts its priorities. Otherwise, all these systems would be bouncing up against the all-controls-all-the-time security glass ceiling—that strategy may seem reasonable at first, but the resulting security overhead and cost do not support doing so. Why is that? Largely it is due to security being incorporated as more of an afterthought than as a business enabling design element. Frankly, it can be difficult to find the technical expertise, vision, and breadth of Information Technology (IT) experience in security engineers. Secondly, the underlying trade-offs between protection, cost, and reduced functionality can be difficult to navigate when the business neither values security as a real need nor when the building blocks do not make composing safer systems easier. These are perennial factors, but they are also routinely surmounted by some enterprises. Lastly, the sad truth is that the way most security controls are conceived or implemented does not lend itself to building both useful and secure systems.

NOTE

As defined by FIPS 199:

"The potential impact is LOW if—The loss of confidentiality, integrity, or availability could be expected to have a limited adverse effect on organizational operations, organizational assets, or individuals."[4] FIPS 199 goes on to define a limited adverse effect as it might: "(i) cause a degradation in mission capability to an extent and duration that the organization is able to perform its primary functions, but the effectiveness of the functions is noticeably reduced; (ii) result in minor damage to organizational assets; (iii) result in minor financial loss; or (iv) result in minor harm to individuals."[4]

"The potential impact is MODERATE if—The loss of confidentiality, integrity, or availability could be expected to have a serious adverse effect on organizational operations, organizational assets, or individuals."[4] It goes on to define a serious adverse effect: "(i) cause a significant degradation in mission capability to an extent and duration that the organization is able to perform its primary functions, but the effectiveness of the functions is significantly reduced; (ii) result in significant damage to organizational assets; (iii) result in significant financial loss; or (iv) result in significant harm to individuals that does not involve loss of life or serious life threatening injuries."[4]

"The potential impact is HIGH if—The loss of confidentiality, integrity, or availability could be expected to have a severe or catastrophic adverse effect on organizational operations, organizational assets, or individuals."[4] And, a severe or catastrophic adverse effect might: "(i) cause a severe degradation in or loss of mission capability to an extent and duration that the organization is not able to perform one or more of its primary functions; (ii) result in major damage to organizational assets; (iii) result in major financial loss; or (iv) result in severe or catastrophic harm to individuals involving loss of life or serious life threatening injuries."[4]

Classified Model

Another approach which associates security controls with categories of perceived risk comes from the arena of national security information. Chapter 5 presented an overview of the use of such information categories (Unclassified, Confidential, Secret, Top Secret, and Compartmented) in the context of data labeling and how they should be handled. But here we are considering the security controls that are generally associated with protecting such data in information systems. Although the specific details of security requirements and technical controls in this realm are largely classified, there are several fundamentally different or unique security controls.

As discussed in Chapter 5, the implementation of information categories is achieved by adding new structures and mechanisms that are used to label and enforce separation by the operating system (OS). In part, these mimic the rigorous policies and document controls that are enforced by organizations dealing with paper or other physical information representations. One way to visualize how these controls operate is as separate containers that are labeled at the highest level of information that resides within a container. Although individual elements or files may be marked with Media Access Control (MAC) style labels, as individual files are added to a container (for instance a directory), the container *floats* its high-level label upward to reflect the upgrading of classification of the overall container. The astute reader will wonder how information can be downgraded: only users with special privileges may perform a downgrade operation, and then this is often considered an exception to policy.

Although there are many tricky situations that arise in how to perform useful work while operating under very restrictive security policy enforcement, the fact is that such multi-level capable systems can replace numerous individual systems with a single implementation. Multi-level systems are more sophisticated and advanced in terms of the range of policy enforcement capabilities, but they are far from trivial to comprehend by the typical user. The use of this technology would be more widely adopted if user interfaces and user tools allowed easier operations.

Another set of security controls that are sometimes used in the classified world have to do with the concept of "originator controlled" data. An example of this is an email that the original sender addresses to a set of trusted recipients. However, the original sender may wish to control the resending of those emails to other potential recipients. This is hard to implement, but has great utility for many of us who would like to have systems enforce constraints around information.

The emphasis with national security data is on the degree of rigor by which separation of different data classification levels is effected and by the equal rigor by which only cleared and authorized individuals are granted access to such data. The commercial world would do well to adopt what is a similar serious approach to maintaining confidentiality over data where it is warranted.

The Cloud Security Alliance Approach

The Cloud Security Alliance developed a Controls Matrix which is a framework of nearly 100 distinct control specifications. The CSA Controls Matrix emphasizes business information security controls in a form that provides structure and detail for matching information security to cloud industry needs. An overview of the scope and controls covered by the CSA Controls Matrix is shown in Figure 6.4.

The CSA Controls Matrix effort is still new (version 1.0 was released in April 2010), and we can expect that it will be expanded over time. But it is a good start and it will serve as one of the models that this book builds on in Chapter 9 Evaluating Cloud Security: An Information Security Framework. For now, the broad approaches we detailed in this section (NIST 800-53 and its applicability to unclassified systems, MAC-MLS approaches, along with the CSA Controls Matrix approach) all serve as background toward implementing security in a structured and planned manner.

In Figure 6.1 we saw that security controls are defined in the *Plan* stage of the life cycle. They are then *Implemented* and then *Evaluated* to verify their appropriateness and implementation correctness. Subsequently, in the *Maintenance* stage we periodically review their currency and adequacy. The remainder of the section focused on security controls and how they are selected for different realms. The

Control area	Control specs	Applicability
Compliance	Auditing activities/reviews, assessments, intellectual property, ...	
Data governance	Data ownership, classification, handling, risk assessments, ...	Applicability to service delivery models {SaaS, PaaS, IaaS}
Facility security	Policies for work environment, authorizations, equipment, ...	
Human resources security	Background screening, termination, ...	
Information security	Infosec mngt prgm, full spectrum policies, technical controls, ...	Applicability to {service provider, customer}
Legal	Nondisclosures and third party agreements	
Operations management	Policies and procedures, capacity planning, eqpt maintenance, ...	Compliance cross reference {COBIT, HIPAA, ISO/IEC 27002-2005, NIST 800-53, PCIDSS}
Risk management	Security assessments, mitigation, policy change impacts, ...	
Release management	New development, production changes, quality, ...	
Resiliency	Impact analysis, BCP, environmental risks, power, comms, ...	
Security architecture	Customer access rqmts, User ID, integrity, network security, ...	

FIGURE 6.4

Overview of the CSA CM.[5]

next section examines the limits of security controls and gets us closer to defining best practices and other strategies for achieving effective cloud security.

THE LIMITS OF SECURITY CONTROLS

There are many reasons why security is often ineffective. From a software perspective, we often face several issues:

- Software development practices are typically not rigorous or focused on engineering principles and verification. To complicate this, software development often tends toward initial releases that saddle the user or administrator with bugs and vulnerabilities followed by patching and wholesale rewrites. In other words, security is inherently challenged by cycles of vulnerable functionality followed by effort expended on fixes.
  Developers are generally not very concerned about the platform that they deploy their software to (admittedly a notable exception to this being mobile platforms). When this is combined with feature sets being the emphasis in development (again, with notable exceptions), the frequent result is that security is an afterthought.
- Software frameworks and functionality scaffolding have grown to be huge. Many of these are based on open source builds that are subject to continual changes, making for dynamic implementations even when application code is static.
- Installation and configuration of software is usually not performed following a rigorous and defined process that brings identical results even when performed by the same installer.
- The discovery of new vulnerabilities extends over time to include even older and mature software.

Starting thus from an often software security challenged position, assembling cloud systems and achieving security is already encumbered with exploitable flaws. Of course, security goes well beyond software, and the situation is not always much better outside software. Procedures and operations processes are hard to design in a manner that is at the same time encompassing, reliable, and flexible enough to meet unpredictable challenges over time. One simply expects flexibility in operation, but one also expects predictable and repeatable results. This takes us back to the topic of the Capability Maturity Model (CMM, Chapter 1) and the Information Technology Infrastructure Library (ITIL) with its best practices for IT service management.

So, on the one hand we have the dangers of vulnerable and exploitable software components and on the other hand we have the dangers of poorly managed systems. Fortunately, much progress has been made in both areas—at least from the standpoint of having the tools to avoid much of the consequence of both areas. But success in security also entails adopting training, process maturity, and initial investment. Both these areas are beyond an in-depth discussion for this book, but the reader is encouraged to investigate the use of ITIL and lighter weight system management. Whether one uses ITIL, COBIT, or a lightweight set of homegrown best practices is less the point. The key is that a cost effective and secure cloud demands reliability, maturity, and agility in system and infrastructure management proficiency.

Where compensating controls are used to manage software, system, or network vulnerabilities, it is important that this be done without introducing new vulnerabilities. Implementing compensating security controls around poorly designed applications or systems does not guarantee any result other than greater complexity. Good security exhibits several qualities and one of them is certainly a tendency to simplicity versus complexity.

A goal for cloud security is ease of use and easy adoption of security controls. Unfortunately, this is seldom the case. The impact on security is such that even when adopting proven approaches in incorporating security controls in a system, the results are often too difficult for end users or administrators to operate reliably. Security controls must not only be appropriate but also be effective and easy to comprehend and navigate by users and administrators.

TIP

Many small and medium sized enterprises lack a chief security officer. In addition, they may not have staff with appropriate insight or background to plan or guide a cloud security strategy. In such cases, the simplest choice is to take the default choices that the CSP provides and trust that these are appropriate to your specific data security needs. Unfortunately, that approach will probably not maximize your chances of getting it right.

A typical approach to filling a gap, such as not having trained security staff, is to hire experienced consulting talent to guide your entire security strategy. When addressing cloud security decisions and the development of a security strategy, such consulting support can not only lead to better security, it can also save time and effort. However, consider extending such a consulting relationship beyond the initial phases of a cloud effort. Having a long term relationship with several security consultants who are familiar with your organization's specific needs may prove very useful as you proceed to subsequent phases of operations.

Security Exposure Will Vary over Time

As discussed in Chapter 1, Introduction to Cloud Computing and Security, risk is viewed in terms of the probability that threats would exploit vulnerabilities and compromise the value of information assets. Thus, we want to implement security controls that are appropriate and cost effective. However, not only is risk management a *Goldilocks* problem (*Not too hot, not too cold: Just right*) but new vulnerabilities and exploits will appear and challenge existing controls. Consequently, we need to continually improve security by exposing new vulnerabilities and mitigating them. Likewise, security controls and procedures must continually be reviewed and when necessarily improved to support mission changes and evolving threat capabilities.

At different stages of a cloud life cycle, the security of the cloud will alternate from higher risk to lower risk between the time that exploitable vulnerabilities are exposed and patches or new controls are put into effect. It is unlikely that most cloud implementations can eliminate all potential risks, but what can be done is to focus on the kinds of risk that meet certain defined thresholds. Different industries have made progress in that regard, notably by following regulatory requirements such as for privacy in health care (HIPAA) and integrity where it comes to internal controls over preventing fraud as required by Sarbanes-Oxley.

Exploits Don't Play Fair

An exploit is like a badly behaved dinner guest who steals the especially delicious bits of food from your plate when you are busy sipping wine. (Well, maybe not exactly a dinner guest.) The fact is that exploits tend to take advantage of borderline circumstances that otherwise do not cause issues. Likewise, the interfaces between applications make a fine target for manipulation by sending them data or control values that are not gracefully handled. One can make the case that applications or systems really should be more resilient in how they manage the unwanted and vexing attentions by hackers and exploits.

The point is that no amount of prior planning can anticipate either a profoundly wicked vulnerability or a decidedly insidious scheme to twist up your controls and thereby gain elevated privilege. What can you do? Well, first you should expect these things in a very general sense and second, have a plan in place to detect and respond to them.

So, what can be done about all this? Monitor! Scan for vulnerabilities! Circle the wagons! Despite the limits of security controls and the increase in exploit sophistication, achieving cloud security is certainly not hopeless, far from it in fact. This book presents security monitoring as a key strategy and a best practice for cloud computing.

BEST PRACTICES

This section presents several best practices for cloud security. Traditional security best practices still apply to cloud computing, but CSPs and cloud consumers may be challenged in adopting such practices when they are more general rather than specific to the cloud space. Fortunately, the area of best practices has seen some productive work, which has important value and continues to mature.

Best Practices for Cloud Computing: First Principals

In this section we identify several key strategies and best practices for security in cloud computing. These form a foundation for the remainder of the chapter where we review the security state of the practice per the broader cloud community.

Policy

The need for a sound security policy cannot be over emphasized. Policy is the true foundation for all security activities. The scope of a policy will vary according to the type of cloud, there will be some overlap between SaaS, PaaS, and IaaS policies, but largely these will become increasingly broader moving from SaaS to IaaS. Likewise, the scope of a corporate policy that guides the use of public cloud will vary from than the same organization's policy guiding a private cloud.

It is a best practice for a cloud provider and for cloud consumer organizations to create and define a clear policy for cloud security. This policy should cover all security-relevant aspects of information security, including personnel, information, facilities, hardware, and software. Policies are important to set organizational direction, but to be successful they must be visible throughout the organization, they must carry the weight of management, and they must assign responsibilities.

Policies should be updated as needed, and they should be supplemented by the use of standards, procedures, and related guidelines that enable implementation of policy. Briefly, where security policy states the reasons and identifies the rules, standards go further in explaining the specifics behind what must be done. Guidelines more generally state how it should be done.

Risk Management

This book has discussed risk management at several points. In Chapter 1, we explained how risk is quantified and described risk management as a *Goldilocks problem*. In Chapter 3, we described risk management as involving *Threat Categorization*, *Threat Impact*, *Threat Frequency* along with the *Uncertainty Factor* of getting the first three right. In Chapter 4 we presented architectural principles that were motivated to mitigate and manage risk. And earlier in this chapter we looked at how to effectively manage risk along with the common stages or activities associated with risk management. Clearly, risk management is a core goal for cloud computing security and as such, we must build on security policy to define a framework or strategy for effectively achieving this goal.

The objectives of risk management best practices are to assess, address, and reduce security risks in a cloud initiative—and to do so in the context of weighing the risks from a business perspective. Selecting security controls and monitoring their effectiveness are part of risk management. Undergoing a formal business process to accept residual risks is an often-ignored step in this. Such a formal process would involve stakeholders from across the organization, and it would certainly need to include the cloud security and operations group. Among the considerations for residual risk are not only actual damages but also damages to the organization's brand or reputation. Indemnification is a viable consideration for some classes of damage, but it probably has limited value when brand or reputation is at risk.

Taken together, a best practice for risk management is to begin with an understanding and assessment of the risks one faces (risk analysis) and orient the selection of security controls (security life cycle framework, Figure 6.1) along with appropriate security practices and procedures toward managing risks. In other words, make risk management the core activity around which your security practice revolves.

Configuration Management and Change Control

It is a best practice to implement a configuration and change management process that can:

1. govern proposed changes,
2. identify possible security consequences, and
3. provide assurance that the current operational system is correct in version and configuration.

The relationship between configuration management and security control procedures is an often-neglected one in commercial implementations of Internet-facing systems. Evidence of this periodically appears in the form of older and vulnerable configurations making their way back into production even months after they have been patched or upgraded. How does this happen?

- The root cause is typically a process failure in configuration management (CM) or change control (CC). The nature of such process failures too often has a great deal to do with a desire to push a new release into production. Without disciplined change and configuration processes, security controls are subject to the introduction of vulnerabilities or the erosion of necessary controls. This is critical to security during the operational phases of the life cycle. One excellent recognition of this is found in NIST SP 800-64, *Security Considerations in the Information System Development Life Cycle*, which states: "Changes to the hardware, software, or firmware of a system can have a significant impact on the security of the system…changes should be documented, and their potential impact on security should be assessed regularly."[6]

If CM or CC processes are to truly support the operation and security of systems, then:

- CM and CC must be well defined and provide a structured method for effecting both technical and administrative changes. When these processes are effective, they provide organizational controls—with input from appropriate stakeholders.
- CM and CC must provide assurances that the IT resources in operation are correct in their version and configuration.
- Planning for CM should take place as the system itself is planned or designed. When a system moves into operation or maintenance, CM and CC activities become operational controls around the overall security of the system.
- CM and CC are essential to controlling and managing an accurate inventory of components and changes.

All that is fine, but systems are simply too large and too complex for purely manual processes in CM and CC to support ongoing security evaluation of the various changes that an operational system is subject to. What this leads to is the need for automation in configuration and deployment—and a coupling between such operational automation and CM and CC processes.

Auditing

In auditing we seek to verify compliance, review the effectiveness of controls, and validate security processes. Some key audit best practices are as follows:

- Follow a regular schedule in using tools (like Nessus, Cenzic's Hailstorm, or Jack the Ripper) to identify newly exposed vulnerabilities, configuration issues, weak passwords and to perform patch level verification (See Vulnerability Scanning, below).
- Periodically review the security controls that are in place, assess their effectiveness and ascertain if they are appropriate to the current or anticipated risks.
- Use automated tools and manual procedures to verify compliance to policy. This should be performed by a CSP or even IaaS or PaaS tenants. (The CSA and CloudAudit are working toward the community development of exactly such tools, existing compliance checking is best illustrated by NIST's Security Content Automation Protocol—or SCAP—tools.)
- Periodic use of an independent penetration testing service to determine if the system can withstand representative exploits.
- System logs should also be manually reviewed on a periodic basis to verify the correct operation of security monitoring and to identify enhancements to monitoring.

Given the various tools and sources of audit data, the process of verifying compliance can involve correlating, comparing, and assessing a vast volume of multiple bits and pieces of data. This hardly lends itself to manual processes, yet it is often the case that the most sophisticated tool in the auditor's kit is a spreadsheet into which data is cut and pasted from various source reports. Clearly, that is less than effective for a large system such as a cloud.

There are many commercial products for performing these far ranging audit tasks, and many can be used by cloud IaaS customers in the same way they would be used for traditional infrastructure. For PaaS the adoption of such tools becomes a bit more problematic as the tenant has less control, but it is still tenable. Meeting the needs of auditing in cloud computing, the CloudAudit community states: "The goal of CloudAudit (also known as "A6") is to provide a common interface and namespace that allows cloud computing providers to automate the Audit, Assertion, Assessment, and Assurance (A6) of their infrastructure (IaaS), platform (PaaS), and application (SaaS) environments and allow authorized consumers of their services to do likewise via an open, extensible and secure interface and methodology."[7]

Vulnerability Scanning

It is a best practice to perform regular cloud infrastructure vulnerability scanning. This should include all cloud management platforms, servers, and network devices. The goal of vulnerability scanning is to identify any new or residual vulnerabilities so that the associated risk may be mitigated. The objectives of vulnerability scanning are:

- Catalog all components so that the resulting list can be used to verify configuration management data. Where devices are identified that are not previously catalogued, a more thorough investigation is necessary.
- Identify any new or previously known vulnerabilities, this will typically involve identifying risky services (such as ftp or telnet) for which there are well-known exploits and ineffective countermeasures. Other vulnerabilities will be identified by verifying patch levels, as vulnerabilities are typically addressed with server or network device OSs patch levels, if a patch has not been applied, then the associated vulnerabilities are still in effect.

In general, there are two classes of scanning. The first is performed from the outside of a machine and can be performed against any target. These scans do not require any access permissions whatsoever and are often performed by hackers to catalog a potential target's vulnerabilities. Much can be learned about the target, but a more thorough scan requires that the scanner authenticate to the target to take a complete inventory of the system from the inside. Authenticated scans can take a considerable amount of time, but when such scans use a tool such as Nessus, the security staff can augment stock scan tests that are inherent to the tool with additional custom scan plug-ins that perform many checks tailored to the needs of the organization.

> **WARNING**
>
> When a scan is performed by an attacker, much can be learned about a target machine just from how it responds to different service requests and packets. This constitutes *reconnaissance* allowing an attacker to enumerate services and the presence of vulnerable applications.
>
> The knowledge that is gained from such scans can be very useful for the attacker to plan a structured attack against the target. Such scans can be blindingly obvious and generate alarms, or they can be very discrete and even performed at an extremely low level of activity and slowly over time. Scanning in this way is well known to security administrators, and consequently there have been many different approaches for attackers to attempt undetectable *low and slow* attacks. (For a more in-depth treatment of port scanning attacks the reader is referred to any of several excellent books and to the documentation around two open source products: Nmap and Metasploit.)
>
> Leaving vulnerable services active rather than hardening a device, and allowing packets from St. Hackingsville to be routed into private infrastructure amount to an open invitation to be scanned. But not all such scans will originate from outside the infrastructure, and this is certainly the case with public cloud services, specifically IaaS or PaaS. There are several strategies that can be pursued when facing a scan.
>
> A common response is to reply to the requestor regardless of whether the port being scanned is open or closed. However, when the port is closed and a requestor receives this response then they know that they have found a device. So, a different approach is to ignore packets from unknown addresses. This is known as stealth mode. However, this strategy only works if all port requests are not acknowledged, otherwise it becomes apparent that you are half-heartedly hiding a device. Some network devices and firewalls use adaptive behaviors to block previously open and closed ports when they detect that an IP address is probing them. But, if the scan is in a low and slow mode, the adaptive behavior will not be very successful if the scan time window is large enough.

Vulnerability scanning has additional benefits. If one collects scan data against the same targets and stores the scan results in a data base, configuration errors and attack trends can be detected by analysis of this data over time. Likewise, use of a database to store scan results makes these immediately available to auditors and automated tools for compliance and other security checking. As with CM and auditing, the scale of scanning a cloud infrastructure really does lend itself to use of greater automation in managing the process and analyzing the data.

Segregation of Duties

It is a best practice to limit the privileges that users have to as small a set which is necessary for the user to perform their work. This stems from the concept of separation of duties, which comes from the business notion that no individual should have privileges that exceed what they need in performing their role. In finance, this translates into *the well-formed transaction*, and would preclude any given employee from creating, approving, and subsequently authorizing payment for a purchase order. Failing to separate such linked functions plays into the hands of the worst in human nature, and is irresponsible in business.

In the cloud, the segregation of duties will already be partially implemented by the nature of the model itself, namely IT will be responsible for managing all aspects of the physical infrastructure. Requests for changes by the cloud provider for the cloud itself will go through a configuration management process where they will be vetted by all the major business functions—security included. And, depending on the cloud deployment model—public, community, or private—the tenant will have a varying degree of responsibility for and opportunity to effect service, software, and other configuration changes. Likewise, the nature of the service models increasingly limit the scope of control the tenant or user has from IaaS to SaaS.

Especially sensitive functions should entail a two-person rule to assure that the function is not only properly invoked but done so under proper circumstances. Similarly, different roles should be defined to configure and manage computer and network security controls. By example, resetting a user's credentials or privileges. Where such actions are performed without organizational process controls, management over user access rights is not reliable. In addition, with cloud services, there are multiple areas of responsibility with the potential to mismanage resources (human error is legendary). These different areas include roles that lie with the CSP and roles that a tenant has responsibility for. By dividing the levers of control enables faster changes and also more informed decisions over privileged management operations. It does bear mentioning that many of the configuration changes that a tenant of a public IaaS service can make can have a significant impact on both the security of their service and on the metered costs.

There is another aspect to segregation of duties and different roles and responsibilities. Not all processes can be fully automated, and even for those that should be automated it is not always the case that this can be achieved given overall budgets, schedules, and competitive pressures. On the path toward automation one will often start by employing people following well-defined steps and processes, eventually converting these to automated processes. And it is also often the case that automated processes have backup manual procedures. Again—whether automated or manual—cloud administration and operational processes must be controlled to meet the goals of segregation of duties and maintain security.

Best Practices across the Cloud Community

The Cloud Computing Use Case Discussion Group is focused on best practices for building clouds or IaaS and PaaS. In July 2010, they published version 4.0 of their *Cloud Computing Use Cases White Paper*. Besides detailing a number of use cases for cloud computing, this group also identified a number of security controls for cloud computing. The following summarizes these[8]:

- **Asset Management** All assets including hardware, network, and software that comprise the cloud infrastructure must be managed.

- **Cryptography: Key and Certificate Management** They advocate for an infrastructure to manage keys and certificates, and encourage the use of standards-based cryptography.
- **Data/Storage Security** They identify the need to support encrypted storage of data and they recognize that some users will need separate storage from others.
- **Endpoint Security** Secure endpoints for cloud resources, along with end point restrictions by protocol and device types.
- **Event Auditing and Reporting** This entails visibility by consumers into security-relevant events and breaches.
- **Identity, Roles, Access Control, and Attributes** Effective implementation of access controls and security policy enforcement depends on defined identity, roles, and privileges.
- **Network Security** Network traffic must be able to be secured at the level of switches, routers, and packets.
- **Other controls listed by the Cloud Computing Use Case Discussion Group** Service Automation, Workload and Service Management, and Security Practices.

Also active in the best practices area, the CSA's *Security Guidance for Critical Areas of Focus in Cloud Computing*[C] identifies a broad range of best practices. These include a number in each of the following areas: Governance and Enterprise Risk Management; Legal and Electronic; Compliance and Audit; Information Lifecycle Management; Portability and Interoperability; Traditional Security; Business Continuity and Disaster Recovery; Data Center Operations; Incident Response, Notification and Remediation; Application Security; Encryption and Key Management; Identity and Access Management; and Virtualization.

The CSA's work is oriented toward practices in both building a cloud and using one. The reader is encouraged to review the CSA security guidance document for detailed recommendations for each of those areas.

Taking a similar approach, the European Network and Information Security Agency developed a comprehensive look at risks and recommendations for information security in cloud computing. Their report *Cloud Computing Benefits, Risks and Recommendations for Information Security*[D] presents a broad review of cloud risks and benefits and does so by aligning the benefits of cloud computing with recommendations for information security practices and requirements. It is an excellent report for planning purposes and governance, both for building clouds and using clouds.

[C]Brunette, G., Mogull, R., The Cloud Security Alliance, Security Guidance for Critical Areas of Focus in Cloud Computing V2.1, December 2009.
[D]Catteddu, D., Hogben, G., Cloud Computing Benefits, Risks and Recommendations for Information Security, European Network and Information Security Agency (ENISA), 2009 http://www.enisa.europa.eu/.

Other Best Practices for Cloud Computing: Cloud Service Consumers

Beyond the CSA's Best Practices, NIST has offered a relatively short set as well. Distilling guidance from traditional security best practices, the CSA's list and a range of NIST sources the following is representative of practices for a cloud consumer:

- **State-of-the-Practice** Select a CSP based in part on their attention to security and how their overall security compares to current practices.
- **Transparency** Select a CSP based on their willingness to offer transparency into key security practices, including risk assessment and incident response. CSPs who meet this will also likely have a customer-facing CSO or CISO.
- **Security Controls** A CSP should furnish security control and practice information that the customer can use to map against their policy requirements.
- **Security Standards and Practices** A CSP should view many of their security efforts as not just good security, but also as competitive differentiation. This is especially the case with adherence to secure coding practices, use of security standards and products that have passed independent evaluation.

In general, as a consumer, one does not want to retire all organizational responsibility for security and hand the reins to the CSP. It is thus a best practice for cloud service consumers to define an overall security program that starts with a security policy and includes all life cycle activities. Where an activity or function is performed by a CSP, identify what the CSPs policy or SLAs state for that and regularly track changes by the CSP against their services. This is clearly too much of an effort for the average small business or individual cloud consumer, but it is a critical exercise for any entity that is relying on a CSP for their livelihood. Making this practice actionable: Verify that your Cloud Security needs are inline with the CSPs security.

TOOLS

It is very useful to use the same tools against your cloud infrastructure as attackers would use against it. However, this is a technique that is best left to the official security team acting in their official capacity. Otherwise, make sure you have a *get out of jail free card* because security policy will most certainly define this sort of activity as warranting reprimand or worse.

To begin with, Nmap is a mature and well-known port scanner that can be used not only to probe your infrastructure but also to map it. There are ports of Nmap for all common OS platforms and some include graphical user interfaces or other front ends. However, Nmap is fairly easy to use from the command line and it can generate a huge amount of output that describes your scanned targets. There are other tools that you can use also, including Nessus and even Web-based scan services. But, Nmap is a completely adequate tool that continues to be improved. Download it from www.nmap.org to get the real deal.

When you scan your cloud, do so from several different points. You should scan from outside the cloud, from the Internet but do so with your source IP address in mind. If your cloud whitelists certain IP addresses as being trusted, your scan results may end up being very different than if you scan from a non-whitelisted Internet source IP. In fact, you should compare the results to verify that your network is properly discriminating between such cases.

Also scan from various points inside the infrastructure. The results you will get will again be quite different based on the source IP within the network. From a tenant VM in an IaaS cloud, you should not be able to see the management infrastructure. And, depending on how the IaaS enabling switching rules are implemented, you may or may not see VMs belonging to other tenants.

Other Best Practices for Cloud Computing: Cloud Service Providers

Here we will identify just a few additional best practices above and beyond those that we listed throughout this chapter. There are many best practices for cloud providers that are consistent with traditional IT security best practices. Practices that are important to bring forward include:

- **Network Isolation** Briefly, network traffic that has to do with the CSP managing and controlling their cloud infrastructure should be kept completely separate from networks that cloud tenants or consumers have access to via VMs or their own applications. Likewise, the CSP should also provide for a similar degree of isolation for tenant service control traffic and tenant data traffic. Failing to do so puts the infrastructure at risk the moment a provider's security configuration fails or is misconfigured, of in the case of a tenant puts the tenant's virtual infrastructure at risk. Network isolation should be seen as a foundation for defense in-depth from a CSP network standpoint. It is thus a best practice to keep control networks separate from data networks.
- **The Use of a CMDB** The use of a CMDB is central to maturity and reliability in operation of the cloud. In addition, the CSP must efficiently manage their resources especially in terms of automated processes that allocate and deallocate, as well as provision and deprovision customer-facing resources. Automated processes must operate against a valid representation of the infrastructure.
- **Configuration Integrity** To identify unauthorized changes, additions, or deletions to any platform's system files, an integrity checking software should be installed at the appropriate level (guest or host VM file system, for instance).
- **Identity** A CSP must implement a scalable and robust Identity and Access Management (IAM) system that provides the following: identity provisioning and deprovisioning, authentication and federation, and authorization and profile management. In addition, the system should support compliance needs.

EPIC FAIL

A security colleague (John) once recounted a story that drives home the need to grasp the importance of taking risk and threats seriously. John had returned from a security consulting engagement with an Asian-based bank which had one of its Internet-facing systems hacked. After he has done a thorough investigation of the system, he met with the customer. John explained that the compromise had occurred because the hacker had exploited an unpatched vulnerability. The customer stated that this sounded like a very bad situation. John replied it was and that the customer simply had to patch the system. The customer replied that they could not patch because it would break necessary functionality. After a long pause they asked: "If we do not patch, what are the odds that another hacker will find the same vulnerability and exploit it again...?" That mere posing of that question evidences the difficulty that many system owners have in grasping the certainty of security risks.

NOTE

From a security standpoint, cloud providers are not all alike. Not only does the nature of cloud services vary from CSP to CSP but so also the degree of security. To begin with, the use of controls is not consistent for providers even for those offering essentially the same services. Likewise, cloud service providers are more or less transparent about their practices and customer support for incident resolution.

The CSP industry has reached the point where vetted community scorecards and reviews of CSP security would be very helpful for prospective adopters. Those should also be used as input to more formal reviews and independent assessments.

SECURITY MONITORING

It is a best practice to automate the collection of security events from all security-relevant network devices, servers, and applications. These events should be archived in raw form to preserve a legal record of all security-relevant activity and being assessed via automated means to detect situations warranting alerts.

Security monitoring in cloud infrastructure and services is based on the generation, collection, analysis, and reporting of security-relevant event data. We can refer to the source events as *security instrumentation data* or *security telemetry*. This amounts to any security-relevant data that is generated by a system, network, or application, along with any other data that may be developed by observing the security-relevant behavior of a system. The scope of what can be collected is broad and the level of detail can be overwhelming. Collection probes can be used to instrument every aspect of a cloud, gathering information on user, application, and system activity, as well as observing data in motion as packets cross-observation points.

The range of possible security events that can be generated, collected, and assessed generally exceeds the ability to be fully processed by centralized cloud monitoring services. Therefore, event generation is configured to limit events to those that are necessary for security. Likewise, there are various points in the event stream where generated events can be filtered before the remaining events are assessed.

Collection of security event data is generally performed using a hierarchical or centralized collection strategy whereby event data is collected as soon as possible after the time it is generated by originating devices. These events are gathered at a security collection and analysis capability where data is archived, assessed, and reported (Figure 6.5).

At a high level, what we seek to do with security monitoring is to provide a feedback loop for the system that is the operating cloud infrastructure. In security monitoring, this feedback is based on three sets of information:

- Knowledge about the infrastructure, such as that which is maintained in a CMDB or similar information about the monitored infrastructure.
- Event data that is a form of output from the cloud infrastructure.
- Security rules and heuristics that are used to assess the event data.

As depicted in Figure 6.6, these three kinds of information sources are used to some extent in modern security monitoring systems. Admittedly, there is no published use of a CMDB to illuminate monitoring and guide automated analysis, but this section (Security Monitoring) will discuss the potential for this in greater detail. Figure 6.6 also makes representations about *the effectiveness of a security feedback* loop. Again, although there are few published descriptions of using security monitoring with feedback loops, doing so is to embrace a forward edge of the field. What this figure seeks to convey is the relationship between cloud security, output from the cloud that enables security monitoring, the role of the CMDB as an additional source of monitoring input, and an automated means to effect feedback to control the cloud.

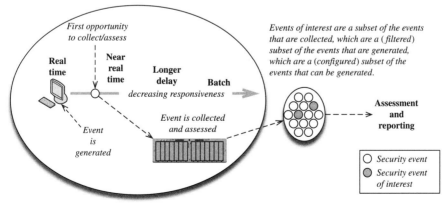

FIGURE 6.5

Security monitoring and security feedback.

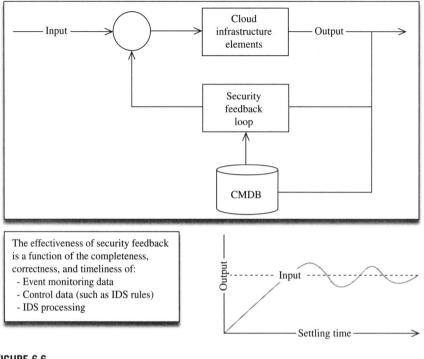

FIGURE 6.6

Security monitoring and security feedback.

Security monitoring needs to become more sophisticated in the near term and largely so because of the demands of complex cloud computing solutions. As this happens, greater automation will likely be required for tuning of analysis functions (automated tuning is depicted as *settling time* in Figure 6.6). The rest of this section will go into greater detail on monitoring in cloud computing.

The Purpose of Security Monitoring

Security monitoring is a key cloud security strategy that has several important purposes for CSPs and tenants, these include:

- **Threat Detection** Some exploits may not be preventable and some threats may not be anticipated, and in this sense monitoring is the last line of defense. But there is a difference between detecting a security situation and doing something about it.
- **Verification of Security Controls** Although most security controls are oriented toward enforcing security policy, monitoring is used to verify the correct operation of other security controls. If events which indicate actions

prohibited by policy appear in the security event stream, this would indicate that policy is not being correctly enforced by security controls.

- **Exposure of Bugs** Security monitoring has identified vulnerabilities or security bugs that were previously unknown. This can take several forms, including the triggering of monitoring rules, which when they are subsequently reviewed against the monitoring record simply does not make sense.
- **A Legal Record of Activity** Security event data can form a legal record of actions that users or processes performed. To be used in a legal proceeding, this data must have verifiable integrity (records have not been altered and they comprise a complete record) and the organization must be able to demonstrate chain of custody over the data.
- **Enabling Forensics** Security event data has great value in gaining an understanding of the steps involved in an exploit along with discerning the scope of any resulting damage.

In multi-tenant cloud computing, security monitoring has additional importance beyond serving as a means for infrastructure control. By the very nature of a multi-tenant infrastructure, monitoring is necessary on an ongoing basis for near-real-time verification of security.

But the other side of that coin has to do with timely provider response to security incidents or alerts that are generated by the monitoring system. Effective security monitoring is a necessary capability if security intervention or incident response is to be effective. In other words, monitoring, detection, and response must be closely tied together to effect a timely response. Finally, by adopting or implementing a robust and advanced security monitoring capability, a CSP has the opportunity to present security monitoring as a service.

Transforming an Event Stream

It is vital that the security instrumentation functionality is correctly deployed and maintained. However, security instrumentation data poses many challenges from generation to transmission and from centralized collection to analysis and response. Achieving a valid security perspective in a complex system like a cloud entails trade-offs in multiple dimensions.

The sheer amount of raw security event data that is generated in even a small cloud infrastructure demands that the collection, handling, analysis, and storage of data be efficient. The density of VMs on physical servers with limited network capacity is a significant concern in this, especially as security is often viewed by the business as important, but more notably a resource and performance drain.

Generation of Security Events

To begin, security-relevant data can be generated at every level of a cloud infrastructure, starting with each hardware platform such as a server chassis.

(The Service Availability Forum has developed extensive standards for service specifications in this area.[E]). Here we are referring to the hardware platform itself. Commonly used data center class servers usually allow for management of their hardware through a separate network interface.

Likewise, carrier or enterprise grade networking gear also has such platform interfaces, and these can also be used to gather some security-relevant information about the platform itself. Although platform level information is not what we are really focused on when we monitor security, including this category of information sources allows us a greater degree of confidence in the integrity and availability of cloud security monitoring.

All modern OSs are capable of generating security event data such as audit or syslog events.[F] To generate the security events OSs need to be configured, how this is done is a function of the OS but it is essentially trivial in nature. The set of possible events is also a function of the OS. By example, labeled OSs, such as Trusted Solaris, will generate an additional set of events based on instrumentation from label-enforcing MAC controls. The kinds of events that are generated by an OS can be very broad. Syslog by example, can be configured to generate event messages based on a facility (auth, authpriv, daemon, cron, ftp, lpr, kern, mail,...) and priority/level (Emergency, Alert, Critical, Error, Warning, Notice, Info or Debug).

Applications and middleware also generate their own data streams, which can all be aggregated into a single event stream or a collection of streams. Although applications are a rich potential source of security data for monitoring, it is unfortunate that few applications are instrumented to any extent. One can hope that cloud applications change this as it is especially valuable for SaaS and PaaS.

Other sources of data include storage systems, network switches, routers, and other network equipment. Network devices used in cloud infrastructure are likely to be capable of a rich and complete set of security instrumentation data.

There are other network-based data sources for events, these include traffic analysis and network traffic monitoring using Snort or other tools. These are primarily focused on assessing traffic to detect inbound attacks or exploit situations. But, this category of event sources is also very important to maintain the internal integrity of domains in a multi tenant cloud or a public cloud solution. By detecting attempts by users in one domain or virtual local area network (VLAN) to access adjacent domains the cloud provider is using monitoring as an active security control.

But network-based events also have great value in detecting several categories of information leakage from inside an infrastructure. Misbehaving insiders or misconfigured processes can be interdicted if they are found to be sending data from a cloud infrastructure to an external location. There is another scenario that has serious consequences for the operators of infrastructure and that has to do

---

[E]Application Interface Specification: Log Service, Service Availability Forum SAI-AIS-LOG-A.02.01 (Date unknown) http://www.saforum.org/
[F]We will discuss audit and syslog in greater detail in section "Collection of Security Events"

with internal systems that are used to attack, spam, or launch denial of service attacks against external Internet-based targets. Snort in particular is an excellent tool to detect such situations. In such a case, Snort can detect an outbound attack and send appropriate alerts or events to reporting components. Failing to stop such outbound attacks can be very damaging to the functionality of a public cloud as CSP IP addresses that are marked as originating attacks can end up on black-lists, thus rendering them either suspect or shunned by other Internet hosts.

It is important to verify that the events selected for any class of device (hardware, OS, network device, application, and so on) are generated properly and include all necessary information. Correct time stamps on data are a critical requirement, as it can become impossible to correctly assess a sequence of events related to a security incident if clocks for different event sources are not synchronized to a common and correct time server.

Taken together, the range of cloud security event sources can generate an overwhelming volume of data that can easily overrun capture buffers thereby resulting in collection gaps and detection blinding. Milder impacts can result in queues becoming saturated and thus delaying detection and alerting until well after a response can be launched. Also, malfunctioning components can send an unbelievable volume of traffic and even worse, they can cause other closely coupled components to themselves run amok, in the process generating even more event traffic. When this happens, it is not uncommon for event buffers to become overrun or for detection to fall behind. If this is possible, it represents not only a security failure but an exploitable vulnerability. In all cases, it is critical that security event generation and collection is properly sized for worst case scenarios—in peak operation the generation and collection should be well below 90% of buffer and network capacity. Testing against various scenarios is a good strategy to follow for such sizing.

The right amount of event granularity is not necessarily known in advance. One strategy is to generate more data than is needed, both filtering it at the source and if necessary at a central collection point. Another strategy is to generate a core set of data and dynamically adjust additional generation and collection filters in response to operational needs. There are complications to each of these strategies, but the fact is that when you are in the midst of an unfolding attack or when you are conducting a forensics investigation, the more data you have available to help assess the situation the faster you can draw sound conclusions and the better your understanding will be.

Collection of Security Events

The state of the practice in security monitoring is to generate data in different realms, collect the data, normalize it as necessary, and then archive and assess the data against a view of what is normal or acceptable versus what is unusual or reportable.

Although many tools are available to collect, forward, and manage security events, syslog is the most common. Syslog gathers events from the OS and forwards them to a syslog host or syslog relay that is located in close network proximity to the event source. Other commercial products are available to collect and manage the event stream, but these are all proprietary in their formats.

In a cloud implementation, platform network interfaces should really be networked out-of-band from the data network(s) to isolate management of server hardware infrastructure from the cloud networks that are used for tenants and users. Besides supporting better security through such isolation, a separate network also reduces the bandwidth requirements for conveying hardware platform telemetry. However, doing so undermines the desire for low cost. Other than bandwidth separation, use of VLANs is acceptable for low to moderate risk applications. But the amount of traffic on a cloud customer-facing network can be significant at times. If syslog and snort traffic are mixed in with customer traffic on the same server to switch interconnects, then under peak loads the security monitoring data can result in unacceptable performance for users.

This situation will be even more of an issue as VM density increases on increasingly more capable servers. Network traffic will increase for hardware servers to the point where it makes great sense to separate the security traffic for each physical server from the public data traffic. Since server class machines for cloud computing will have multiple high speed interfaces—Gigabit Ethernet (GbE), 10 GbE or even fibre—allocating a separate link to security monitoring is reasonable. Other network strategies for ensuring performance with high rates of event traffic include bonding multiple ports—or links—together as a higher aggregate virtual link, and then instantiating VLANs over that link to separate security traffic from public traffic.

As security events are collected in streams and as these are forwarded via the network to a central collection point, there are a range of different strategies that one can pursue. There are several considerations in doing this, these include:

- Ensuring the continual collection and archiving of event data even when analysis and monitoring services are unavailable.
- Minimizing the impact of security events on public portions of the infrastructure network.
- Enabling reporting of time-critical alerts even under periods of peak load and while under attack.

Collecting data also involves normalizing it into a format that allows for the data to be conveyed through a common mechanism such as syslog.

Correlation and Analysis Strategies

Looking at the event stream we have bits of data that singly are called *events*. Some of the events that we gather arrive as *alerts*, other events are purely informational, and many events can be examined in multiple dimensions—alone or in context—and thus serve as raw data for analysis. Having generated and collected events, we now seek to make something out of them. Using the language of military analysis, when we collect security events in a centralized manner, our goal is to illuminate, assess, and escalate indications and warnings that represent situations—rather than just reporting events. In doing so, we also need to minimize false positives (Type I errors) and false negatives (Type II errors). A false positive is a warning we might escalate that is in error, whereas a false negative is a warning we failed to detect.

Real time analysis fits the need for time sensitive detection and response. Typical real time analysis is based on simple alerts, which often requires human review. More sophisticated analysis can be performed via batch analysis or near-real time correlation and combinations of techniques. Attack signatures can be used to match events of interest against known scenarios, but this matching becomes very complex when detection or analysis time windows are made longer to catch *low and slow* attacks. More sophisticated analysis involves assessment of complex and broader windows of time and focuses on establishing context among seemingly unrelated individual events or changes over periods of time. A more sophisticated detection capability would involve complicated situational awareness, which would require layers of analysis and analysis results and indicators that can be sliced and diced in multiple dimensions to identify behavior associated with security attacks that have yet to have signatures or to identify attacks that cannot be described by simple signatures. Figure 6.7 depicts the event stream

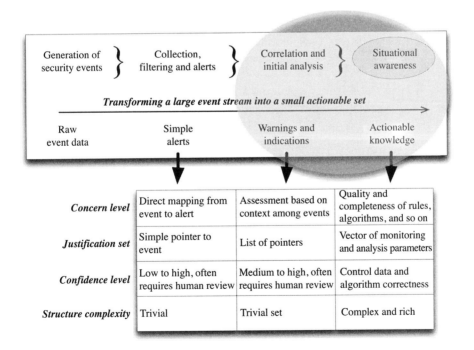

FIGURE 6.7

From raw events to situational awareness.

from generation, collection, analysis, and up to situational awareness. Figure 6.7 also relates how a concern level can be established starting with simple alerts to alerts based on context between events and up to higher degrees of confidence with more capable detection in the situational awareness realm. Also depicted Figure 6.7 are the characteristics of the structures and analysis at these levels.

In this section, we have seen how security events are the lifeblood of security monitoring. To be effective in interdicting an active threat, security monitoring must have a feedback capability. Figure 6.8 shows the same event stream from Figure 6.7, but now we also show how simple alerts and higher level indications and warnings are reported via monitoring interfaces. It is the goal to make human security analysis productive rather than a game of responding to the blinking red light. Therefore, the presentation of alerts and monitoring situations to a security analyst is more of an art than a science at this point in time. The addition of automated means of response by situational awareness capabilities will take away some of the repetitive and drudgery aspects from security analysts. Figure 6.8 depicts this view of the evolving nature of security monitoring. It is noteworthy that much of this functionality can be achieved through use of available open source components today. What does not exist can be created with some additional effort.

Figure 6.9 shows the relationship between functional components involved in security scanning, security monitoring, and automated response. Security monitoring is shown as including the following processes: event management, event filtering, correlation, assessment, and response. Note that the use of a CMDB is depicted at

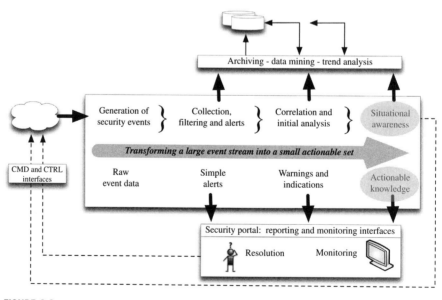

FIGURE 6.8

The future of security monitoring in cloud infrastructure.

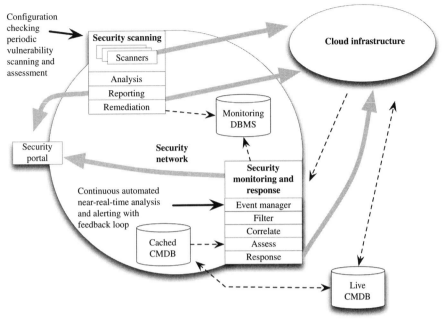

FIGURE 6.9

Implementation of security monitoring in cloud infrastructure.

two levels, with a cached CMDB used by the security system for high-availability and reliability in operation. In this model, the cached CMDB is continually updated from the infrastructure-facing CMDB. Also depicted Figure 6.9 is the role of security scanning. It should be pointed out that besides the use of a separate and isolated network for the security, a portal is also depicted for virtual access to monitoring and scanning functions.

The Need for C.I.A. in Security Monitoring

It is a best practice in cloud security to assure the security of monitoring and the integrity and availability of the event stream. If monitoring is insecure, then monitoring will produce results that are not trustworthy. Monitoring is only as reliable as event data is complete and correct. This drives the requirement for strong assurance and appropriate security controls for all aspects of monitoring: Monitoring probes, data collection, data transmission, data analysis, and data archiving must all meet well-defined requirements and they do so at a trust level that is commensurate with the mission value of the overall system and at a level of data assurance that meets the highest level of data that is processed. In other words, the security around monitoring must meet or exceed that of the system and its data.

At a minimum, if monitoring probes produce suspect data then monitoring is worthless. If monitoring data is corrupted, destroyed, or subverted then we have failed to achieve a basic and necessary level of operational security. It may not be possible to reliably collect monitoring data from within a tenant's VM, but we should always be reliably generating monitoring data, conveying it, and centrally collecting it for audit, analysis, monitor, and archive purposes. Appropriate security monitoring, or security event management (SEM), or security event incident management (SEIM) must be a high priority.

The Opportunity for MaaS

Cloud providers can be expected to offer broader and richer security monitoring and alerting capabilities for their tenants. Since the provider will already need to perform security monitoring of infrastructure as part of their normal operation, it makes sense for providers to utilize that same infrastructure as a means to implement monitoring for their customers. What would this look like?

To the customer: Tiered services most likely. The appeal of CP monitoring services for customers will vary according to the nature of the cloud delivery model (public to private), the nature of the service delivery (IaaS to SaaS), the sensitivity of the information and processing, regulatory and compliance requirements, as well as the degree of customer risk acceptance or aversion.

Alternatively, tenants using IaaS and PaaS services models may assume all monitoring within their service boundaries or they may perform monitoring using a hybrid model. When monitoring is done within a service boundary, its value will be constrained to the service management or users within that space. In contrast, if monitoring is performed at each level and monitoring information from a lower foundational level (for instance IaaS) is made available to monitoring at a higher level (for instance PaaS or SaaS), then more information is available and a more complete understanding can be discerned.

SUMMARY

For a CSP, effective security represents an opportunity to reduce ongoing costs and provide a competitive service. Over time, CSPs can be expected to increase their use of security controls, obtain independent certification and accreditation, and even express more security functionality in the form of tiered services or add-ons for customers.

As a customer of a cloud service, if a CSPs security practices are not inline with the value of our information, then that cloud service does not meet our security needs. If no other CSP will meet our cloud security needs, we probably need to consider building a private cloud or implementing a more expensive and sophisticated custom IT infrastructure. This is a cloud trade-off—you can live with a public solution (and the cost is compelling), or you turn inward and build a private solution. However, today this paradigm is already changing as CSPs and communities of interest are starting to recognize that there is opportunity for higher entrance-cost clouds that cater to communities of specialized security and privacy needs.

One can easily envision cloud service customers of PaaS or IaaS preferring to use a CSP security information event management (SIEM) capability as long as the customer's event stream is not accessible to other customers. This sort of capability would be a competitive advantage for a CSP as the cost of expressing such a service to a customer would be a fraction of the cost for a customer to develop or install a commercial capability.

This chapter also advocates that there is an important difference between security monitoring and a monitoring system that can reliably trigger an effective response in the same time domain as the threat itself. Complex multitenant cloud infrastructure requires a monitoring solution that can automate certain responses in the time domain of threats.

Endnotes

1. NIST Special Publication 800-53 Revision 3, Recommended Security Controls for Federal Information Systems and Organizations; 2009.
2. Ibid.
3. NIST Federal Information Processing Standards Publication 199 (FIPS Pub-199), Published February 2004. Available at: http://csrc.nist.gov/publications/fips/fips199/FIPS-PUB-199-final.pdf [accessed 22.03.11].
4. Ibid.
5. CSA Cloud Security Controls Matrix, R1.1_Final, The Cloud Security Alliance, December 2010.
6. NIST SP 800-64, Security Considerations in the Information System Development Life Cycle.
7. http://www.cloudaudit.org/page3/page3.html [accessed 22.03.11].
8. Ahronovitz M, et al. The Cloud Computing Use Case Discussion Group "Cloud Computing Use Cases White Paper" Version 4.0, July 2, 2010. http://cloudusecases.org [accessed 22.03.11].

Security Criteria: Building an Internal Cloud

Although one should acknowledge that the mainframe computer has more than a little in common with private cloud computing, a great deal has changed since the mainframe ruled corporate Information Technology (IT). The cost of computing has plummeted, mobile computing devices have redefined what a computer is, advances in networking allow high speed and pervasive access, and the explosion of mobile devices and apps makes even recent era PC applications seem stodgy. More elemental similarities between cloud computing and the classic mainframe involve the potential to recentralize compute and storage resources, the return of operating discipline to internal IT, and the abstraction of IT to a series of services only recently imagined.

Today, building your own private cloud can be as simple as virtualizing a few servers and as complex as refactoring your entire IT infrastructure. But doing so both within budget and with results that enable security requires planning and an appreciation for what will be faced when the cloud is in operation.

PRIVATE CLOUDS: MOTIVATION AND OVERVIEW

Why would an enterprise invest in a private cloud when the field of public cloud offerings is expanding? In essence: flexibility and security. Public clouds offer an ease of access and financial incentives that are compelling. But private clouds can address the combined desire for greater flexibility in defining cloud services along with a need to physically control information resources. However, keep in mind that the advantages to be gained with a private cloud will be limited by its scale and by how the enterprise manages it.

With public cloud offerings, you will typically not have much success getting a cloud security provider (CSP) to cater to unique requirements for cloud services, compliance, or security. In such cases, or where there is a need to maintain complete physical and electronic control over an organization's information resources, a private cloud can be the wisest cloud-based option. This is an

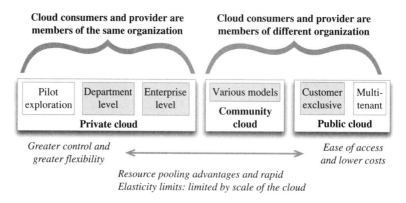

FIGURE 7.1

Decision: public or private cloud?

evolution in traditional in-house hosting, the principal difference being the use of the cloud IT model. Figure 7.1 depicts these issues surrounding public or private cloud decisions: the cost benefits and ease of access when using public utilities versus the greater flexibility and control with private clouds.

This is not to say that public cloud suppliers will not offer customers exclusive and separate sections carved out of overall infrastructure to implement a remotely hosted private cloud, just that doing so undermines their economic model. If such exclusive sections of a public cloud infrastructure can be securely carved out of the combined hardware, storage, and network fabric and if these exclusive sections can be forced to fall on sufficiently *safe* boundaries, then this may well make such a practice cost effective. Although this is a hybrid model of delivery on top of raw cloud infrastructure, it can be made to be cost effective for both the CSP and the consumer. Regardless of the potential for customizable customer exclusive public cloud offerings, there are other motivations that will drive many customers toward private clouds.

TOOLS

An organization can implement an exploratory cloud as a proof of concept or to develop skill and experience. This can be very useful to develop a hands-on understanding of technical issues and possible complications that might be faced before making a larger commitment to an operational cloud. Engaging in a realistic proof of concept cloud can also inform all enterprise parties as to their responsibilities as consumers, providers, and stakeholders. If such an activity is pursued as a serious endeavor, it can lead to the development of valuable artifacts and learning.

1. **Plan** Before embarking on a cloud prototype, define the scope and gather requirements for the cloud prototype. It also makes sense to declare what you believe will be gained from using the cloud model.

2. **Develop a Business Case** Identify a group to pilot or area to investigate. Gather cost data and perform a cost/benefit analysis. Identify the expected business benefits and prepare a test that will provide information against some notable risk.
3. **Prototype** Develop a proof of concept or small-scale implementation using the same basic technology or products that you expect to use if you subsequently decide to embark on a fully funded cloud project.
4. **Assess Results** Analyze the findings of the pilot or prototype and if necessary, revisit the assumptions and business case. Report or review the findings.
5. Repeat as necessary.

Security Implications: Shared versus Dedicated Resources

One of the major ways that cloud computing achieves cost savings is by eking greater utility out of shared (pooled) resources. What does this mean for security? That depends on how the organization implements, manages, and operates their overall cloud infrastructure. But the potential for better security with a private cloud is greater at a lower overall cost than with traditional private IT.

The trend with private cloud computing is in contrast with how organizations traditionally resource their individual IT needs: individually and on a per need basis. Before the recent rise of virtualization and more powerful servers, individual business applications were apt to reside on individual servers—resulting in a chaotic and undisciplined landscape: server sprawl. With the rise of virtualization, this situation has evolved into one where the number of physical servers can be reduced, but without enforced discipline, server sprawl has become VM sprawl. With fewer physical servers, more applications and functions have come to depend on fewer hardware resources—and typically without much margin for tolerance in terms of server outages.

Return to the Mainframe?

At the department level, the move to server virtualization is somewhat of a return to the mainframe mix of pooled and centrally managed resources. With mainframes, you could dynamically allocate more resources if you needed them; this is similar to cloud computing. Cloud computing brings back the pooled, elastic, and centrally managed model that marked the mainframe era—but in an evolved manner that is more server failure tolerant than mainframes and more readily resource augmented as well.

One take on this was published at www.googlegazer.com:

So while the technology may be different, updated, and certainly faster, cheaper, more pervasive, and much more scalable, at the end of the day, Cloud Computing is a centralized mainframe-like core with distributed nodes, in a prettier, sexier new miniskirt. But hey, we like the pretty dress, and the GoogleGazer believes that Cloud Computing not only is not a fad, but it presages a fundamental paradigm shift that will have as powerful an effect on society as the Internet itself, and will turn out to be truly disruptive technology.[1]

But, while there is a good deal of overlap between mainframe and cloud computing, cloud is still unique in several ways. To begin with, cloud computing is far more services oriented than the mainframe model itself is. Although users can pay for these cloud services in a manner that is similar to mainframe charging, the overall model is very different. As discussed in Chapter 2, the National Institute of Standards and Technology (NIST) essential characteristics—broad network access, rapid elasticity, measured service, on-demand self-service, and resource pooling—together go far beyond the core mainframe cloud-like characteristic of *resource pooling*. Likewise, the service models in conjunction with virtualized hardware, network, and storage leave the mainframe model behind.

Considerations for Achieving Cost Savings

When it comes to savings from a private cloud, the bottom line is twofold: First, most enterprises will not be able to achieve savings to the degree that can be realized by adopting a public cloud service. But second, by adopting a private cloud mode versus a traditional IT model, significant savings should be achieved.[2] If the private cloud is sized to both minimize excess capacity and to allow for peak demands, then ongoing cost reductions will be evidenced by lower equipment charges, along with lower than typical data center-related costs and somewhat lower power (equipment and cooling). This makes sense because there needs to be less equipment in a cloud pool versus in a traditional model. Further, if a private cloud is built at a huge scale, then the reduction in power can actually represent significant savings.

Last but not least, expect to achieve a reduction in IT staff in contrast to a non-centralized traditional enterprise where multiple server rooms are spread over multiple departments. There are many possible cost variations here, and while overall cost may not achieve the reductions with a public utility, if the organization values maintaining physical control as much or more than it does the private public cost differential. Private cloud economics can approximate a public service when the scale of an organization's compute and storage needs are substantial enough to achieve deep discounts for equipment. In addition, there are other compelling cost advantages even with private clouds; to begin with, the patterns that form the building blocks of the infrastructure will bring repeated savings through the life cycle as will the reduction in operations costs versus traditional computing services.

Trade-offs with Customization in a Private Cloud

Along with the motivation for greater control with a private cloud, a second motivation is the degree of flexibility and customization that can be achieved. In general terms, the fact that computing and information resources are pooled and centrally managed will bring several kinds of opportunities. To begin with, the overall organization can centrally manage and offer basic IaaS and PaaS services to individual departments. This is an evolution on IT services delivery within an enterprise. But, while central cloud services can offer a greater degree of variation than would be expected by a public cloud, additional customization and services can still be performed by the consumers upon receiving such service delivery. In this example, SaaS will likely be delivered at several levels in the organization: as a basic enterprise service (such as e-mail and storage) and at individual business function levels for specialized services.

While a private cloud can be more flexible than a public cloud in delivering customized cloud services to organizational groups, the realization of savings depends on how this is done. Examining where savings are achieved with the cloud model will prove helpful for such planning.

Where such customizations are numerous or where customizations deviate from a core set of offerings that the private cloud presents to its internal custo-mers, this will drive up costs for cloud management and operations. By reviewing the essential characteristics of cloud computing (especially on-demand self-service, resource pooling, and rapid elasticity), we can understand that if savings are to be achieved over time, all IT operations need to be carefully defined and maintained to support that goal. Where a private cloud is small in implementation and where the cost is also small compared to the organization's overall budget—cost is going to be less of a factor than other trade-offs will be. Where the private cloud is very large in implementation, cost factors will likely drive the architecture and the IT discipline in service delivery toward allowing customization, but only doing so if there is a sufficient business case.

It is worthwhile to characterize infrastructure deviations to support the needs of internal customers. These will fall into the following categories:

- **Hardware Platform Variation** A good part of the cost savings with the cloud IT model comes from the multiplied efficiencies in how pooled hardware is managed. Where users require different hardware for computing or storage, this cannot be economically supported unless these needs are sufficiently common (that is, it achieves the scale where it is economical) to warrant dedicating a pool of identical resources. It will probably be more cost effective to upscale all compute servers rather than support a difficult to manage number of variations. The trade-off here has to do with the scale of demand for needed hardware features. Having a standardized platform will enable security as hardware variations can lead to misunderstanding and errors that can have profound security implications.
- **Network Variation** Just as with hardware patterns, where the network pattern is altered or customized for small sets of servers, the cloud will give up some of its cost savings. If there is enough need for a different network expression to deviate from the norm, it may prove economically reasonable to dedicate a number of racks or more of a different network implementation. But all such variation should be done at rack or *pod* (a group of racks) boundaries. A different set of

needs may drive isolation of users and departments by effecting either physical or virtualized network isolation. One such driver may be data or processing sensitivity or classification. It would be possible to build a single hardware cloud that is both physically and virtually isolated at well-demarked physical rack boundaries—in such a case, all traffic for one sensitivity level would be contained by a completely different network than that for another level.

- **Software Platform Variation** It is going to be significantly less difficult to support users who need a specialized operating system (OS) or software stack than it is to add memory or additional physical network links to actual hardware. Expect variation with software, but seek to drive such needs toward common golden images that can be security tested once rather than testing numerous minor variations of the same essential OS release or services stack. Build once, use often should be the mantra here.

- **Allocation Boundaries** Where the security confidentiality principle is a primary concern, allocation, and provisioning of user and department usage may argue for segregating user, or department or sensitivity level. This form of isolation will not achieve the same degree of isolation as the example above for physically separate networks, but it can be used to isolate pools of related users from others at the server hardware boundary.

It is also important to note that any variation from a small set of patterns increases the opportunity for error. By example, human error in operation can easily lead to routing traffic across network segments that should be separated to maintain security, or by comingling user polls or storage in violation of security policy. Where such variation is necessary, it will be important to take additional precautions by implementing multiple reinforcing defense-in-depth measures.

Finally, for every pool of systems, storage, or network service, a fraction of the capacity is always unutilized to handle failure reallocations and peak usage needs. At a small scale, this reserved capacity is a significant fraction of the pool size. The cost of the spares is amortized across the utilized fraction of the pool.

With an increase in the number of pools, each needs spare capacity while the size of each pool is shrinking. The cost of unutilized capacity increases and the support costs are multiplied. Unfortunately, the likelihood that the size of each pool will be chosen correctly drops with each new pool type. Keeping focus on the cloud benefits and the need to avoid proliferation of pool types may be one of the hardest discipline exercises for IT departments.

Costs: More Than Meets the Eye

The hardware and operational costs of computing involve numerous factors. Scaling a private cloud will involve an understanding of current and future computing and storage needs. Architecting a private cloud will entail understanding the individual needs of multiple internal cloud users and establishing the parameters for flexibility in delivering IT resources that will be either dynamically or statically cut from the whole cloth of the entire cloud infrastructure.

To begin with, it is useful to analyze the use of existing servers in an internal data center and discern the level of usage at various times of the day, week, or month. In a traditional data center, simply turning off such servers at unused times can reduce the usage of power and cooling system. There is much argument regarding the pros and cons of this approach, but in this situation, recent CPU trends largely obviate the need for such power-on power-off cycles. For instance, Sun SPARC chips have had this capability built into their hardware thread processing for several years now—with other CPU makers following suit. This is actually noticeable in a data center when walking down the hot aisle of a row of server racks in off-peak use hours: Servers that manage their power consumption based on actual workload simply run cooler because they actively manage their power consumption by moving processing to a fewer number of hardware threads.

The point of this discussion has to do with the cost of running servers, and the range of strategies in managing cost has expanded with newer hardware and the newer IT model of cloud computing. Because of the smaller population of cloud consuming users and applications in a private enterprise, a private cloud may not meet the advantages that a public cloud may. Simply stated, unless there is off-peak load to consume otherwise idle cloud resources, a private cloud may need to be scaled for maximum peak periods and lie largely idle for the remaining hours. Depending on the nature of the business, this may very well present opportunity for traditionally compute strapped organizations—such as analytics or R&D.

Cost-based Advantages to Security

When individual servers are pooled together into a centrally managed private cloud, there are going to be opportunities to improve security. The benefits of multiplied efficiencies alone will present advantages for operational security as well as for implementing future security capabilities. Identifying and implementing architectural and operational patterns for a cloud can have powerful enabling advantages for security.

In addition, with scale comes the opportunity for bigger and better security tools. For instance, identity and access management solutions can be far more effective if they are enterprise-wide versus done at a server or department level. When identity is implemented at an enterprise level, more robust and capable solutions can be used. The trend toward multifactor authentication with an electronic access card is almost unthinkable at a departmental level—but it becomes cost effective at the enterprise. Likewise, centralized security monitoring is more cost effective across a larger space of platforms.

Private Clouds: The Castle Keep?

There are many reasons why a private cloud would have appeal even when the organization uses other computing models. To begin, an enterprise might use a public cloud for the bulk of its computing needs but still run a small in-house private cloud for secure applications. In such an approach, less sensitive applications and data could be moved to a public or community cloud, whereas more sensitive information resources enjoy the greater control of a private cloud.

Although most enterprises generally update and move their applications to supported hardware and software platforms, one can find a few older applications that require an older OS version. Or, applications might require nonstandard servers and operating systems that are generally not available in a public cloud. These might best be kept in-house, in some form of data center, or in an accommodating private cloud. Unfortunately, such nonstandard servers can require the kind of individualized IT support that the cloud IT model seeks to avoid altogether. Another approach to be explored would be the use of virtualization or emulators to implement the nonstandard virtualized hardware platform that the application requires.

> **NOTE**
>
> Although the commonly accepted cloud delivery models are public, private, community, and hybrid, a private cloud can be implemented at any level within an organization. The private cloud can be developed as an enterprise-wide capability, as a departmental capability, or even as a capability to express (in part or whole) to customers.
>
> The enterprise-wide cloud will likely be supplied by an IT organization that is separate from the consumers of the cloud. This model optimizes the enterprises investment in IT and enables individual business functions to rapidly deliver services build on top of centrally provisioned resources.
>
> The departmental level cloud will be supplied by the same organization that consumes the cloud's services. This model can also maximize the department's use of computing and storage resources.

Analysis to Support Architecture Decisions

One of the fundamental questions that private cloud planners must ask is how much authority will IT have to make decisions for regularization versus the almost certain user requests for individual customizations. IT is often asked to accommodate applications in an endless number of ways that undermine the multiplied simplification and regularization of the cloud model. But users and their applications usually have more flexibility in their network and system requirements than is typically requested. This is a negotiation for cloud implementation in which many IT departments do not have a strong enough position.

Before building a private cloud, a thorough analysis of the required infrastructure should answer basic questions, such as:

- Are there requirements for specific hardware architectures (Intel, Sparc, and so on) or platforms?
- Are there requirements for specific Operating Systems or versions?
- Does the planned application mix entail hardware or networking requirements (memory, direct attached storage, and nonstandard networking)?

- Will existing servers or other gear be repurposed for the cloud?
- What is the anticipated load or traffic?
- Are there reliability or availability requirements that will drive the network, storage, or processing aspects of the architecture?
- Will the cloud be based in one physical location or will it exist in multiple locations?
- What are the requirements for continuity of operations and disaster recovery, and will these drive the architecture?

When building a private cloud, you need identify applications that require unique or nonstandard cloud hardware—assuming there are different hardware platforms. The bottom line is that without commonality for the hardware and storage platforms the private cloud cost savings will be undermined.

The deployment of mission critical systems warrants considerable advance planning. Applications must to be analyzed to ascertain how they should best be provisioned. Even on virtualized hardware, you want to ensure that you do not overload physical systems, or colocate all your mission critical applications on servers that will be subject to dynamically hosting additional VMs for nonmission critical servers. Likewise, VMs that serve for high availability of services should probably not be colocated on the same physical server. Finally, placing mission critical failover services in the same physical rack is probably not an effective strategy either—from the standpoint of power failure to a rack or localized fire.

SECURITY CRITERIA FOR ENSURING A PRIVATE CLOUD

A private cloud will likely serve many sets of internal users. These various user groups will often operate against sets of information that need to be isolated from each other. When there is no business need for making data from one group accessible to another group, the private cloud must enforce separation. Likewise, the private cloud must maintain whatever sensitivity labels or levels. This can easily complicate the design and operation of storage, networking, and other shared resources. A private cloud may also express some services to external users on the Internet, for instance, customers of the enterprise. Such connectivity for customers must be secured in and of itself, but overall the private cloud must also enforce various kinds of separation between sets of internal users and between internal users and any external Internet users. In other words, there will be several different security boundaries even within a private cloud.

> **WARNING**
>
> Despite the fact that enterprise clients can be infected by the same malware that is commonly found on the Internet, the Internet still represents a larger magnitude threat. Although many internal enterprise security efforts amount to mere attempts at preventing
>
> *(Continued)*

(*Continued*)

threats to internal information resources, the reality is that containing threats and resulting damage is generally the best one can hope for. This is not to say things could not be better, just that most enterprises pursue a dated approach to security that does not help their cause. For instance, despite corporate prohibitions against broad classes of activities, many users find that using social media sites is more important than following official policy—policy needs to be smarter about security, and enterprise network security needs to be better architected. All that said, it would be ridiculous to simply open corporate networks or private cloud networks to the Internet without fundamentally changing these private networks.

Network Considerations

A private cloud can be networked to support delivery for internally and/or externally facing services. Supporting this is the overall network infrastructure that the private cloud is built upon. There are three choices here: Network the cloud to present its services to the Internet, to private networks, or to both. Based on the mission of the cloud and data sensitivity, the security criteria for these cases may be different and they should be defined by the security policy.

Limiting Access at the Edge

So, it comes down to what should be different between securing a cloud from Internet users versus from internal enterprise users? Probably not as much as one might think, the biggest differences will typically be the degree of robustness of the cloud-edge network and server gear and the nature of security strategies for responding to the frequent magnitude of attack attempts that originate on the Internet. Where we are exposing the cloud to either Internet users or to internal enterprise users, we are going to do so in response to a business case and a solid understanding of the risk factors.

Whether from internal users or from the Internet, the cloud represents resources that must be protected. To do so, one must limit external interaction with these resources in terms of typical security questions: Who (users and IP addresses) should have what form of access, and be capable of which actions and under which circumstances? Doing so, entails use of several categories of countermeasures. To begin, the ingress to the cloud is the best place to filter out unwanted inbound traffic. Blacklisted IP addresses and IP ranges can be filtered or shunned by network devices, such as routers and firewalls. The flip side of this is identifying whitelisted IP addresses, which represent trusted IP sources—such as internal enterprise IP ranges, tenants with fixed IP addresses, or cloud operations and management.

Secondly, we may also use the ingress to authenticate inbound traffic by use of various means, including the use of traffic source certificates or authentication to initiate secure and encrypted connections. There are numerous ways to achieve this, including IPSec tunnels or proprietary VPN solutions (for instance, Cisco VPN). Whatever the approach, use a vetted solution and increase security via the use of two factor authentication. This authenticated inbound traffic is decrypted at the edge of the cloud and forwarded via use of encrypted connections to the internal cloud server destination. Resolving the remaining questions as to user roles and access situations is beyond the scope of this book, but it should be noted that this can be performed for various purposes and at multiple levels in the overall cloud implementation.

There are certainly further considerations for inbound traffic, but insofar as these are not really limited to cloud usage and are typical with Internet facing services, the reader is advised to refer to any number of excellent resources on the topic. It should be pointed out that the ingress is the first point in a cloud where we can instrument traffic and security. One can make a strong case for instrumenting the outside of the ingress, but unless your security monitoring activities will really take advantage of the knowledge of filtered external threats, there is little point to directly tracking this traffic. Certainly it makes sense to monitor at various points in the ingress itself as much value can be obtained by understanding when source IP addresses are actively attempting to penetrate via a VPN—a common response to this might be to shun any further traffic from a source IP address after observing a high rate of failed connection attempts.

Do Not Cross the Streams

Getting back to the question of Internet users versus internal enterprise users, keep in mind that when presenting network connectivity toward both internal and public Internet users it is critical that you do not present opportunity for a nonenterprise user to gain access either to the enterprise data or to the enterprise. This has several aspects:

- Mixing enterprise and external user traffic is fraught with peril and must be avoided. This speaks for defining safe methods for interacting with shared cloud services—in many cases, the risk of exposure will preclude even this. Generally, SaaS traffic is terminated at a proxy or web service with data being passed to other services that are not directly reachable by users.
- Storage of enterprise versus Internet users must be segregated in a defense-in-depth manner. All user data really should be encrypted using at minimum organizational keys if not end user keys. Enforcing cryptographic isolation should be sought by completely storing different classes of users in different storage realms. At minimum, this data should be maintained on separate storage devices, if not in different storage systems altogether.
- How the data is processed will be a function of its sensitivity—it would be an error to mix sensitive enterprise data in the same app instances where you process public Internet users.

Isolation: Network

Considering the need for network isolation within a private cloud, we have already identified two broad categories of connectivity: Internet users and private network users. There may be numerous further subcategories for these, perhaps based on information sensitivity or various functional areas (such as accounting or R&D), and also on the basis of the nature of the service itself. For instance, when users only interact with software interfaces (such as Web pages, e-mail clients, or other SaaSs), they operate at a level of abstraction that usually does not allow for any opportunity to have visibility into the infrastructure. The distinction here is that with SaaS, end users do not directly interact with the infrastructure as they do with either PaaS or IaaS. This tells us that a cloud will need to manage connectivity and isolation in multiple ways depending on factors such as service and the source of the connection.

Where there is a need to segregate networks, this can be achieved in multiple ways. The entry point to the cloud—the ingress—can be used to resolve multiple in-cloud destination addresses. In other words, the ingress routes traffic to the appropriate in-cloud destination. These destination addresses can exist on the same in-cloud subnet, or addresses can be in completely isolated realms of the infrastructure that cannot route traffic to each other. Different security policies can be in effect for these separate realms.

Isolation between such realms can be effected through various means, including physically separate networks or via virtual local area networks (VLANs). The degree of assurance in isolation is generally higher with separate networks, but it is still subject to error or misconfiguration at the ingress, and thus such isolation should be reinforced via some mechanism such as a firewall. (It is unlikely that misconfiguration would occur simultaneously at both the ingress and the firewall.) In any event, all such network configurations need to be verified via regular scans or configuration checking. Figure 7.2 depicts some of these concepts and how separate and isolated in-cloud regions can share a common ingress. In Figure 7.2, we

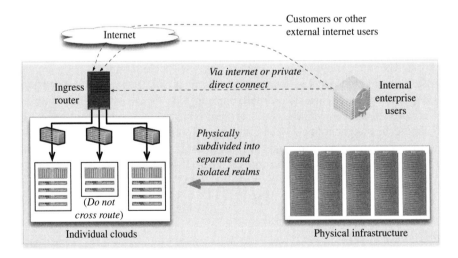

FIGURE 7.2

Cloud infrastructure and subclouds via physical network isolation.

assume that the ingress will inspect and filter all inbound traffic thereby reducing the overall amount of security attacks that the individual realms are faced with.

Figure 7.2 also assumes that identification and authentication takes place either at the *internal enterprise* (via some enterprise-wide directory perhaps) or by individual subclouds via some local or federated identity mechanism. Identity could just as well be managed by an infrastructure-wide identity management solution that serves all of the individual clouds depicted in Figure 7.2.

Network isolation can also be achieved by use of various means of encryption. In general, encryption offers the ability to effectively isolate traffic through common pathways; for instance, the ingress of a cloud can forward all traffic to a common cloud instance within which this traffic is differentiated according to its source and destination, and isolation is effected by use of, by example, IPSec tunnels.

Presenting separate encrypted channel termination points for different categories of information sensitivity is fairly straightforward even in a dynamically shape shifting cloud. Isolation for multiple information sensitivity levels can also be achieved by servicing different destination addresses to separate subclouds at the ingress. However, one complication comes when a single user needs to concurrently access multiple levels.

Another area to consider is the use of wireless access points within the infrastructure to support operations. Installing a wireless network and configuring it with either weak or no encryption would nullify any other network security that is in place.

Isolation: Physical

Rather than mixing different sets of internal private cloud users and applications, or private cloud with external Internet users in the same cloud instance, it is wise to carve up the overall cloud infrastructure into separate zones. These zones can even be segregated along physical boundaries. For a small private cloud, such boundaries should minimally be enforced at a physical server level, but more typically at a full rack boundary.

A best practice in physical isolation is to contain separate categories of use (internal users, public Internet users, and so on) within groups of separate racks (sometimes referred to as pods or compartments). For higher assurance, it is a best practice to isolate these physical zones by physically surrounding them with cages. For even higher assurance, completely enclose these separate cages (top and bottom) and maintain strict physical access control standards.

But what exactly do you need to physically isolate? That will depend upon where processing for these sets of users is performed and whether that processing can coexist. This topic is well beyond the scope of this book, but at a high level the issues can be recast in terms of the following basic question: Can processing and storage for internal and external users be performed from the same instances of applications and storage? If so, then the requirement for physical isolation can be limited to the cloud ingress and inside proxies/services where sessions are managed. From that point, traffic is no longer directed from outside, rather it is now managed, interpreted, and acted upon by edge services that act on the originating user's behalf. If the answer to the question is no, then policy requires full physical isolation and there will be separate cloud instances servicing public Internet users and enterprise users.

Isolation: Logical

An overall production cloud infrastructure will most likely be logically divided for a number of distinct uses:

- Development Cloud(s)
- Test and Staging Clouds
- Production Cloud

Obviously, there could be more divisions of the overall infrastructure, but the point here is that by its nature cloud infrastructure should support such flexible and dynamic carving out of temporary or longer-term realms. Figure 7.3 depicts a scenario where an overall cloud infrastructure is carved up into several realms, one serving production and the others for relatively temporary needs. This diagram shows that the carving out of realms is performed on a server hardware boundary, but this will not necessarily be the case. Access to an individual realm is via routing services either to VMs (IP addresses) or via a service that is expressed by the realm, such as a URL. Separation between realms can be performed through various network means and will be enforced at a minimum by the cloud core switching infrastructure.

When we carve out such realms, we are really creating different domains to enforce security policies that pertain to information processing for each domain. These logical domains have boundaries that are marked by policies specific to each domain. Figure 7.4 depicts the separation between logical domains and the boundary

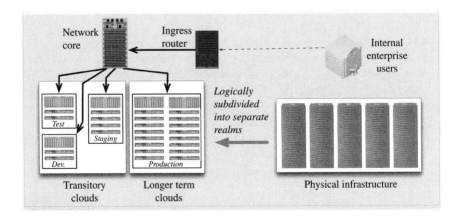

FIGURE 7.3

Cloud infrastructure: logical isolation to support.

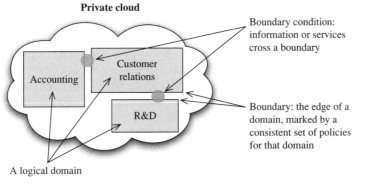

FIGURE 7.4

Logical domains and boundaries.

conditions where information or services might cross a boundary. Information or services do not *magically* cross such boundaries. Rather, information can be shared by one domain (say Accounting) to satisfy the need of another domain (say Customer Relations) to perform its legitimate function. (Today, cross-boundary sharing is increasingly implemented by use of service oriented architecture or SOA.) Effective cross-boundary sharing requires governance structures and assurance that both parties information security needs are met.[A] Once again, an appropriate and effective information security policy is a foundational key to success in meeting both specific functional and broader organizational security needs.

On the other hand, domain isolation may be ineffective or vulnerable to exposure, leading to unintended access to cross-domain information. Cross-domain vulnerabilities can be as simple as a single user having access to multiple domains, thus leading to the potential for information leakage from one domain into another. Or, cross-domain vulnerabilities can present exposure via ineffective or insecure controls.

Physical Management Network

How operations and administrative personnel will connect to the cloud hardware for device setup and platform management needs to be considered. The servers, routers, switches, and so on that comprise the private cloud all need to be managed by IT personnel. Management of these devices can be performed from the same location as the cloud infrastructure or remotely.

Maintaining a separate network for such management traffic is a data center best practice. Routers and switches can be configured to allow their management

---

[A]Cross-domain information sharing is a complex topic, the reader is advised to start with the following sources to gain a more in-depth understanding:

- http://www.mitre.org/tech/xbis/XBIS_Lab_Brochure.pdf
- http://www.ctg.albany.edu/publications/reports/factors_inf_gov_cbi

from specific networks or IP addresses (in other words, whitelisting). An advantage to this is that the risk that a particular device will be exploited is greatly reduced if network access is not accessible from outside the data center.

Even without a separate management network, it is possible to increase security by maintaining access control lists (ACLs) for routers and other network gear to limit the source addresses that are allowed to connect to perform management functions. Again, as with a separate management network, security benefits when you reduce the overall attack surface. With either of these options, one can reduce not only the risk but the opportunity of a security incident.

Management Tools

Among many important initial steps in setting up a private cloud is effectively addressing the need for management tools that will bridge your physical and virtual infrastructure. Not only will you need to manage the physical servers and storage but you will also need to manage the virtual infrastructure that is overlaid on the physical. The software that performs this bridging and management is evolving very rapidly at this point, and you should expect to see fundamental advances in this space. Eventually, there should be some integration points between cloud management software and the world of CMDBs. One should also expect to see integration points with security policy software and with security monitoring capabilities.

It is worthwhile pointing out that not all physical servers may host VMs or be virtualized—security monitoring components and other cloud management servers may be stand-alone physical servers. While this does fly in the face of completely uniform and flexible infrastructure—and there are many reasons for striving for that—the reality may be that some functions may just be simpler to implement as not core to the cloud. In practice, a smaller private cloud would likely lean in this direction more than a very large private cloud.

Data Center Considerations

The physical location of the private cloud and its supporting infrastructure is important to consider for security. Locating a mission critical data center on a flood plain or in an earthquake prone area while implementing world class data and network security makes little sense. Surely data centers are located in marginal physical locations, but this puts more pressure on the organization than may be necessary. In addition, failures of physical security or of parts of the infrastructure can lead to security breaches or denial-of-service situations.

EPIC FAIL

News of a huge Microsoft cloud data loss that affected T-Mobile Sidekick users was released on Saturday October 10, 2009. T-Mobile announced that[3]:

Based on Microsoft/Danger's latest recovery assessment of their systems, we must now inform you that personal information stored on your device—such as contacts, calendar entries, to-do lists or photos—that is no longer on your Sidekick almost certainly has been lost as a result of a server failure at Microsoft/Danger.

Danger blamed the outage on a server crash and promised that service would be restored 100%, but subsequently they stated that the "likelihood of a successful outcome is extremely low."[4]

Eventually, on October 15th, 2009 Microsoft stated that they had recovered the personal data that was earlier believed lost.[5] Confusing, isn't it? The question to ask is: How did that happen? Should a server failure pose such a consequence for a customer's data? Or, did the problem simply stem from an inappropriate name for the provider company (*Danger*)?

The thing that is really interesting about this example is that it happened at all. Surely the server replicated this data to a remote location or at least to another part of the data center? Surely the data could be recovered as soon as the backup data was restored to a redundant server setup? Surely the operations personnel knew that the data would eventually be recovered and would have communicated that certainty to customers early on in the incident.

Acts of Nature

Where the data center is physically located is worth considering, especially when the enterprise spans multiple locations. If the enterprise has offices in geographically distant cities, you may wish to take advantage of this and use these sites as co-processing sites to mitigate the effect of an act of nature.

Business Continuity and Disaster Recovery

Setting up a private cloud may involve replacing multiple individual servers. This consolidation may have a more profound effect if the data center becomes unavailable than if a single server malfunctions. This may not be due just to one or more servers becoming unavailable due to a power outage, but could also include: loss of network connectivity, storage controller failure, natural disaster, or misconfiguration of edge devices such as a router or firewall.

The ability to recover from an outage will vary greatly from one enterprise to another and will depend on many factors. Most large enterprises will have business continuity and disaster recovery plans in place, but they will need to be revisited when the internal cloud architecture is being designed. Existing plans may not be sufficient for the new cloud. If the plans have to change, it is worth ensuring that a test is undertaken afterwards to make sure that these are sufficient for the enterprise.

Physical Security and Access

Physical security and access to the cloud data center also needs to be considered. If it is located on-site, it may be implemented as a room partitioned off from regular office space. This is hardly ideal for many reasons, including the need for multiple high current power circuits, fire suppression, and server noise. A dedicated server room is not easily or inexpensively carved out of existing office space. In either case, how will access be controlled to this on-site space? Access must be limited to those who need it, and this should be implemented with multiple concentric zones. For instance, a building that houses millions of dollars of networking and server gear for a mission critical cloud demands building perimeter security as much as it does data center perimeter security along with cloud floor and cage security. For these reasons alone, it may be most cost effective to locate a private cloud in a professionally staffed and certified hosting center—where only your organization has physical access to your cages.

As well as requiring physical or electronic locks for doors, there needs to be a means to log all physical access to the data center. Logs should be kept for a sufficient period to allow for auditing on a periodic basis or in case of an investigation. Further, if there is any reason to evacuate the building, you need to know who was or is in the data center.

Along with access to the server room or cages, access to individual racks should also be evaluated. It may make sense to segregate racks based on enforcing individual or role access. This is especially important if development or test servers are colocated with production servers. In addition, human error will crop up even in cases of seasoned and knowledgeable staff, making the choice of physical configuration important regardless of other motivations.

Security Cameras and Environmental Sensors

It is common practice within a data center to monitor access points and hallways with video cameras. This ensures that procedures for access are followed, and it also serves as a powerful deterrent. The deterrent factor increases when video feeds for remote cameras are plainly displayed for all employees and visitors to see. As with any logging, video should be saved per security policy—generally 30 to 180 days. Camera video feeds should be sent on separate networks from data as they can require a great deal of bandwidth, and it will also ensure that the cameras are secured from normal users. However, it makes sense to have cameras share bandwidth with other control networks. Full motion video is not used in data centers as often as stop motion is, which is far less bandwidth intensive. Furthermore, many modern IP-based security cameras can generate event messages upon image changes, allowing these events to be injected into the same security systems that perform anomaly and intrusion detection.

Security cameras aren't the only option for instrumenting the physical infrastructure space. Proximity sensors can replace some camera functions for detecting the physical presence of a person, but cameras have greater value for recording and identifying who did what and when. In addition, temperature and humidity sensors are very important sources of information for a valuable private cloud infrastructure as are smoke and other fire detection sensors.

Fire Suppression

For a small on-site cloud in a server closet, fire suppression may be an extension or part of the existing office system. In most cases, this is not an ideal system to suppress the fire as water and computers do not mix well! The best method for stopping a fire without undue damage to the cloud infrastructure is to use a gaseous fire suppression system, often called clean agent fire suppression. Obviously, a comprehensive fire detection system should be in place to ensure that any fire is detected as early as possible. Passive fire protection needs to be in place as well, such as the installation of fire walls around the data center so that any fire in or outside the facility is restricted.

Reliable Power and Data Center Cooling

Modern servers are absolute power hungry devices. Not only do they require lots of clean and reliable power to operate but they also generate a great deal of heat, which also requires power to cool. A hosting data center is likely to have access to multiple separate power supply feeds, with additional mechanisms at various levels to ensure power continuity. To supplement this, there should be uninterruptible power supply (UPS) units, which are essentially large battery units to bridge momentary power dips or losses. UPS units typically have a short supply capacity and a data center will need standby power generation with sufficient fuel capacity.

Unfortunately, an on-site data center may not have all or even some of these. Whatever power mechanisms or backups you have will require periodic testing. Overall, reliable power and backups are a specialized area, so expertise in the field should be sought.

The density of servers that are likely to be deployed for cloud computing will almost certainly generate more heat than the average data center of 10 years ago. If these servers are located in an on-site server room, the heat generated will exceed the cooling capabilities of a normal office environment. In such a case, you should ensure that the current air conditioning units can either handle the additional heat dissipation or you need to upgrade or augment cooling.

TIP

Building a private cloud entails building virtualized pools of computing, storage, and network capabilities—at scale. These IT resources are expressed by IT to cloud consumers in ways that mask the underlying complexity. They must also be delivered in an agile and highly automated manner to meet the needs for greater efficiency and reliability than are commonly associated with IT operations. What does this mean for IT staff?

The range of technologies that go into building a private cloud, along with the complexity of making these work in an automated and coherent manner will lead to an evolution in cloud IT staff skill sets and their roles. IT staff are generally sufficiently skilled for their current roles, but they will probably need to master a deeper and broader set of skills in physical hardware and software technologies, as well as with virtualization technologies. Many of the critical skills that are needed with cloud computing infrastructure are highly specialized, including IT security. If there is a downside to cloud computing, it might be the shortage of such a deeply skilled IT workforce.

On the one hand, the move to cloud computing presents an opportunity not only to consolidate IT resources but also to reduce overall IT headcount; on the other hand, the talent that is needed for a large private cloud commands a premium salary. The bottom line? Expect a smaller but more capable and expensive IT staff.

Operational Security Considerations

Chapter 10 (Operating a Cloud) will address broad operational issues in operating a cloud. In this section, we will look at some of these from the standpoint of putting appropriate controls in place when building a private cloud.

Antimalware

The deployment and updating of antimalware software is also important within a virtualized environment. Where virus-prone operating systems are used for virtual servers in a manner that makes them subject to viruses, an antivirus solution should be used. This should be made part of the template VM images before a VM is instantiated. The virus signature files will often need to be updated on at least a daily basis. Setting virus-prone servers to automatically update their signature files every several hours will not entail undue overhead, but it will ensure that the maximum protection against viruses is deployed. Keep in mind that by using VMs, one achieves an advantage in terms of reducing cost-to-recover from infection—all that is really needed is to stand up a replacement uninfected VM.

A better antimalware approach for a cloud computing infrastructure is one where all input is filtered and examined before it gets to a server. Also, in the case of a mission critical application, one will need to maintain strict control over *any* changes to the system image/applications. For such applications, you really can't afford to get to the point where a production environment is constantly being subject to per-host virus exposure and remediation. One of the cost savings in cloud computing is the possibility to *reduce* repeated operations via better IT processes, and management of virus risk is one.

Device Configuration

As we have seen so far, a cloud infrastructure is more than just a collection of servers in a hardware pool. The infrastructure to connect these together and to other networks is equally important—network switches and routers for instance. If these are not configured correctly, then this would present a vulnerability that could be exploited. Additionally, how each server is configured can also play an important role in overall cloud security. In this regard, if a cloud server is misconfigured, then this can be exploited by either a user who has access to the server or by a service endpoint outside the cloud. Consider the consequences that could result if such a server is trusted by other in-cloud servers. Therefore, it is a best practice in private clouds to verify security relevant server configurations.

Routers and switches are another category of devices that are often installed and then forgotten about until an additional route needs to be added. It is just as important to depreciate and remove unused routes as it is to verify the correct configuration of permitted routes. Broader consideration needs to be given to the setup of routers and other network devices. Weak passwords or authentication mechanisms could lead to these devices becoming a jumping off point for an attacker. By their very nature, a router in your network will be a trusted device and an attacker on this box will be able to see your network and intercept any traffic going through it.

Intrusion and Anomaly Detection

An intrusion and anomaly detection capability will give visibility into the hard to discern events and security situations that are hard to identify in the volume of event traffic and alerts in a cloud. Most likely, the ingress router or cloud network front end will have some such capabilities built into or optional to the equipment. But this is oriented toward detecting inbound—or possibly outbound—traffic in contrast to detecting security incidents or attacks that are taking place within the cloud itself. Therefore, a complete intrusion detection capability will likely involve multiple technologies extending from the front end of the cloud infrastructure all the way down to the internal network and key servers within the cloud complex itself.

To some extent, detection depends on logging of exceptions and errors, and the subsequent process of analyzing data from logs. The amount of information will grow rapidly, and a dedicated event management capability will be required to alert only the most meaningful information to security personnel.

Deploying network intrusion and anomaly detection systems for a cloud should be seriously considered. Although these are generally not deployed throughout an enterprise, they are more common for data center infrastructure. The downside of such detection systems is that, like antivirus systems, they require frequent care and feeding. Signatures will have to be updated on a regular basis, and labor intensive analysis of the alerts will be necessary. The amount of work and the skills involved in this should not be underestimated. Therefore, this is often outsourced to a third party security monitoring company.

The investment of such a capability is cost effective for a medium- to large-sized private cloud. It scales regardless of the number of customers and thus becomes cheaper (per customer) with each new internal customer. This scalability of otherwise expensive technologies is a key benefit with private clouds.

Data Backup and Storage

A separate network can also be used to backup servers and other cloud devices. Attaching backup and storage devices to this network (or to a separate storage area network) can reduce traffic on the main network and provide additional security. Users will rarely need to access the file storage directly as this will normally be undertaken via the application.

The internal cloud infrastructure should be designed to cater for the backup and storage requirements, which may well be larger than normal. Users may want to store different images or keep development snapshots of their servers and be able to enable and disable these as required.

When you are designing the storage requirements of the cloud computing environment, you will need to consider the following forms of storage:

- **Direct Attached Storage (DAS)** This is a traditional method of grouping storage devices together for large SCSI disk arrays directly connected to one or more servers. This solution has ongoing utility for a private cloud, but the disks need to be physically colocated with the servers they are connected to.

- **Network Attached Storage (NAS)** These devices are connected via an Ethernet network and can provide data storage services to a multitude of clients. Since NAS devices can be located further away than DAS devices, they can be grouped and located in a more secure part of the data center.
- **Storage Area Network (SAN)** A SAN provides a way to attach storage devices to servers such that they appear to be locally attached to the operating system. As with NAS, storage is typically located away from the client servers. The difference with SAN is that they utilize a Fiber Channel topology, which provides fast access to the storage devices. Another SAN-style approach is iSCSI, which is important because it offers the control of SANs and the lower expense of IP networks.
- **Internal Disk** The typical server configuration includes internal disk. Although internal disk is good for system performance, there are several drawbacks to it in cloud computing. First, as VMs are provisioned to a server, the isolation between VMs may be compromised via disk pathways. The big risk here is that one VM may gain access to the hardware disk and thus be able to see files belonging to another VM.

There are security advantages to using a SAN, particularly in terms of disaster recovery. Servers can boot from a SAN, which can shorten the time from provisioning to booting a server. An additional advantage is that a SAN can be configured to span multiple locations, even remote locations. This means data can be replicated to remote locations and can be retrieved quickly for disaster recovery.

Regulation

The laws and regulation of a state or country must be considered when considering a private cloud. This was explored in Chapter 3 Security Concerns, Risk Issues and Legal Aspects, but a few points should be made here as some legal and regulatory requirements involve important security criteria to consider when you are building your cloud. Some of this regulation applies mainly to one country, such as the Sarbanes–Oxley Act (SOX) in the United States, whereas others will apply internationally. The Payment Card Industry Data Security Standard (PCI DSS) is a worldwide standard that has strict compliance rules.

Location of Data

Although you may not consider the location of the data center where you are going to install an internal cloud important, a number of considerations need to be made. The location of the data center and data will be governed by laws just as if the data were handled by a third party. Sometime during the transition to a private cloud, it will be worth looking at this aspect as it may not have been addressed in the past.

There are many laws governing what personal data can be collected and where this can be transferred to, even if this is for backup purposes. Building two data centers, one in the United States and one in a country located within the European

Union (EU) and backing up each data center to the other may seem a secure and strategic option. However, there are strong privacy laws within the EU and these may well prohibit the moving data to a country not in the EU, even if just for backup purposes.

Data Retention

The retention time for certain data will also need to be considered. A consolidation of the data center into a cloud architecture may also have led to the modification of the data storage regime in place, perhaps to SAN environment. The data must still be archived, probably at an off-site location, to the requirements set out in law. Finance data in particular has strict rules and regulations governing it and failure in this area may be very damaging.

SUMMARY

In this chapter, we examined several security considerations specifically for those who intend to develop and deploy their own private cloud. While many of the same considerations should be taken into account for implementing a public cloud, there are differences. The chapter reviewed several of the primary motivations for building a private cloud—chief among these is a desire for greater control over information resources and a need for greater flexibility over how the cloud may be built and what it offers in terms of customization. Overall, when getting your cloud with custom services and SLAs is the driving factor, or where maintaining control over your data is a primary concern, the private cloud is the likely delivery approach.

In summary, it is worthwhile to revisit the topic of isolation for a private cloud. As stated in this chapter, a private cloud will likely serve the needs of multiple internal tenants. Most likely, security policy will require that there be appropriate controls to enforce limiting access to specific categories of information across departments within an organization and even within a single department. Many of these controls will involve the notion of isolation of user sessions and data from other users and data at different levels of sensitivity. As depicted in Figure 7.5, effective isolation requires a coherent strategy that implements defense-in-depth. Such a strategy starts by limiting access to the physical infrastructure that comprises the private cloud and extends to the use of OS controls, virtualization-based isolation, network isolation (VLANs), and even application controls. Different physical controls will be present at the building perimeter, server room, cloud cage, pod (a physical grouping of server/storage racks), and a single rack.

The chapter also examined many security criteria that will be involved in building and deploying a private cloud. Again, these generally have a good deal in common with public cloud security criteria. In Chapter 8 (Security Criteria: Selecting an External Cloud Provider), we examine some of those.

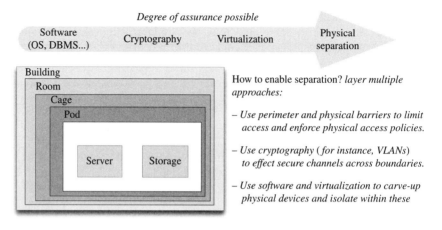

Degree of assurance possible

Software (OS, DBMS...) — Cryptography — Virtualization — Physical separation

Building
Room
Cage
Pod

Server   Storage

How to enable separation? *layer multiple approaches:*

– *Use perimeter and physical barriers to limit access and enforce physical access policies.*

– *Use cryptography (for instance, VLANs) to effect secure channels across boundaries.*

– *Use software and virtualization to carve-up physical devices and isolate within these*

FIGURE 7.5

Multitenancy and isolation.

Endnotes

1. Googlegazer.com, posted on August 3, 2008 by dsarna http://googlegazer.com/2008/08/03/cloud-computing-is-it-old-mainframe-bess-in-a-new-dress/ [accessed 23.03.11].
2. Morton G, Alford T. *The economics of cloud computing: Addressing the benefits of infrastructure in the cloud.* Booz Allen Hamilton, Inc.; 2009. Available from: http://www.boozallen.com/media/file/Economics-of-Cloud-Computing.pdf [accessed 23.03.11].
3. Wingfield N. Microsoft, T-Mobile stumble with sidekick glitch. *The Wall Street J.* http://online.wsj.com/article/SB10001424052748703790404574467431941990194.html; 2009 [accessed 23.03.11].
4. Keizer G. Sidekick users livid over microsoft server failure. *PCWorld.* http://www.pcworld.com/article/173498/sidekick_users_livid_over_microsoft_server_failure.html; 2009 [accessed 23.03.11].
5. http://www.microsoft.com/presspass/press/2009/oct09/10-15sidekick.mspx [accessed 23.03.11].

Security Criteria: Selecting an External Cloud Provider

8

INFORMATION IN THIS CHAPTER

- Selecting a CSP: Overview of Assurance
- Selecting a CSP: Overview of Risks
- Selecting a CSP: Security Criteria

Up to this point, we have developed an understanding of the security issues and countermeasures for cloud computing. In Chapter 2 (Cloud Computing Architecture), we reviewed current cloud service and delivery models. In Chapter 3 (Security Concerns, Risk Issues and Legal Aspects), we examined the major outstanding concerns with cloud computing. In Chapters 4, 5, and 6, we detailed the various aspects of Securing the Cloud, namely architecture, data security, and best practices. In the preceeding chapter (Chapter 7, Security Criteria: Building an Internal Cloud), we identified specific criteria that one needs to consider when building a private cloud. This chapter builds on that information to detail security criteria for selecting a public cloud or cloud service provider (CSP).

When adopting a public cloud, the consumer does not need to be operationally concerned with the details of the underlying cloud infrastructure. However, there are several open questions for customers that have to do with security and governance of the cloud service. Keep in mind that in Chapter 3, we delineated the responsibilities that a data owner has with the SaaS, PaaS, and IaaS. Also, in Chapter 5 (Securing the Cloud: Data Security), we discussed several residual responsibilities that the data owner has when using a public cloud. But before we exercise any responsibilities, we need to select an appropriate CSP.

SELECTING A CSP: OVERVIEW OF ASSURANCE

As discussed in Chapter 2, public clouds come in different services forms—IaaS, PaaS, and SaaS. These forms of public clouds share common criteria for securing them. The goal of this chapter is to cover those criteria in a way that allows a cloud adopter to make informed vendor decisions.

Vendor Claims and Independent Verification

Generally to this point, when organizations adopt public clouds, they do not take on the effort of evaluating the security of their vendors. And frankly, CSPs have not exactly been keen on repeatedly incurring the cost of answering customer's detailed security questions. Too often, a vendor may state that they are SAS70 or ISO 27002 *compliant*, but simply stating that a CSP is compliant only amounts to *self-certification*. (Self-certification is no more reliable in effect than the old New Yorker cartoon with the two dogs sitting in front of a computer, and one says to the other: "On the Internet, no one knows you're a dog.")[1]

In this regard, the increase in third party audits by some CSPs is a positive trend, but these audits are not always performed against common test sets. For instance, one has a great deal of leeway in a SAS70[A] audit—being able to specify the *controls* and *control objectives* that will be verified isn't sufficiently meaningful when performing CSP comparisons. What we want to know is does a given CSP meet our requirements for security and how do they stack up against other CSPs?

TOOLS

Selecting a CSP should also involve some research including reviews from other customers and industry groups. These sorts of reviews will only go so far, but they can be valuable for identifying observed issues or problems with established providers.

Some current online reviews of existing providers can be found here:

* www.cloud-hosting-providers.com
* www.bestcloudserver.com/reviews
* www.cloudhostingreviewer.com

But keep in mind that free information is sometimes worth what you pay for it. Expect to spend a good deal of time in online searching for reviews of your primary CSP candidates and in reviewing a rapidly expanding set of online resources.

A Role for Government

But this is changing, and one of the largest Information Technology (IT) consumers in the world is behind it. The U.S. federal government has been adopting public cloud computing to process nonclassified data in lieu of building new systems. Supporting the federal government, the National Institute of Standards and Technology (NIST), General Services Administration (GSA), the Federal CIO Council along with working bodies such as the Information Security and Identity Management Committee (ISIMC) and The American Council for Technology (ACT), Industry Advisory Council (IAC) have addressed the problem of cloud security assurance from multiple directions. In doing this, these groups have

---

[A]Statement on Standards for Attestation Engagements (SSAE) No. 16, will effectively replace SAS70 as of June 15, 2011. For more information on SSAE 16, see: http://ssae16.com/SSAE16_overview.html

developed guidelines including the Federal CIO Council's *Proposed Security Assessment and Authorization for U.S. Government Cloud Computing.*[2] Known as the *Federal Risk and Authorization Management Program* (FedRAMP), this effort has several goals including developing a government-wide risk and authorization management program for cloud computing.

The approach taken by several groups—the Federal CIO Council, the Cloud Security Alliance (CSA), and the European Network and Information Security Agency (ENISA), included—is to either adopt or otherwise leverage NIST 800-53R3 or similar controls (introduced in Chapter 6) and thereby define a security baseline or benchmarks for assessing the security of a cloud implementation or service. The federal government with its immense buying power stands to make a significant difference in how CSPs represent the security or their services in a manner that is consistently verified across CSPs.

Information Security Management Systems

Information security management systems (ISMS) are organizational programs whose scope covers every aspect of policy through specific security controls and procedures. The adoption of ISMS has been furthered by ISO/IEC 27002. As discussed in Chapter 1, ISO 27002 outlines control objectives and controls that should be implemented to address requirements that are identified by a risk assessment. By organizing these as guidelines and general principles for security, they can also form a common basis for evaluation criteria for CSPs. ISO 27001 identifies the following categories of security control objectives[3]:

- **Security Policy** A comprehensive information security policy provides clear direction and demonstrates management commitment to security. The policy should be consistent with business objectives and meet business requirements, and it should comply with laws and regulations.
- **Organization of Information Security** Establish a management framework to implement security, assign security roles, and coordinate implementations across the organization. Control third party use of your organization's information by use of appropriate security controls.
- **Asset Management** Establish responsibility for and protect your organization's assets. This includes the use of an information classification system.
- **Human Resources Security** Employees must understand their responsibilities for security. This includes all aspects of personnel, including contractors and third party users, as well as all phases of employment.
- **Physical and Environmental Security** Physical security is a necessary component of information security and involves every aspect of ensuring a controlled and protected environment for information facilities and equipment.
- **Communications and Operations Management** Define responsibilities for information processing facilities and establish procedures for their operation and control. This entails backups, media protection, future planning activities, third party service delivery, and protection against malicious and mobile code.

- **Access Control** Control access to information and ensure that controls meet organizational requirements. This entails all forms of information and associated processing systems.
- **Systems Development and Maintenance** Identify security requirements before starting the development process or any other aspect of implementation or acquisition. Verify that applications and controls operate correctly and are appropriate.
- **Information Security Incident Management** Report security events, incidents, and all weaknesses. Establish formal processes and procedures for managing incidents and situations.
- **Business Continuity Management** Establish and use a business continuity management process to counteract interruptions and protect critical processes, the goal being to minimize impact to the business and to enable expedient recovery.
- **Compliance** Comply with legal and regulatory requirements. Perform compliance reviews and regular audits.

The ISO 27000 series recognizes that people, processes, and technology are equally important aspects of effective security. ISO 27001 and ISO 27002 can form the foundation for verifiable security in public cloud services, and with third party accreditation, these serve to address the need for CSP selection criteria for cloud consumers.

Independent Verification

But don't expect to waltz in and start asking a CSP detailed questions per an ISO 27000 series accreditation. Obtaining accreditation is both time consuming for a CSP and expensive—but doing this is becoming a cost of a CSP doing business. Without third party accreditation of vendor security claims, cloud consumers can only trust that CSPs security claims and representations of their security policies and infrastructure are accurate. In contrast to private cloud security, public cloud users do not have the luxury of being able to review details of or examine the security implementation, processes, and procedures of a public cloud. Not only is it not prudent for a CSP to expose technical details of cloud security, it also isn't cost effective to meet the needs of individual consumers by sharing such information to win their business. As a result, the best method of addressing this is to place value in trusted third party accreditations.

Listed below are the most relevant third party accreditations or certifications that may be used by CSPs:

- **SAS70, Type II** Statement on Auditing Standards (SAS) No. 70 Type II Certification developed by the American Institute of Certified Public Accountants (AICPA). This certification focuses on a CSPs infrastructure, policies, and procedures to assure that it follows best practices in minimizing the risk of service disruption and to ensure security of data. This is a widely used form of accreditation adopted by many public cloud providers today. (As mentioned earlier in this chapter, SSAE No. 16 will effectively replace SAS70 as of June 15, 2011.)

- **ISO 27001/2** ISO 27001/2 are generally thought of as more holistic for information security as compared to SAS70 as it is more detailed in examining how an organization manages information security management.
- **PCI** A standard developed by the Payment Card Industry that is a requirement for any service that manages credit card data. It outlines standards and requirements for securing sensitive information, including personal information, credit card numbers, and so on.
- **Cloud Security Alliance (CSA)** In late 2010, CSA revealed an initial program for accreditation/certification that is oriented toward certifying individual competency in cloud security practices.
- **FISMA, FedRAMP, and NIST 800-53R3** These are all U.S. federal government processes or programs to measure security for federal IT systems. However, due to the buying power of the federal government in the public cloud space, certifications that use these may be adopted by the private sector as alternatives to other commercial certifications.

Selecting a CSP: Vendor Transparency

Customers of a pubic cloud service have expectations that the data they put into the service will have integrity and be protected. In essence, customers trust that the CSP will offer the appropriate level of security and governance. Unfortunately, vendor claims about security are often made without sufficient justification—as the reality of vulnerability exposure and often poor security practices evidence. In addition, many cloud service providers may make vague representations of their security while also transferring all liability to customers. For a provider to follow through with their security representations, security controls must be properly implemented and maintained in daily operation. In this, customers need more than trust, they seek a degree of understanding of what the provider actually does and would do under various circumstances. This includes information about the CSPs security policies, their practices, and incident response.

The term transparency is used to describe the degree of visibility into security policy and operations that a CSP offers to its customers. Although customers should not expect a CSP to detail how security is implemented, a customer expects a CSP to be open and accountable about security practices—especially during or after security incidents. The term *transparency* is used to encompass these actions, and includes such areas as disclosure, process, and audit. In practice, this is demonstrated when a vendor immediately acknowledges that there is a security issue or incident when such events might affect customers. Transparency involves a commitment to communicate relevant information to a customer and to advise customers as to risk or risk mitigation actions.

As a white paper from Sun Microsystems put it[4]:

Governance, information security, and transparency are inter-related concepts. Together, they can turn an otherwise confusing and shifting information-based commercial landscape into a pragmatic framework. "Governance" in this context is the superset of security, privacy, and regulatory requirements, and commercial imperatives that can help an organization assess risk, manage day-to-day processes, and move forward with some degree of control over assets and ethics. "Information security" is the collection of people, processes, and technology that help an organization provide confidentiality, integrity, and availability for its precious information assets. Finally, in this context, "transparency" is viewed as revealing enough information to enable reasonable strategic business decisions while respecting an organization's need for confidentiality.

But revealing extensive information about security is often prohibited by organizational security policy, and even if it is not, it goes against the grain of typical security practice. This sounds a little like security-by-obscurity, and in fact today, there are fewer secrets about security techniques than organizations would like to believe. What should be kept close to the vest are specific implementation details that can be exploited by a hacker—such as IP addresses of security devices or their exact placement on a network diagram. Figure 8.1 depicts one such aspect of transparency, namely the technical details of a security implementation that it would be imprudent to disclose.

So, what should be disclosed under transparency? CSPs should disclose enough information to empower customers and users to make informed decisions about choosing a CSP or implementing additional security procedures or measures. Overall guidance for disclosure includes the following:

- **CSPs Security Policies** The CSP should disclose sufficient details of their security policies and standards to allow customers to be informed in their security expectations and to guide their behavior in using the service.
- **Security Implementation and Procedures** A CSP should provide enough detail about the security implementation and operational practices to allow customers to decide if the CSP should be entrusted with customer data. The kind of information that should be provided does not need to be deeply technical, but it should be ample for a customer to gauge that the provider not only understands the need for appropriate security but has also implemented it and is capable of maintaining it in all aspects of operation.
- **Liability and Risk** The CSP should not be expected to disclose any information that would result in liability for the CSP, its business, or its data

FIGURE 8.1

The limits of prudent disclosure.

center and operations. Likewise, the CSP should not disclose any information that may result in risk to customer data, customer privacy or business, or third parties.

- **Service Issues** Security or availability service issues should be disclosed in a timely manner to allow customers to implement contingency plans. Specific information about security incidents should include their scope and how the CSP is rectifying the situation. This can allow customers to gauge their exposure and respond as per their own service level agreements (SLAs). In addition, customers and users should have the means to report vulnerabilities, security incidents, or security concerns to the CSP.
- **Regulatory and Legal** A CSP may be required to disclose some information based on regulatory or legal mandates. Likewise, some disclosures may result in breach of a regulatory or legal requirement, so they should be avoided.
- **Division of Responsibilities** The CSP should delineate areas for which they are and are not responsible, particularly where this involves customer responsibility or expectations of responsibility.

SELECTING A CSP: OVERVIEW OF RISKS

From a cloud consumer's perspective, your data is only as secure as the cloud in which it exists. CSP claims are easy to come by, but hard to verify without evidence. Achieving third party certification or accreditation gives the CSP credibility that appropriate processes and procedures are in place to meet the security needs of customers. When the CSP is transparent and reveals information, customers can make an informed selection. But more is required by a customer to assure security on an ongoing basis.

Risk Will Vary by Customer and by CSP

In Chapter 1 (Introduction to Cloud Computing and Security), we introduced the concepts of risk and risk management. We saw that risk can be expressed as a relationship between threats, vulnerabilities, countermeasures, and asset value. In Chapter 3 (Security Concerns, Risk Issues, and Legal Aspects), we looked at various perceived cloud computing risks, and we examined how one can assess and mitigate risk. Then, in Chapter 5 (Securing the Cloud: Data Security), we looked at risk from the standpoint of data in motion and data at rest for public SaaS, PaaS, and IaaS.

With that background on cloud computing risks, one next should consider the requirements of individual organizations. Consider the relationship between the likelihood of an incident versus its expected business impact: some incidents are highly unlikely yet if they took place, they have a very high impact; other incidents are highly likely, but have a very low impact; and, others are highly likely and have a very high impact. Figure 8.2 depicts this relationship and shows where

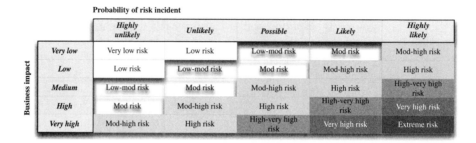

Probability of risk incident

Business impact	Highly unlikely	Unlikely	Possible	Likely	Highly likely
Very low	Very low risk	Low risk	Low-mod risk	Mod risk	Mod-high risk
Low	Low risk	Low-mod risk	Mod risk	Mod-high risk	High risk
Medium	Low-mod risk	Mod risk	Mod-high risk	High risk	High-very high risk
High	Mod risk	Mod-high risk	High risk	High-very high risk	Very high risk
Very high	Mod-high risk	High risk	High-very high risk	Very high risk	Extreme risk

FIGURE 8.2

Probability of incident versus business impact.

we have the greatest concern based on the high potential for an incident and a high business impact.[5]

Assessing Risk Factors

Selecting a public CSP should entail an assessment of the risk that a customer or data are subject to. The nature and level of risk will vary according to many factors; among them are the CSPs cloud architecture and security measures. Overall, risk can be broadly classified into several categories, these include:

- **Technical Risks** These include isolation failure (technical or physical), control interface manipulation, compromise of accounts, data interception, data leakage, data remanence, and malicious probes or scans.
- **Policy and Legal Risks** These include loss of governance, compliance failures, jurisdictional issues, subpoenas, and also licensing issues.
- **Operational Risks** These include malicious insiders, errors and misconfiguration, bandwidth problems, modification of network traffic, social engineering, compromise or loss of confidential logs, loss of backup data, physical security compromise, loss of encryption keys, and natural disasters.

Going through an exercise in evaluating individual risk factors can be tedious, but it does contribute to a better understanding and it makes for a more informed CSP selection process. As shown below, Table 8.1 details a broad range of such representative risk factors and identifies examples of affected assets. (This table is largely derived from analysis by the European Network and Information Security Agency.[6])

The risks that are listed in Table 8.1 are representative and do not form a complete set. However, by developing a list which details the specific risks that your organization is especially concerned about can be very helpful as a start when evaluating a prospective CSP. The resulting list can be used as the basis for a checklist to use in identifying areas of residual concern or areas that may warrant additional security measures.

Table 8.1 Risk Factors and Assets in Cloud Computing

Risk	Probability	Impact	Affected Assets	Factors
CSP fails or business changes affect tenant	Unknown	High	Reputation and customer trust; personal and sensitive data; service delivery	Economic conditions; poor business practices; CSP acquired by off-shore owner or tenant competitor; data moved to new jurisdiction; lack of transparency
Subpoena and e-discovery	High	Medium	Reputation and customer trust; personal and sensitive data; service delivery	Lack of resource isolation; data stored in multiple jurisdictions; lack of transparency
Lock-in	High	Medium	Company reputation; personal and sensitive data; service delivery	Lack of transparency; absence of standard solutions
Multitenancy	Low	High	Reputation; data exposure; service delivery; IP address blacklisting	Isolation failure (technology or procedural); indirect: other tenant fails in their security responsibility in which unfairly taints reputation of CSP and by transference other tenants; multitenancy complicates intervention and remediation
CSP outsourcing	Low	Medium	Reputation and customer trust; personal and sensitive data; service delivery	Hidden dependencies on third party services; lack of transparency
CSP insider threat	Medium	High	Reputation and customer trust; personal and sensitive data; service delivery	Unclear or ineffective roles and responsibilities; inadequate technical or physical security; failure in applying need-to-know; lack of transparency
Ineffective incident management	Medium	High	Reputation and customer trust; personal and sensitive data; service delivery	Inadequate procedures do not meet needs in light of exploits
Governance loss	High	High	Reputation; customer trust, personal and sensitive data; service delivery	Unclear or ineffective roles and responsibilities; inconsistent responsibility between CSP and tenant; lack of access by tenant to provider audits; lack of transparency; absence of standard solutions; unclear asset ownership/custodianship

Continued...

Table 8.1 Risk Factors and Assets in Cloud Computing (*Continued*)

Risk	Probability	Impact	Affected Assets	Factors
Compliance challenges	High	High	Certification	Lack of access by tenant to provider audits; absence of standard solutions; jurisdiction where data is stored; lack of operational information; lack of transparency
CSPs systems are tainted with regulated or classified data by a customer	Low	High	Storage; backup data; operational or security logs	A regulated company uses a public cloud without the cloud provider being aware that data that is subject to regulation is now in the cloud. Or, classified data is inadvertently introduced into a public cloud
Loss or compromise of logs	Low	Medium	Operational or security logs; forensic review	Inadequate policy or procedures; technical vulnerabilities (authentication, authorization); unclear or ineffective roles and responsibilities; procedural failures; misconfiguration; failure in applying need-to-know
Loss or compromise of backups	Low	High	Reputation and customer trust; personal and sensitive data; backup data	Inadequate physical security; technical vulnerabilities (authentication, authorization)
Unauthorized physical access	Low	High	Reputation and customer trust; personal and sensitive data; backup data	Inadequate physical security and/or procedures
Theft of equipment	Low	High	Personal and sensitive data; physical computing or network hardware	Inadequate physical security and/or procedures
Inadequate resources	Low/ medium	Low/ high	Reputation and customer trust; personal and sensitive data; service delivery	Inaccurate planning; inadequate infrastructure/ provisioning; lack of supplier redundancy
Data Remanence or media destruction failure	Medium	High	Reputation and customer trust; personal and sensitive data; credentials	Procedural failures (lack of rigor in handling media in erasure or destruction process); inadequate data erasure measures (lack of verified multipass)

Risk				
Common service failure	Low	High	Service delivery	Time service, directory or other common enabling service fails
Isolation failure	Low–Medium	High	Reputation and customer trust; personal and sensitive data; service delivery	Technical vulnerabilities in hypervisors, network, storage, or systems software; inadequate security/penetration testing; failure to maintain physical separation between customers who warrant such
CSP customer interface compromise	Medium	High	Reputation and customer trust; personal and sensitive data; service delivery	Technical vulnerabilities (authentication, authorization, interface, systems software); procedural failures
CSP service management compromise	Low	High	Credentials; reputation and customer trust; personal and sensitive data	Technical vulnerabilities (authentication, authorization, encryption); procedural failures; CSP credential exposure
Privilege escalation	Low	High	Personal and sensitive data; access control; service delivery	Technical vulnerabilities (authentication, authorization, encryption, hypervisor); unclear or ineffective roles and responsibilities; procedural failures; misconfiguration; failure in applying need-to-know
Tenant failure to secure IaaS or PaaS	Low/ medium	Medium/ high	Reputation and customer trust; personal and sensitive data; credentials	Unclear or ineffective roles and responsibilities; tenant procedural failure; lack of transparency
Social engineering	Medium	High	Reputation and customer trust; personal and sensitive data; service delivery	Lack of security training; inadequate physical security
Loss of network connectivity	Low/ medium	High	Service delivery	CSP network failure; CSP ISP failure; tenant network failure; tenant ISP failure
Co-tenant performs network probes or malicious scans	Medium	Medium	Reputation and customer trust; personal and sensitive data; service delivery	CSP network or virtualization configured to allow cross-tenant network traffic; Higher assurance tenants not physically isolated from high risk behavior tenants; tenant resources (PaaS/IaaS) compromised

Continued…

Table 8.1 Risk Factors and Assets in Cloud Computing (*Continued*)

Risk	Probability	Impact	Affected Assets	Factors
Network failure	Low	High	Service delivery	Misconfiguration; hardware failure; systems vulnerabilities; inadequate or failed business continuity
Network management	Medium	High	Reputation and customer trust; personal and sensitive data; network connections	Misconfiguration; hardware failure; systems vulnerabilities; inadequate or failed business continuity
Modified network traffic	Low	High	Reputation and customer trust; personal and sensitive data; service delivery	Inadequate or failed encryption; provisioning or systems vulnerabilities
Loss of encryption keys	Low	High	Credentials; reputation and customer trust; personal and sensitive data	Procedure failures
DDoS	Low/medium	High	Reputation and customer trust; personal and sensitive data; service delivery	Ingress filtering/detection inadequate; misconfiguration of network or platform controls; systems/network or protocol vulnerabilities
Data exposure (in motion)	Medium	High	Reputation and customer trust; personal and sensitive data	Technical vulnerabilities (authentication, authorization, encryption); procedural failures; key exposure; lack of transparency

Risk: A Deeper Look at CSP Business Viability

Many of the cloud security risks in Table 8.1 should be familiar to a security professional. But one area lies far outside the typical realm in which the typical security expert works. Simply put: A CSP may fail as a business or be subject to adverse circumstances—any of which could be a risk for a customer who comes to rely on a cloud service. The viability of the CSP is an important factor when choosing a public cloud. The CSPs ability and interest to operate has much to do with their profitability. Since CSPs are for profit businesses, if the CSP can't manage their business, then the cloud service is in jeopardy.

The capacity of a CSP to provide adequate security can be undermined if the CSP can no longer appropriately fund security or security relevant aspects of cloud operations. Various scenarios are possible, including:

- **Staff Reductions** Segregation of duties is part of effective information security. Among other unfortunate consequences of laying off personnel, such *personnel actions* can leave remaining staff to assume the duties of departed staff. This can result in the loss of checks and balances in an organization. Likewise, staff who previously had no expertise in technical security may find themselves implementing configuration changes without understanding their broader impact.
- **Security Infrastructure Relevancy** Information security can be a moving target, especially the nature of vulnerabilities and threats. Deployed technology might not necessarily be effective or relevant tomorrow. If a CSP can't keep their security technology relevant, its security will become ineffective.
- **Business Model** A CSP might initially advertise that their service maintains information privacy, but if the business model evolves that agreement may be null and void. This is common with SaaS providers when they are provide a free service and initially commit to keeping data private or never selling information to third parties about your activities. But a change of ownership or management team changes can alter the business model such that it might compromise former privacy understandings.
- **Accountability** Employee moral can have a negative impact on the security of the cloud service. For example, insuring that patches are applied in a timely manner might suffer if the administrators applying them aren't overly concerned with doing so or might not put in the extra effort to test, follow quality assurance checks, and then deploy. It is not uncommon for unhappy employees to provide unsatisfactory results.

Risk: A Deeper Look at CSP Business Continuity

It is also equally important to understand CSPs business continuity capabilities. If there was a disaster that would impact the cloud, the provider should have a formal disaster recovery plan that is kept relevant and periodically tested. It is especially important to understand the procedures and design the cloud provider has in place to ensure its viability. Disaster recovery not only includes natural issues like earthquakes, fires, or tornadoes but also includes how you recover from man-made issues like human error. Even if the CSP has a disaster recovery plan in place, does the plan itself compromise the security of the cloud?

NOTE

When selecting a cloud storage provider, there are several considerations beyond security. First, there may be a significant degree of latency between your processing and your in-cloud storage. Depending on the volume of data being processed, this can cause unacceptable performance. Likewise, if users interact with in-cloud data, this may also result in an unacceptable user experience.

It may be possible to manage such performance issues with a combination of ample bandwidth or even by traffic management. Another approach is to use a cloud storage gateway device. Various vendor solutions are available, and many options exist for this. One factor to consider with these devices is the difference between caching and tiering. Those that use the caching approach use in-cloud storage as the primary storage. Those that use the tiering approach, on-premise storage is your primary storage and the in-cloud storage is secondary storage.

SELECTING A CSP: SECURITY CRITERIA

Beyond considering risk factors, there are many security criteria to consider when selecting a CSP. Following is a list of some criteria that are specific to security:

- **Security Policies** Any security conscious organization will have carefully considered and enforced security policies. The quality of a CSPs security policy is indicative of how seriously they take their responsibility for security.
- **Security Staff Independence** Security operations staff should report independently but operate in close cooperation with the operations staff of the cloud. The security team's responsibility is to assure the continuing security of the service, a responsibility that cannot take a backseat to operational pressures.
- **Change Management** Changes to the infrastructure must be documented, reviewed, and approved. The authority to make what changes must be clearly delineated.
- **Upgrades and Patch Management** Upgrades and patches should be applied in a timely and safe manner to limit exposure and to provide appropriate security on an ongoing basis.
- **Scans** The CSP must perform regular vulnerability assessments and scan the infrastructure. Any issues must be evaluated for their potential impact and be promptly rectified.
- **Forensics** Security relevant logs must be retained long enough to assure their availability to meet forensic and legal requirements. Such logs contribute to knowledge of how an incident or breach occurred and also to understand the scope of its impact.
- **Incident Management** A security incident response process should be documented and transparent to the customer. Not only is a customer interested in the response time frame (detection, incident disclosure, remediation, review,

and public disclosure), but customers may also require responsive cooperation from a CSP to support resolution of customer identified incidents.

- **Business Continuity** Recovery point objective (RPO) is the maximum amount of data loss that is acceptable after a data loss incident. This is expressed in terms of time, namely the point in time before the event back to which data can be successfully recovered. In other words, the time of the most recent reliable backup. Recovery Time Objective (RTO) is the maximum amount of time that is acceptable for restoring and regaining access to data after a disruption. Factored into RPO and RTO are loss of revenue and the extent to which a disrupted process impacts business continuity. RPO and RTO will vary widely, depending on the requirements of the business function.

Security Criteria: Revisiting Defense-in-depth

As discussed earlier in this chapter (Selecting a CSP: Overview of Assurance), if a customer is to accept the security claims around a public cloud, then it is not necessary to know product and configuration details, but it is necessary to have an understanding that such mechanisms are in place. Below (and depicted in Figure 8.3) is a list of some of the key layers that make up a defense-in-depth model for any network and should be in place for a public cloud:

- **Hardened Routers** Routers are not primarily meant to implement security, but they are usually the first point of entry to the network. They should be hardened to prevent against common threats like spoofing, malformed packets, protocol-based attacks, and denial of service attacks.

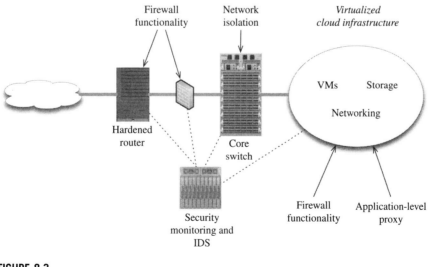

FIGURE 8.3

Defense-in-depth example.

- **Firewalls** Firewalls have many forms, including hardware based and software based. Hardware firewalls should be installed at the edge of the network as well between critical security zones that might exist within the infrastructure. Firewalls should also be used in software form by customers of IaaS.

- **Application-level Proxy or Firewall** Inside a perimeter firewall, some hardened networks today deploy a proxy at the application level. The primary reason for this is to adhere to the principle of deny everything and explicitly permit only what you want to permit. Although a firewall will almost always have a policy similar to this, a proxy inherently applies the same principle at the application layer. Deep packet inspection or layer 7 aware device scans can also be used to secure against application level threats where proxies might not be feasible.

- **Security Information and Event Management (SIEM) sometimes also known as Security Event Management (SEM)** SIEM can be very expensive, but it addresses several key security needs. Security monitoring was covered in Chapter 6, where we detailed security event generation, event collection, event analysis, and the alerting process. But there is more behind the utility of a SIEM than just the realm of monitoring and alerting. Although a SIEM is a critical operational component for ongoing security awareness, it is also necessary for compliance. In addition, there are synergies that can be achieved between other security related infrastructure and a SIEM—for instance, when information from an identity management system (IMS) is made available to a SIEM, alerting can improve because detailed knowledge of user roles can reduce the number of false alarms and improve the quality of detection. Likewise, detection can be improved when information of the infrastructure—as may be managed by a CMDB—is made available to a SIEM.

- **Host and Network Intrusion Detection/Prevention** IDS implements an added layer of security within the infrastructure to assist in detecting potential intrusions, misuse, or insider threats. IDS can be a consumer of information that is managed by a SIEM or it can be a completely separate system such as Snort-based appliances.

Many of these components—a SIEM, IMS, and CMDB—are expensive and complex to operate. As a security-conscious consumer of cloud services, the fact that a CSP uses such capabilities to assure ongoing security is as important as knowing that in doing so, the CSP follows processes and procedures that meet standards and or are consistent with best practices. But how does one measure this?

TIP

To see how well cloud computing can be described to customers, take a look at http://heroku.com/.

This CSP has figured out how to graphically explain how their architecture and pricing works. Remarkably, they have done so in a manner that makes sense to both the Über geek and the casual researcher. With a dark background and blue and purple text, this site can be described as cool and informative. Sliders and interactive tools let the prospective client understand what they will need and how much it will cost.

In contrast, most other cloud service providers are rooted in text-based detailed explanations of this sort of information.

Security Criteria: Other Considerations

Beyond its physical infrastructure, cloud architecture can also impact its security. Specific details for the architecture or the information security management system might not be obtainable, but subscribers to the cloud should still obtain a basic understanding of the underlying technology.

Patch Management

A formal patch management process is a key to ongoing security. With a public cloud you are relying on the cloud provider to patch their systems, but your data may be at risk until they do. This is of paramount importance when you are talking about patching the foundation, such as virtualization-level vulnerabilities. But operational VMs may also require patching, and that can become interesting. The sheer number of VMs in a virtualized cloud makes patching all VMs unrealistic. Virtualization brings new opportunity to the traditional patch process since it is easier to patch a golden image and then copy customer components to a copy of that image.

Device Configuration

How does the cloud provider handle device configuration management? A key area to focus on is how changes are tracked and how delegated administration works. A malicious CSP employee is one of the great risks to an otherwise properly secured cloud. As a result, basic protection like managing changes to production equipment is paramount to its security.

Security Operations Center

The equipment protecting an infrastructure often is only as good as the engineers managing it. From a security point of view, management of a public cloud also entails the ability to adequately respond to incidents as they occur. In the event of a critical security issue, there needs to be a team of qualified engineers in place to assess the threat, diagnose its impact, and react accordingly. These engineers need to have a primary responsibility of security and not operations, as often the two roles can conflict. As a result, this team is often called a security operations center (SOC) and not a network operations center (NOC).

The CSP should also be responsive to requests that you submit since this will have a bearing on your ability to secure your use of the cloud. For instance, if you are suffering from a denial of service attack that is affecting your cloud application but is not large enough to affect the cloud as a whole.

Infrastructure

Although a customer purchases a service that is abstracted away from underlying infrastructure, the CSPs infrastructure is of great importance when considering security. You might be purchasing a small slice of it, or perhaps just timesharing it, but in the end your data is only as secure as the infrastructure and physical locations are. A CSP is unlikely to provide details such as exact specifications of the servers or their patch levels, but an organization adopting that cloud should have more than just an understanding of the policies that are in place to address these concerns, they should also have a sufficient understanding of the environment in which their business will operate from.

Platforms

The kind of servers that are deployed along with the foundational software that comprises the cloud can be valuable information for customer (and attacker). If a cloud is built on virtualization, an understanding of how virtualization is accomplished is important. There are several common virtualization products available that form clouds, including VMWare, Xen, and Microsoft's Hyper-V. If virtualization is used, it is an important area to focus on in an information security management system, as it basically is creating the foundation or platform for the cloud. Virtualization security is still an evolving science, of which there is a tremendous amount of research and development still occurring—including how to best secure it. An understanding of what kind of platform is used allows the subscribing organization to know what threats might exist as new vulnerabilities are discovered. It also allows the organization to assess whether or not the security of their cloud has been compromised by a new development in this space.

Data Backups

A basic element of any disaster recovery plan is data backups and moving those backups off-site. This can take the form of backing data up to high capacity storage tapes and moving those tapes off-site. The same can be done with disk-based storage or remote network-based backups as well. Depending on the details of how the backups are occurring, the mere act of backing up the cloud might compromise security, for instance: Is encryption used as backups are created? When the backups are physically being moved to another location is there a chain of custody? Are there any measures in place to insure that the data has not been tampered with during the move?

EPIC FAIL

In an article published on www.enterprisestorageforum.com, Henry Newman[7] warned of the limits of cloud-based storage. Newman points out two factors: bandwidth limitation and data integrity issues. Newman's point about data integrity is that most CSPs use storage media that isn't designed for the expected level of usage.

Newman explains that the two disk failure measures are *hard error rate* (average number of bits before an error) and *annualized failure rate* (AFR), which are based on the number of hours a device is used. He points out that although these rates have improved in the past decade, disk density has increased even more and this will lead to problems, especially for archival data that is not accessed often.

If Newman is correct, then we are rapidly approaching the point where many of the disks used in cloud-based storage are about to fail. The result may not be one giant epic fail, but a series of smaller failures impact a subset of users and thus may well undermine the general experience of reliable use of cloud storage.

Security Practice

One of the most important aspects of a CSPs security policy is to understand how one subscriber's data or instance is kept separate from another user's data. Platform segregation from other subscribers is a significant threat vector to consider. An understanding of how the segregation is accomplished can influence just what kind of data gets stored in the cloud.

To this point, an MIT paper *Hey, You, Get Off of My Cloud: Exploring Information Leakage in Third-Party Compute Clouds*,[8] described how security researchers found a way to breach the segmentation that Amazon had in place in their Elastic Compute Cloud such that they were able to successfully prove that exploitation was possible from within one virtual machine to another virtual machine simply by existing on the same host instance within the cloud—a concept called coresidence. They were able to successfully exploit how Amazon attempts to randomize the hosts selected to house VMs and ended up with two machines running on the same host to then prove that information leakage between two independent VMs was possible. Theoretically these two VMs could have belonged to two different organizations—perhaps one legitimate and one malicious.

Protecting against such threats can be difficult, but making sure that your ISMS policy is aware that they are potential threats is the key, as well as knowing that the provider is aware of research and exploits in this area. In the example above, Amazon very quickly reacted to the vulnerability and further randomized their host selection process, along with other changes.

Additional Security-relevant Criteria

As we saw in the section Risk: A Deeper Look at CSP Business Viability, not all security criteria are specific to security. The remainder of this section presents a number of other such criteria.

Service Level Agreements

Service level agreements (SLA) are a critical component of a public cloud's availability. A cloud must be available and network reachable to provide any value to its tenants or customers. Service-impacting issues put the cloud subscriber at the mercy of the CSP to resolve it. An SLA is the primary means a customer has of assurance that availability will be maintained or the failing to do so the CSP will incur penalties.

As an alternative or adjunct to third party certification, similar SLAs can apply to security. What good is the cloud if it is available but insecure? Although a security SLA will not guarantee security, it does provide assurances that appropriate policies and procedures are in place. And, if they are not met then there is a penalty to the CSP.

Elasticity

The elasticity, or on-demand ability for a cloud to increase capacity dynamically and without reasonable limits, affects the availability of the cloud. Availability is core security property, and availability is subject to DDoS and numerous factors including misbehaving processes that attempt to consume all available resources. Consequently, when considering the elasticity capacity of a cloud, you must take a holistic view. Don't look at scalability from the perspective only of how much storage or CPU cycles your particular instance can consume. Make sure you understand the overall limits and how the cloud provider scales their cloud. How do they accommodate customer growth? Make sure to get an understanding of load balancing, how load is shared among nodes, and how that affects your adoption of the cloud with your particular application. Usually this can be quantitatively tracked in the form of a SLA with availability metrics as well.

WARNING

With all the computing power and network bandwidth that is available to lease from a public cloud, we can easily imagine ways to use that to perform a great deal of on-demand work—say, being able to rapidly standup a compute capability that a cloud customer can use to perform on-demand research and analysis that scales across hundreds or thousands of elastically provisioned VMs. But consider how all this power can also be used by crime syndicates, hackers, and even nation states to find a witness, sift through huge stolen data sets, and disrupt competitors Internet businesses or propagate nation-wide denial of service attacks.

Using clustered or grid computing to crack passwords has been done for several years, so using cloud-based computers to do the same thing was expected since the start of cloud computing. The fundamental difference is the universal access to public clouds to gain access to vast computing resources. With IaaS, the CSP can't really detect that the tenant is performing password cracking, breaking weakly encrypted files, or performing any other illegal action within a cloud instance. (In fact, using Amazon cloud services in such ways is an infringement of its conditions of use.) By using many computers in parallel, weakly encrypted content stands no chance if someone wants access to the content. As reported in *The Local*, a German hacker cracked a W-LAN password in 20 minutes using Amazon cloud.[9] In that report, German IT security expert, Thomas Roth, spent approximately $2 in an Amazon GPU instance to crack the WPA password of his neighbor's wireless network (with his neighbors permission). Similar cracks have been previously reported, and there has been at least one well-reported service *WPACracker* that used 400 Amazon cloud VMs to achieve the same thing.

But the real concern in this space has to do with using cloud VM instances to attack Internet-based web sites or to hack external networks. Not only is the potential magnitude of such attacks concerning but also the ease of performing such an attack is remarkable. But along with the ease of such attacks comes the difficulty of responding to such attacks and the consequences of blacklisting a CSPs IP addresses in the wake of such attacks. CSPs must perform egress filtering and detection if IP addresses associated with their service are to avoid being shunned by being included in blacklists. But even if CSPs perform such detection and monitoring, a cloud-based attack can be well underway and achieve its goals by the time the CSP shuts down the offending instances. By using multiple CSPs in a coordinated manner, an attacker can launch a crippling attack against numerous targets with very little cost or risk.

Data Center Location

The location of the data center(s) that implement the service utility has both direct and indirect implications. These include laws that govern data and its jurisdiction. A prospective customer should have many questions about this, including: Would the CSP store sensitive information (customer names, addresses, credit card numbers, medical records, and so on) that are not allowed to be stored outside certain borders? Is the cloud made up of multiple data centers, perhaps in multiple countries? Where will data be stored? How stable is the country or region in which the data center operates? Is it at risk to law enforcement without due process? Does the stored information (that is, data that is at rest) require encryption?

At the very least, a customer should know in which jurisdictions the nodes are that form the cloud. Be wary of organizations that cannot guarantee at least the national or regional level where the data will be stored.

Staff

As a hallmark of cloud computing and the economics of such a service, a cloud customer will have very little (if any) direct exposure to the personnel managing that cloud. This is certainly true for most SaaS and it is largely true for PaaS and IaaS. Nevertheless, the organization is still at the mercy of those personnel even though they are not directly managing them. In terms of security, it is important to understand the hiring policies and procedures of the public cloud provider for key personnel involved in the development and management of the cloud.

At a basic level, several questions should be answered: Are background checks performed on CSP personnel? What are their minimum required credentials to be considered? What system of checks and balances is in place to prevent a rogue or malicious employee from compromising the integrity of the cloud?

Change Management

How individual device configuration changes are recorded is important, but the process of reviewing and approving such changes is equally important. Again, from a security point of view, this is to help mitigate potential threats to a secure cloud infrastructure from malicious or rogue employees. It naturally also provides availability and reliability to the cloud by properly reviewing and approving changes, but it also creates a natural layer of checks and balances. The key point to make is that a change management system needs to have not only the administrative approval from those involved in the operations side for the provider but also from those involved in the security side. All changes should be looked at from both points of view.

SUMMARY

In summary, selecting a public cloud should include consideration of potential risks. A thorough understanding of the cloud provider's architecture, infrastructure, policies, and procedures may not be possible, nor is that necessary as long as the CSPs security claims are independently verified to a level of assurance that meets the customer's needs. In this regard, a number of standards exist, notably the ISO 27000 series. Just as important as such verification is the CSPs willingness to be transparent about their security practices.

This chapter examined a number of security criteria that prospective cloud service customers should consider. These include criteria that clearly fall into the realm of security, as well as others that are security relevant—such as SLAs, data center location, and cloud elasticity. The goal of this chapter was to present an overview of how to select a CSP based on security requirements. In the next chapter, we present a framework for cloud information security. That framework can also be used to more exactingly detail out the security requirements that a customer has in selecting a cloud provider.

Endnotes

1. Steiner P. The New Yorker 1993;**69**(20):61.
2. Proposed Security Assessment & Authorization for U.S. Government Cloud Computing, Draft version 0.96, CIO Council, US Federal Government; 2010.
3. ISO/IEC27002:2005, http://www.iso.org/iso/catalogue_detail?csnumber=50297, International Organization for Standardization (ISO) and the International Electrotechnical Commission (IEC) [accessed 24.03.11].
4. Building Customer Trust in Cloud Computing with Transparent Security, Sun Microsystems White Paper; 2009 https://www.sun.com/offers/details/sun_transparency.xml [accessed 20.02.10].
5. Cloud Computing: Benefits, risks and recommendations for information security. *European Network and Information Security Agency* 2009:22.
6. Ibid.
7. Newman H. Why Cloud Storage Use Could Be Limited in Enterprises, http://www.enterprisestorageforum.com/technology/features/article.php/3843151 October 9, 2009 [accessed 24.03.11].
8. Hey You. Get Off of My Cloud: Exploring Information Leakage in Third-Party Compute Clouds. Ristenpart T, et al., ACM Conference on Computer and Communications Security, 2009.
9. Published Jan 16 2011, http://www.thelocal.de/sci-tech/20110116-32461.html [accessed 24.03.11].

Evaluating Cloud Security: An Information Security Framework

INFORMATION IN THIS CHAPTER

- Evaluating Cloud Security
- Checklists for Evaluating Cloud Security
- Metrics for the Checklists

Cloud security represents yet another opportunity to apply sound security principles and engineering to a specific domain and to solve for a given set of problems. Up to this point in the book, we have surveyed a number of aspects of cloud security. In Chapter 4, we examined the architectural aspects of securing a cloud. In Chapter 5, we considered the requirements for cloud data security. Chapter 6 presented key strategies and best practices for cloud security, Chapter 7 detailed the security criteria for building an internal cloud, and in Chapter 8, we presented security criteria for selecting an external cloud provider.

This chapter builds on that previous material and presents the foundation for a framework for evaluating cloud security. This material is intended to go beyond and augment the security criteria we introduced in Chapter 8. It should benefit activities that precede the evaluation, certification, or accreditation of a cloud. We start by reviewing existing work in this area, and then we will put forward a set of checklists of evaluation criteria that span the range of activities that together support information security for cloud computing. The goal of this chapter is to provide the reader with an organized set of tools, which can be used to evaluate the security of a private, community, public, or hybrid cloud. Evaluating the security of a hybrid cloud may best be done by managing the evaluation of the two or more cloud instances using one set of checklists per instance. By example, if the hybrid consists of a private cloud and a public cloud, simply evaluate the private components using one set of checklists and evaluate the public components into their separate realms. When done in this manner, you can more readily compare public cloud alternatives.

EVALUATING CLOUD SECURITY

Most users of a cloud, whether it is a private or a public cloud, have certain expectations for the security of their data. Similarly, the owner and operator of a cloud share responsibility for ensuring that security measures are in place and that standards and procedures are followed. We can capture our expectations and responsibilities for security by stating them formally in documented requirements. By example, the NIST 800-53 security controls (these were discussed in Chapter 6) detail specific requirements for federal government systems. Systems that are fielded by government agencies must generally comply with these and related NIST requirements. The Cloud Security Alliance *Controls Matrix* takes a similar approach in detailing security requirements for cloud implementations, and there is a growing trend by commercial users to adopt such generally accepted requirements. A good starting point when you need to measure the presence and effectiveness of the security of a cloud includes having a list of required or recommended security controls.

To begin, there are two aspects to security controls in cloud implementations. The first has to do with the presence of the control. The second aspect is the effectiveness or robustness of the control. In other words, it is not enough that a security control is present—but that control also needs to be effective. Going further, one can describe this as the degree of trust (or assurance) that can be expected from these controls. For instance, a cloud may implement encrypted communications between the cloud and an external user—but if we are evaluating the effectiveness of encrypted communications, then we also need to verify that the control is properly designed, implemented, and verified.

Measuring the presence and/or effectiveness of security controls (against security requirements) is largely what security evaluations are intended to do. Security evaluations have broad value as guidance for planning or developing security and for verifying that required controls are properly implemented. But evaluations also have utility for procurement of cloud services; for instance, a CSP may choose to publish the high-level results of a third party security evaluation. In addition, if we are to compare the security of two or more clouds, then that will entail having a common set of criteria for evaluation.

On the basis of the sensitivity of data or the expected risk of a system, we should undergo an initial requirements phase where appropriate security controls are identified. If we subsequently perform a thorough assessment of the decision process that led to identifying those controls and couple that assessment with a security evaluation of the effectiveness of those controls that were implemented, then we should have a fairly good understanding of whether an overall cloud service has a sound security posture versus the risk it is subject to.

Figure 9.1 depicts the relationship between requirements, security evaluation of a cloud, the cloud implementation, vulnerability remediation, and continuing configuration management controls.

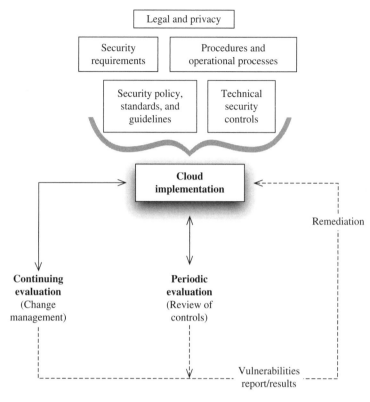

FIGURE 9.1

From requirements and evaluation to ongoing security remediation.

Existing Work on Cloud Security Guidance or Frameworks

In the few years since cloud computing arrived as a new model for IT, several efforts have already taken place to offer guidance for cloud security. These include:

- **Cloud Security Alliance (CSA)** The CSA has been very active in various efforts, including:
- **Cloud Controls Matrix (CCM)** This is "designed to provide fundamental security principles to guide cloud vendors and to assist prospective cloud customers in assessing the overall security risk of a cloud provider. The Cloud Controls Matrix provides a controls framework that gives detailed understanding of security concepts and principles that are aligned to the Cloud Security Alliance guidance in 13 domains."[1]
- **Consensus Assessments Initiative Questionnaire** This effort is "focused on providing industry-accepted ways to document what security controls exist in IaaS, PaaS, and SaaS offerings, providing security control transparency."[2]

- **Security Guidance for Critical Areas of Focus in Cloud Computing** V2.1 published in December 2009 presented security guidance for a number of areas in cloud computing; these include architecture, governance, traditional security, and virtualization.
- **Domain 12: Guidance for Identity & Access Management** V2.1 published in April 2010 discusses the major identity management functions as they relate to cloud computing. This work forms a cornerstone of the CSA's *Trusted Cloud Initiative*.
- **CloudAudit** Seeks to give cloud adopters and cloud operators the tools to measure and compare the security of cloud services. It does this by defining "a common interface and namespace that allows cloud computing providers to automate the Audit, Assertion, Assessment, and Assurance (A6) of their infrastructure (IaaS), platform (PaaS), and application (SaaS) environments."[3]
- **European Network and Information Security Agency** Leading the security guidance efforts in Europe, ENISA has produced several guiding publications for securely adopting cloud computing, these include:
- **Cloud Computing: Information Assurance Framework** Published in November 2009. Presents a set of assurance criteria that address the risk of adopting cloud computing.
- **Cloud Computing: Benefits, Risks and Recommendations for Information Security** Published in November 2009.
- **The Federal CIO Council's** *Proposed Security Assessment and Authorization for U.S. Government Cloud Computing.*[4] The core importance of this document is that it adopts the NIST 800-53R3 security controls for cloud computing in low- and moderate-risk systems.
- **The Trusted Computing Group (TCG)** In September 2010, the TCG formed the *Trusted Multi-Tenant Infrastructure Work Group*, which is intended to develop a security framework for cloud computing. The Trusted Multi-Tenant Infrastructure Work Group will use existing standards to define end-to-end security for cloud computing in a framework that can serve as a baseline for compliance and auditing.

All of these efforts are relatively new and have yet to gain broad acceptance. More so, they are either initial activities that are intended to serve as a starting point for more formal work or the product of community efforts toward a common framework for cloud security. In other words, there is a great deal of uncertainty in this area. That presents a difficulty for cloud adopters who need to evaluate the security of their private or community clouds and also for users who need a means to evaluate the security of a cloud service.

Today, users do not yet have a common and standard means to evaluate cloud security. In fact, much of the pre–cloud computing world has not adopted security evaluation frameworks outside those realms where regulation requires a security benchmark or where evaluation is mandated. But cloud security is a fast moving area, and all of the above efforts have taken place between 2009 and the end of 2010. The adoption of these efforts is accelerating in several ways, especially in the government space with FedRAMP. By its very nature, adoption of public clouds is a change agent in security. There is a fast shaping trend here, and one can expect to see real progress in the near term. This is an example of how cloud computing is stimulating better security in business areas where otherwise there was great concern over security but little improvement until the rise of public clouds.

TOOLS

Many tools are used for security testing. These include the following categories:

- Port scanning for open and responding services
- SNMP scanning
- Device enumeration or cataloging
- Host vulnerability scanning
- Network device analysis
- Password compliance testing and cracking

There are several basic tools that have stood the test of time; these include NMAP for port scanning and Nessus for host vulnerability scanning. In addition, there has been a more recent crop of powerful tools that allow for extensive defense testing to identify quality, resiliency and related security vulnerabilities. These tools offer test suites for a broad range of cloud network security needs.

CHECKLISTS FOR EVALUATING CLOUD SECURITY

The intent of developing a cloud security evaluation checklist is to have a uniform means to verify the security of a cloud and also to obtain assurance from a CSP about their security. However, as stated in this chapter's introduction, such checklists can also be used by prospective customers or users to compare cloud security for different providers.

The remainder of this section presents checklists that form the heart of a framework for evaluating cloud security. The questions in these checklists are derived from several sources that include the CSA Cloud Controls Matrix,[5] the ENISA Cloud Computing Information Assurance Framework,[6] and NIST's 800-53R3.[7]

WARNING

Security testing, especially penetration testing and vulnerability testing, can easily produce a false sense of security. The problem is twofold:

- First, such tests are based on current knowledge of vulnerabilities and can't account for zero-day exploits that periodically arise. New vulnerabilities are discovered on a daily basis. Every once in a while, vulnerabilities are even exposed for very mature systems. Again, multiple layers of defense—defense-in-depth—is the best strategy against exposure to a zero-day exploit.

(Continued)

> (*Continued*)
> • Second, a sound bill-of-health in penetration or vulnerability testing cannot be taken as a measure of overall security—including procedures and the broad range of operational controls that any information security program depends on.
>
> In other words, security testing—and especially penetration testing—only test the target system at a point in time and only to a limited extent. Systems and configurations tend to change over time, and new vulnerabilities can become exposed years after a system is fielded, tested, and approved. The bottom line is that these sorts of tests should be viewed as very superficial and should not be relied on to ascertain security. Which begs the question: Should they be performed at all? Security engineers generally agree that such tests have value. But, remember this: your opponents may have more time and interest in "testing" your systems than you do, so take testing seriously but don't rely on it.

One application for the checklist is that a cloud owner can use it to guide a security evaluation of their cloud. If cloud providers use such a checklist as a framework to report on the security of their clouds, then prospective tenants and users could compare the relative security of multiple clouds. The checklist can also be used by a public cloud customer to ask a series of questions that are relevant to their business needs. Not all these questions will be relevant for all uses or business relationships.

Each of the following sections is organized around a set of closely related controls or requirements. Figure 9.2 presents an overview of the evaluation checklist sections and lists the groups of controls or requirements for each section.

Foundational Security

A security *policy* defines the organization's requirements or rules for security. Security policy delineates the constraints and requirements that individuals and groups must operate under, and it serves as a statement of management's intent for security. Actions that are taken in regard to security should be clearly traceable to the security policy. Several classes of policy may exist, including an overall security policy as well as additional policies that address more limited areas (such as an *acceptable use policy*). Policy is focused on achieving desired results, and not on specific implementations.

Foundational security	*Defense in depth*	*Operational security*
Policy, standards, and guidelines	Software assurance	Data center: Physical security
Transparency	Network security	Data center: Power and networking
Personnel security	Host and VM security	Data center: Asset management
Third party providers	PaaS and SaaS	Operational practices
	Identity and access management	Incident management
Business considerations	Authentication	
Legal	Key management	
Business continuity	Cryptography	
Resource provisioning		

FIGURE 9.2

Overview of evaluation checklist.

Augmenting such policies are other statements of requirements for specific areas. These are usually defined as *standards* and cover such specific areas as technical controls or specific hardening requirements. Standards state mandatory actions that support policy. *Guidelines* are a third class of documentation that is less formal and more oriented toward procedural best practices. These are recommendations or descriptions of practices that support the objectives of a security policy by describing a framework to implement procedures. In other words: A policy states *why*, a standard states *what*, and a guideline states *how*. Checklist 9.1 covers foundational security elements related to policy, standards, and guidelines.

Checklist 9.1 Policy, Standards, and Guidelines[8-10]

Policy, Standards, and Guidelines

- Has a security policy been clearly documented, approved, and represented to all concerned parties as representing management's intent?
- Has the security policy had legal, privacy, and other governance review?
- Has the security policy been augmented by security standards and/or guidelines?
- Has the policy been augmented by a privacy policy?
- Are the security and privacy policies, as well as standards and guidelines, consistent with industry standards (such as 27001, CoBIT, and so on)?
- Are third party providers held to the same policies and standards?

Checklist 9.2 covers evaluation criteria that are focused on CSP transparency.

Checklist 9.2 Transparency[11-13]

Transparency

- Does the CSP provide customers with a copy of the governing policies, standards, and guidelines?
- Are customers notified of changes to governing policies, standards, and guidelines?
- Does the CSP provide customers visibility into third party compliance audits?
- Does the CSP provide customers visibility into penetration tests?
- Does the CSP provide customers visibility into internal and external audits?
- Does the CSP provide customers visibility into CSP asset management and repurposing of equipment?

Personnel security for a cloud is a foundation upon which operational security resides. The intent of personnel security is to avoid several classes of security risk and to create an environment that reinforces the objectives that are stated in security policy. Checklist 9.3 lists evaluation criteria related to personnel security.

Checklist 9.3 Personnel Security[14-16]

Personnel Security

- Are there policies and procedures for:
- Hiring employees who will have access to or control over cloud components?
- Pre-employment checks for personnel with privileged access?

- Are personnel security policies consistent across locations?
- Do they apply to online cloud systems and data as well as to offline systems that either stored data or to offline systems that will be provisioned for online use?
- Is there a security education program, and if so, how extensive is it?
- Is personnel security frequently reviewed to determine if employees with access should continue to have access?
- Are personnel required to have and maintain security certifications?
- Does physical access to the CSP's facility require background checks?

The use of subcontractors or third party providers can create undue risk for customers unless such providers follow and operate in accordance with CSP policies. Checklist 9.4 details criteria for third party providers.

Checklist 9.4 Third Party Providers[17–19]

Third Party Providers

- Are any services or functions provided by a third party?
- If any part of a cloud is subcontracted or otherwise outsourced, does the providing party comply with the same policy and standards that the CSP enforces?
- If used, are third party providers audited for compliance with the CSPs policies and standards?
- Does the CSP security policy (or equivalent) and governance extend to all third party providers?

Business Considerations

Various business considerations bring with them the need for security consideration. Business considerations include legal, business continuity, and resource provisioning. Evaluation criteria for these are listed in Checklists 9.5, 9.6, and 9.7; Checklist 9.5 covers legal criteria.

Checklist 9.5 Legal[20–22]

Legal

- Where—in which jurisdiction—will data be stored?
- Where—in which jurisdiction—is the CSP incorporated?
- Does the CSP use third party providers who are not located in the same jurisdiction?
- Does the CSP subcontract any services or personnel?
- Does the CSP use a customer's data in any manner that is not part of the service?
- Does the CSP have a documented procedure for responding to legal requests (such as a subpoena) for customer data?
- In the event of a subpoena, how does the CSP produce data for a single customer only without providing non-subpoena data?
- Is the CSP insured against losses, including remuneration for customer losses due to CSP outages or data exposure?

Business continuity can be critical for customers who use cloud-based services in a mission critical manner. Criteria associated with business continuity are listed in Checklist 9.6.

Checklist 9.6 Business Continuity[23–25]

Business Continuity

- Does the CSP have a formal process or contingency plan that documents and guides business continuity?
- What are the service recovery point objective (RPO) and recovery time objective (RTO)?
- Is information security integral to recovery and restoration?
- How does the CSP communicate a disruption of services to customers?
- Is there a secondary site for disaster recovery?

Business continuity is a complex topic that warrants far greater coverage than possible in a cloud security book. The interested reader is encouraged to research several related topic areas; these include business continuity planning along with contingency and disaster recovery planning. There are many sources for these areas, including:

- ANSI/ASIS SPC.1-2009 Organizational Resilience: Security, Preparedness, and Continuity Management Systems—Requirements with Guidance for Use American National Standard
- The National Institute of Science and Technology (NIST) Special Publication 800-34 *Contingency Planning Guide for Information Technology Systems*
- Good Practice Guidelines can be downloaded from: www.thebcicertificate.org/bci_gpg.html
- And the Business Continuity Institute is located at www.thebci.org

---

EPIC FAIL

As reported by the German online newspaper *Zeit Online* on February 18, 2011,[26] an error in the cloud provider's payment system paralyzed a German company's access to their public cloud SaaS e-mail and online documents. Although the actual facts in this case are not fully clear at the time this chapter was written, it should serve as a warning: Any cloud provider's accounting or customer management systems could be in error and in an extreme case this might result in a *business* denial-of-service.

Such an accounting error is certainly not unique in the world of billing and debt collection, but in a communications system—such as the Internet—or in a cloud services situation, the error can conceivably occur, and the consequences felt very quickly without the victim having any prior billing warning. The cloud services model brings a second complicating factor: Many cloud services largely rely on self-service interfaces, with little recourse from traditional human customer service representatives.

In the radio.de case, it appears that the CSP abruptly cut off access to radio.de's office software and relevant documents. Radio.de apparently could not reach the CSPs regional office in Dublin, and e-mails to the CSP did not solve the problem for a few days. The facts

(Continued)

> (*Continued*)
> in this specific case are not at all clear, so the CSP will go unidentified here. However, if you outsource your critical business functions, make certain that any similar situation can be more quickly resolved with the CSP. That will entail doing your homework before you form a business relationship with a CSP, and it will entail maintaining contact with the provider so that you are always aware of any changes in contact methods or details. Finally consider this: If your disaster recovery plan is stored on the CSPs systems, you really don't have a CSP disaster recovery plan at all.

Resource provisioning has to do with assuring that the cloud service will be sufficiently resourced as customer demand increases. To do this, a CSP would need to take certain measures to successfully deliver on their SLAs. For instance, the CSP might have procedures in place to add servers or storage as demand increases. Checklist 9.7 lists evaluation criteria for resource provisioning.

Checklist 9.7 Resource Provisioning[27–29]

Resource Provisioning
- What controls and procedures are in place to manage resource exhaustion, including processing oversubscription, memory or storage exhaustion, and network congestion?
- Does the CSP limit subscriptions to the service in order to protect SLAs?
- Does the CSP provide customers with utilization and capacity planning information?

Defense-in-depth

The integrity and security of an operational cloud depends on the integrity of components that comprise it. Software is a primary vector for vulnerabilities and exploits. To begin, Checklist 9.8 lists evaluation criteria for software assurance.

Checklist 9.8 Software Assurance[30–32]

Software Assurance
- What controls are in place to maintain integrity of operating systems, applications, firmware updates, configuration files, and other software?
- What industry standards, guidelines, or best practices are followed?
- What controls or guidelines are used to obtain or download software and configuration files?
- What guidelines or procedures are used to maintain software integrity?
- Is penetration or vulnerability testing used on each release?
- How are identified vulnerabilities remediated?

One very powerful technique for improving software security is to empower developers during the development process itself by giving them access to security testing tools. Such tools range from static code analysis through web security testing. A best practice is to have the development environment closely mirror the eventual testing, staging, and production environments. With development, this is not always easy, but the fewer deltas between environments the better the transition and the fewer security surprises your developers will encounter. (When test, staging, and production environments vary widely, errors and costs will rise dramatically as well.)

TIP

One software testing technique is known as *fuzzing*. This technique involves injecting invalid and unexpected data to the input of a program or system. Using this technique, even random data can result in program crashing or entering a state whereby a security control can be made to fail. Two areas are especially fruitful for this testing, one is file formats, and the other is network protocols. Fuzz data can be sent as events, command line input, or mutated packets. One of the strengths of using fuzzing is that it can illuminate severe and exploitable bugs.

The most significant aspect of a cloud's security may well be the network implementation. Architectural and isolation choices that are made here will have far reaching benefits or consequences. Network choices start with the physical network, equipment functionality, and extend to network virtualization and monitoring. The degree of isolation between different classes of traffic (customer access, customer-to-customer, operations and management, external access, and so on) will drive other security requirements at the systems and VM levels. Checklist 9.9 lists criteria for network security.

Checklist 9.9 Network Security[33-35]

Network Security
- What controls are in place to manage externally sourced and internally sourced attacks, including distributed denial of service (DDoS)?
- For customers, how is isolation managed between VMs by the hypervisor?
- For customers, how is isolation managed between VMs by network hardware and routing?
- What standards or best practices are used to implement virtual network infrastructure?
- How are MAC spoofing, ARP poisoning, and so on protected against?
- How is isolation managed between customer accessed/routable systems and cloud management systems and infrastructure?
- Is cloud customer processing dependent on off-cloud tenant components such as LDAP?
- Does the CSP perform periodic penetration testing against the cloud?
- If so, is penetration testing done both from external to the cloud and from inside the cloud and the cloud infrastructure?
- Does the CSP perform vulnerability testing of the cloud infrastructure, cloud management, and also customer accessible components?
- How are identified vulnerabilities tracked and addressed?
- Is vulnerability information made available to customers?
- Does the CSP allow customers to perform vulnerability testing against the customer's own VMs or other containers?

The kinds and degree of security controls that are required to protect hosts and VMs are to a large extent driven by the network architecture. There are trade-offs on the one hand between extreme network isolation and control and on the other hand with the desire for maximum flexibility in operation. The greater the flexibility, the more compensating controls are needed at the host and VM levels. Checklist 9.10 lists evaluation criteria for host and VM security.

Checklist 9.10 Host and VM Security[36–38]

Host and VM Security
- Are customer VMs encrypted and/or otherwise protected when stored?
- Are VM images patched before they are provisioned?
- How and how frequently are VM images patched after being provisioned?
- To which standards or guidelines are VM images hardened before being provisioned?
- What are the procedures for protecting hardened and patched VM images?
- Can a customer provide his/her own VM image?
- Does the CSP include any authentication credentials, and if so, what are they used for?
- Do hardened and patched VM images include operating firewall instances by default? (And if so, what are the allowed services/ports?)
- Do hardened and patched VM images include operating IDS or intrusion prevention systems (IPS)?
- If so, does the CSP have access to these in operation (and if so, how)?
- Do hardened and patched VM images include any form of network, performance, or security instrumentation that the CSP or tenant has access to?
- How is isolation ensured between server colocated VMs for different customers?
- How is communication implemented between VMs for the same customer?
- How is security ensured for user data in storage systems?
- How is security ensured for user data in motion between storage systems and customer VMs?
- How is security ensured for user data and user interaction between a VM and a non-cloud user system?
- Does the CSP provide information to customers to guide customer security so that it is appropriate for the virtualized environment?

CSPs are generally responsible for the platform software stack, including security. Although a CSP may be reluctant to provide details about the security of a PaaS stack, a CSP should be transparent about their security practices and the scope of security controls. Checklist 9.11 lists evaluation criteria for PaaS and SaaS security.

Checklist 9.11 PaaS and SaaS Security[39–41]

PaaS and SaaS Security
- How does the CSP isolate multitenant applications?
- How does the CSP isolate a user's or tenant's data?
- How does the CSP identify new security vulnerabilities in applications and within the cloud infrastructure?
- Does the CSP provide security as a service features for PaaS (such as authentication, single sign on, authorization, and transport security)?

- What administrative controls does the CSP provide to a tenant/user and do these support defining/enforcing access controls by other users?
- Does the CSP provide separate test and production environments for customers?

Identity and access management are critical elements of security for a cloud. Checklist 9.12 lists evaluation criteria for identity and access management, along with authentication.

Checklist 9.12 Identity and Access Management[42–44]

Identity and Access Management
- Do any CSP controlled accounts have cloud-wide privileges (if so, which operations)?
- How does the CSP manage accounts with administrator or higher privilege?
- Does the CSP use 2-man access controls, and if so, for which operations?
- Does the CSP enforce privilege separation (for instance, RBAC), and if so, what roles are used to limit which privileges (security, OS admin, identity, and so on)?
- Does the CSP implement break-glass access, and if so, under what circumstances are they allowed and what is the process for post-clean up?
- Does the CSP grant tenants or users administrator privileges, and if so, what are the limits to this?
- Does the CSP verify user identity at registration, and if so, are there different levels of checks depending on resources to which access is granted?
- How are credentials and accounts deprovisioned?
- Is deprovisioning of credentials and accounts done in a cloud-wide atomic-operation manner?
- How is remote access managed and implemented?

For CSP supplied customer-use identity and access management systems:
- Does this support federated identity management?
- Is the CSP's system interoperable with third party identity provider systems?
- Can a customer incorporate single sign on?
- Does this system support separation of roles and LPP?

How does a CSP verify their identity to a customer under the following scenarios:
- When the CSP communicates out-of-band to a customer or user?
- When a customer interacts with the CSP via an API?
- When a customer uses a cloud management interface?

Authentication
- How is authentication implemented for high-assurance CSP operations?
- Is multifactor authentication used?
- Is access to high-assurance operations limited to only operations cloud-networks and only from whitelisted IP addresses?
- Does intrusion detection/anomaly detection detect multiple failed logins or similarly suspicious authentication or credential compromise activities?
- What procedures are invoked if a customer's credentials or account is compromised?

Key management and cryptography must be handled in precise and correct ways otherwise cryptographic security is quickly undermined. Checklist 9.13 lists security criteria for these areas.

Checklist 9.13 Key Management and Cryptography[45–47]

Key Management

- For keys that the CSP controls:
- How does the CSP protect keys, and what security controls are in place to effect that?
- Are hardware security modules used to protect such keys?
- Who has access to such keys?
- How are those keys protected for sign and encrypt operations?
- What procedures are in place to manage and recover from the compromise of keys?
- Is key revocation performed in a cloud-wide atomic-operation?

Cryptography

- For what operations (and where) is encryption used?
- Are all encryption mechanisms based on third party tested and evaluated products?
- Does security policy clearly define what must be encrypted?

To this point in the checklists, we have covered evaluation criteria for foundational security, business considerations, and defense-in-depth. The final group of checklists addresses operational security issues.

Operational Security

Many concerns around public clouds have to do with the fact that physical security of IT is in a third party's control. With a public cloud, a physical breach will affect multiple customers. Checklist 9.14 lists evaluation criteria for data center physical security and data center power and networking.

Checklist 9.14 Data Center: Physical Security and Power and Networking[48–50]

Data Center: Physical Security

- What are the requirements for being granted physical access to the CSP's facility?
- Do non-employees require escort in the facility?
- Is entry into the facility constrained by function and entry location? (Examples: shipping and receiving, housekeeping)
- Is the facility divided into zones such that each requires access permissions?
- Is strong authentication (for example, multifactor card and pin or card and biometric) required for physical access?
- Is all access monitored and documented?
- Are all entry locations alarmed and monitored?
- Is video monitoring complete for all common areas of the facility?
- How long is video retained?
- How often is a risk assessment performed for physical security?
- Does the CSP require that all deliveries or equipment removals be performed by the CSP within the facility (that is, is there a separate shipping facility outside the physical perimeter of the cloud facility itself)?

Data Center: Power and Networking

- Is power and networking secured within the facility?
- Are environmental systems (lighting, AC, fire detection) implemented to industry standards?

- Is air conditioning sized to withstand extended periods of extreme conditions?
- Is the facility exposed to moderate or higher risk of environmental or weather damage?
- Does the facility receive power from multiple power sources?
- Does the facility provide backup power generation for a period or time that is adequate to recover from loss of a primary power source?
- Does the facility have adequate UPS for short or temporary outages?
- Does the facility have multiple Internet connections, and are these from different tier 1 providers?

A CSP must maintain a current and complete list of all information resources that are used to implement and operate the cloud. The state-of-the-practice (ITIL) is to use a CMDB to maintain such information. The state-of-the-art is to have that process automated by using the CMDB as the centralized repository with which all other cloud management functions interoperate. Checklist 9.15 lists criteria for data center asset management.

Checklist 9.15 Data Center Asset Management[51-53]

Data Center Asset Management
- Does the CSP maintain a current and complete inventory of all hardware, network, software, and virtual components that comprise the cloud?
- Does the CSP automate such inventory tracking and management?
- Does the CSP maintain a record of all assets that a customer has used or on which a customer has stored data?
- Does the CSP support asset categories of different sensitivity levels, and if so, how are these isolated or separated from each other?
- Does the CSP maintain segregation or physical separation of assets at different sensitivity levels?

Effective security is an ongoing process that entails well-defined procedures and roles for all personnel. To be effective, such procedures must anticipate various kinds of events. Procedures should offer enough guidance to allow personnel to navigate a broad range of failure in systems, processes, and other circumstances. Such events and responses must be captured with learned lessons integrated into updated procedures. Chapter 10 will provide a deeper treatment of this topic, but here we will outline the kinds of controls that guide operational practices and security. Checklist 9.16 lists evaluation criteria for operational practices.

Checklist 9.16 Operational Practices[54-56]

Operational Practices
- Is there a formal change control process, and are the procedures clearly documented?
- Does change control include a means to guide decisions as to what changes require a reassessment of risk?
- Are operating procedures clearly documented and followed?
- Are there separate environments for development, testing, staging, and production?

- What system and network security controls are used to secure end user or tenant applications and information?
- What security controls are used to mitigate malicious code?
- What are the backup procedures (who does this, what gets backed up, how often is it done, what form does it take, and are backups periodically tested)?
- Where are back ups stored, and for how long are they kept?
- Will the CSP securely delete all copies of customer data after termination of the customer's contract?
- Under what circumstances are customer resources sanitized using industry best practices (for example, degaussing)?
- Does the CSP have documented security baselines for every component that comprises the cloud infrastructure?

The goal of incident management and response is to minimize or contain the impact of events. Incident management should be well defined in order to support and guide the CSPs and the customer's ability to reduce the consequence of unanticipated events or situations. Checklist 9.17 lists evaluation criteria for the area of incident management.

Checklist 9.17 Incident Management[57–59]

Incident Management
- What information is captured in audit, system, and network logs?
- How long is it retained, and who has access to it?
- What controls are used to protect these logs from unauthorized access and to preserve the chain of custody of such materials?
- How and how often are logs reviewed?
- How and how often are logs checked for integrity and completeness?
- Are all systems and network components synchronized to a single time source (NTP)?
- Does the CSP have a formal process to detect, identify, and respond to incidents?
- Are these processes periodically tested to verify that they are effective and appropriate?
- Are log and other security data maintained to comply with legal requirements for chain-of-custody control, and do the data and controls comply with legally admissible forensic data?
- What is the escalation process for incident response?
- Does the CSP use intrusion detection, security monitoring, or SEIM to detect incidents?
- Does a CSP accept customer events and incident information into their security monitoring and incident management process?
- Does the CSP offer transparency into incident events, and if so, what kind of information is shared with customers and users?
- How are security events and security logs protected and maintained?
- How long are security logs retained?
- Who has access to such logs?
- Does the CSP allow customers to implement a host-based IDS in VMs?
- If so, can a customer send such VM IDS data to the CSP for processing and storage?
- How are incidents documented as they take place?
- How are incidents analyzed after the incident has ended?
- Can the CSP provide a forensic image of a customer VM?
- Does the CSP report statistics on incidents to customers?

METRICS FOR THE CHECKLISTS

The checklists alone have utility to judge the security of a cloud, but what prospective public cloud customers and owners of a private cloud want to know are:

- How secure is the implementation?
- Is the CSP meeting best practices for security?
- How well does the CSP meet discrete security controls and requirements?
- How does this service compare with other similar services?

Looking at checklists 9.1 to 9.17, there is a good deal of variation in how controls can be implemented and how they can be measured. This makes it very difficult to identify metrics for each question. Existing approaches for measuring security meet this challenge by both detailing fine grained security controls for specific realms (such as NIST 800-53R3) and specifying which of these controls apply to systems operating at different levels of assurance or sensitivity. But even then, the actual evaluation of the security of an implementation is time consuming and expensive and requires expertise.

The resulting Certification and Accreditation (C&A) of a system is a snapshot in time and must be repeated as the system evolves and undergoes change. Typically, these evaluations are paper exercises that involve a great deal of effort. What is needed is an evolution to this process itself, and cloud computing will demand greater automation simply due to the nature of the contract between IT and cloud consumers.

What would this look like? To begin with, the information and the evidence *artifacts* that are collected about security, systems, and processes must be organized in a C&A repository that is more like a database than a traditional formal document. The importance of collecting and organizing this information is that it supports statements and claims about how discrete security controls are met.

Having such information in database form makes it useful to multiple entities. In a cloud implementation, multiple parties use the same infrastructure and controls. A security evaluation should enable the reuse of information about such controls as well as information about their effectiveness. Cloud computing really does change the game for security, and it is already becoming clear that the adoption of cloud will drive the development of not only better security to meet the demands of elasticity and on-demand self-service but also for the measurement and evaluation of security.

SUMMARY

The rise in public computing utilities has brought increased need for better security. By their very nature, competitive public cloud services are faced with the need to provide cost-effective services and features sets that enable ease of adoption. But equally important is the need for a public cloud service to be seen as an appropriate and safe solution to meeting IT requirements. And in that, CSPs have few alternatives than to undergo evaluation of their product using commonly accepted criteria. Likewise with private clouds, even if security requirements are included from the earliest design stages, and even when sound principles are followed in building and fielding a private cloud, the proverbial proof is still in the *evaluation pudding*.

The security checklists in this chapter are intended to guide readers in developing their own lists for verifying the security of either a CSP or a private cloud. At the time this book was being written, there were several ongoing activities around developing industry or government guidelines around this need. Readers are encouraged to research the state of such work by following the various leading groups that are involved in these activities. It is not at all clear how successful any of these groups will be, and already today there is a good deal of collaboration between groups such as the CSA and CloudAudit/A6. It is certain that this is a rapidly evolving area, and it is very likely that the unique characteristics of the cloud computing model will drive far greater automation in the ongoing verification of such evaluation criteria.

NOTE

Readers who are interested in cloud security evaluation are advised to join the following groups:

- The Cloud Security Alliance:
  - www.cloudsecurityalliance.org
  - www.linkedin.com/groups?mostPopular=&gid=1864210
  - http://groups.google.com/group/cloudsecurityalliance
- CloudAudit:
  - www.cloudaudit.org/
  - http://groups.google.com/group/cloudaudit
- The Trusted Computing Group:
  - www.trustedcomputinggroup.org/solutions/cloud_security
  - www.linkedin.com/groups?mostPopular=&gid=3254114
- CloudSecurity.org (http://cloudsecurity.org/forum/index.php) is not very active but has potential as an independent forum for collaboration in testing cloud security.

It seems that every few weeks, Linked In and Google Groups are adding a new cloud group, and more than a few of these are focused on security. With all these cloud security groups, one of the best ways to stay informed is to join the major high-level cloud interest groups and follow general trends in the field. Periodic research via web searching should identify other specific interest area groups as they arise.

Endnotes

1. CSA-GRC-Stack-v1.0-README.pdf. http://www.cloudsecurityalliance.org/.
2. Ibid.
3. Ibid.

4. Proposed Security Assessment & Authorization for U.S. Government Cloud Computing, Draft version 0.96, CIO Council, US Federal Government; 2010.
5. Controls Matrix (CM), Cloud Security Alliance V1.0; 2010.
6. Catteddu D, Hogben G. Cloud Computing Information Assurance Framework, European Network and Information Security Agency (ENISA). http://www.enisa.europa.eu/; 2009 [accessed 24.03.11].
7. NIST Special Publication 800-53 Revision 3, Recommended Security Controls for Federal Information Systems and Organizations; 2009.
8. Controls Matrix (CM), Cloud Security Alliance V1.0; 2010.
9. Catteddu D, Hogben G. Cloud Computing Information Assurance Framework, European Network and Information Security Agency (ENISA). http://www.enisa.europa.eu/; 2009.
10. NIST Special Publication 800-53 Revision 3, Recommended Security Controls for Federal Information Systems and Organizations; 2009.
11. Controls Matrix (CM), Cloud Security Alliance V1.0; 2010.
12. Catteddu D, Hogben G. Cloud Computing Information Assurance Framework, European Network and Information Security Agency (ENISA). http://www.enisa.europa.eu/; 2009.
13. NIST Special Publication 800-53 Revision 3, Recommended Security Controls for Federal Information Systems and Organizations; 2009.
14. Controls Matrix (CM), Cloud Security Alliance V1.0; 2010.
15. Catteddu D, Hogben G. Cloud Computing Information Assurance Framework, European Network and Information Security Agency (ENISA). http://www.enisa.europa.eu/; 2009.
16. NIST Special Publication 800-53 Revision 3, Recommended Security Controls for Federal Information Systems and Organizations; 2009.
17. Controls Matrix (CM), Cloud Security Alliance V1.0; 2010.
18. Catteddu D, Hogben G. Cloud Computing Information Assurance Framework, European Network and Information Security Agency (ENISA). http://www.enisa.europa.eu/; 2009.
19. NIST Special Publication 800-53 Revision 3, Recommended Security Controls for Federal Information Systems and Organizations; 2009.
20. Controls Matrix (CM), Cloud Security Alliance V1.0; 2010.
21. Catteddu D, Hogben G. Cloud Computing Information Assurance Framework, European Network and Information Security Agency (ENISA). http://www.enisa.europa.eu/; 2009.
22. NIST Special Publication 800-53 Revision 3, Recommended Security Controls for Federal Information Systems and Organizations; 2009.
23. Controls Matrix (CM), Cloud Security Alliance V1.0; 2010.
24. Catteddu D, Hogben G. Cloud Computing Information Assurance Framework, European Network and Information Security Agency (ENISA). http://www.enisa.europa.eu/; 2009.
25. NIST Special Publication 800-53 Revision 3, Recommended Security Controls for Federal Information Systems and Organizations; 2009.
26. Asendorpf D. "Ab in die Wolken", Zeit Online, 2011; http://www.zeit.de/2011/08/Cloud-Computing; 2011 [accessed 24.03.11].
27. Controls Matrix (CM), Cloud Security Alliance V1.0; 2010.
28. Catteddu D, Hogben G. Cloud Computing Information Assurance Framework, European Network and Information Security Agency (ENISA). http://www.enisa.europa.eu/; 2009.
29. NIST Special Publication 800-53 Revision 3, Recommended Security Controls for Federal Information Systems and Organizations; 2009.
30. Controls Matrix (CM), Cloud Security Alliance V1.0; 2010.
31. Catteddu D, Hogben G. Cloud Computing Information Assurance Framework, European Network and Information Security Agency (ENISA). http://www.enisa.europa.eu/; 2009.

32. NIST Special Publication 800-53 Revision 3, Recommended Security Controls for Federal Information Systems and Organizations; 2009.
33. Controls Matrix (CM), Cloud Security Alliance V1.0; 2010.
34. Catteddu D, Hogben G. Cloud Computing Information Assurance Framework, European Network and Information Security Agency (ENISA). http://www.enisa.europa.eu/; 2009.
35. NIST Special Publication 800-53 Revision 3, Recommended Security Controls for Federal Information Systems and Organizations; 2009.
36. Controls Matrix (CM), Cloud Security Alliance V1.0; 2010.
37. Catteddu D, Hogben G. Cloud Computing Information Assurance Framework, European Network and Information Security Agency (ENISA). http://www.enisa.europa.eu/; 2009.
38. NIST Special Publication 800-53 Revision 3, Recommended Security Controls for Federal Information Systems and Organizations; 2009.
39. Controls Matrix (CM), Cloud Security Alliance V1.0; 2010.
40. Catteddu D, Hogben G. Cloud Computing Information Assurance Framework, European Network and Information Security Agency (ENISA). http://www.enisa.europa.eu/; 2009.
41. NIST Special Publication 800-53 Revision 3, Recommended Security Controls for Federal Information Systems and Organizations; 2009.
42. Controls Matrix (CM), Cloud Security Alliance V1.0; 2010.
43. Catteddu D, Hogben G. Cloud Computing Information Assurance Framework, European Network and Information Security Agency (ENISA). http://www.enisa.europa.eu/; 2009.
44. NIST Special Publication 800-53 Revision 3, Recommended Security Controls for Federal Information Systems and Organizations; 2009.
45. Controls Matrix (CM), Cloud Security Alliance V1.0; 2010.
46. Catteddu D, Hogben G. Cloud Computing Information Assurance Framework, European Network and Information Security Agency (ENISA). http://www.enisa.europa.eu/; 2009.
47. NIST Special Publication 800-53 Revision 3, Recommended Security Controls for Federal Information Systems and Organizations; 2009.
48. Controls Matrix (CM), Cloud Security Alliance V1.0; 2010.
49. Catteddu D, Hogben G. Cloud Computing Information Assurance Framework, European Network and Information Security Agency (ENISA). http://www.enisa.europa.eu/; 2009.
50. NIST Special Publication 800-53 Revision 3, Recommended Security Controls for Federal Information Systems and Organizations; 2009.
51. Controls Matrix (CM), Cloud Security Alliance V1.0; 2010.
52. Catteddu D, Hogben G. Cloud Computing Information Assurance Framework, European Network and Information Security Agency (ENISA). http://www.enisa.europa.eu/; 2009.
53. NIST Special Publication 800-53 Revision 3, Recommended Security Controls for Federal Information Systems and Organizations; 2009.
54. Controls Matrix (CM), Cloud Security Alliance V1.0; 2010.
55. Catteddu D, Hogben G. Cloud Computing Information Assurance Framework, European Network and Information Security Agency (ENISA). http://www.enisa.europa.eu/; 2009.
56. NIST Special Publication 800-53 Revision 3, Recommended Security Controls for Federal Information Systems and Organizations; 2009.
57. Controls Matrix (CM), Cloud Security Alliance V1.0; 2010.
58. Catteddu D, Hogben G. Cloud Computing Information Assurance Framework, European Network and Information Security Agency (ENISA). http://www.enisa.europa.eu/; 2009.
59. NIST Special Publication 800-53 Revision 3, Recommended Security Controls for Federal Information Systems and Organizations; 2009.

Operating a Cloud

10

INFORMATION IN THIS CHAPTER

* From Architecture to Efficient and Secure Operations
* Security Operations Activities

Throughout this book, and in several ways, it was stated that cloud computing is an evolution in IT models whose adoption has far-reaching consequences. On the one hand, we gain advantages such as ease and speed of deployment along with radically lower capital costs. Therefore, cloud adopters can face lower risks for new IT projects. Using a public cloud, anyone with an idea that requires IT infrastructure can act on it without actually acquiring infrastructure or hiring a staff. An Internet connection, a laptop, and a credit card and you can gain access to unprecedented amounts of virtual IT infrastructure—and with a wait time that is measured in minutes versus in the weeks or months that it takes to acquire and install traditional infrastructure. On the other hand, the downside with public cloud adoption largely has to do with the reduced flexibility inherent in public cloud services along with concerns related to giving up physical control over information resources. And, there is the *roach motel* or lock-in factor as well, as not all public cloud services will make it easy for a customer to move his/her data to another provider.

Too often, traditional IT does not enjoy a synergistic relationship with other business functions. It often seems that other business departments coerce IT into bending over backward to deliver a botanical garden of unique and difficult to deliver or sustain solutions. Other times, powerful IT departments push back against even reasonable business requests by either delaying or denying requests. But cloud computing is forcing change here, as the catalog of services needs to be clearly defined as will associated SLAs. Consumers of cloud resources won't be filling out triplicate forms only to wait weeks or months for a server to be delivered. Not exactly, in the realm of private clouds, consumers of IT services will expect to get their virtual servers from a private cloud as fast as they can from a public cloud.

With these transitions and with the nature of the self-service contract for cloud services, IT will need to become a greater partner of the business overall—showing the larger organization how to get more for less. But we should also expect that the rise of cloud computing and the changes it brings will likely trend toward

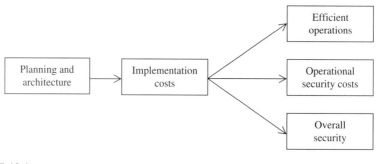

FIGURE 10.1

Overall security and operations are influenced by many decisions.

an overall reduction in infrastructure IT personnel. And that is only natural given the degree of automation in how IT services are delivered with clouds.

In earlier chapters, we defined cloud computing and surveyed current cloud services and delivery models. We investigated security concerns and issues with cloud computing, and we addressed many of those by closely examining cloud security and architecture. At various points, we touched on the importance of security operations and the relationship between architecture, implementation, and ongoing security costs. This chapter is focused on the operation of a cloud from a security perspective.

The goal of operating a cloud is to deliver cloud services in an efficient, reliable, cost-effective, and secure manner. This can be very difficult to achieve, and it depends on many supporting activities. Architecture drives implementation and ongoing costs, including operational security costs. Efficient and secure operation is predicated on sound planning. Reactive security measures are a disruptive and costly consequence of ineffective planning. Figure 10.1 depicts this overall relationship.

Unfortunately, upfront planning and architecture are often given short shrift due to a combination of factors. One common excuse is that it is too expensive in terms of time and resources, and perhaps unnecessary if you already know what you need to do. But experience generally shows that investment in planning and architecture can pay back savings in not only operational costs but in protecting schedules from otherwise unanticipated issues that arise. In an imperfect world, there seem to be two choices: Spend too much time planning and delay efforts from the start, or spend insufficient time planning and experience delays or crisis later in the schedule. Rarely does a team follow a Goldilocks path.

TIP

Consider the following return-on-investment (ROI) goals for security:

- Security should reduce overall required staff time.
- Security technologies and processes should reduce overall costs.
- Security should enable functionality and enable systems management.

> If we were to define some rules to support ROI for security, we might start with these:
>
> - Security should increase revenue through increased desirability by customers.
> - Security should reduce the staff time in emergency remediations.
> - Security should reduce the amount of unavailable (hence unsalable) resources.
> - Security should reduce the cost of indemnification (or its insurance) for breach of SLAs.
> - Security should reduce the possibility of regulatory intervention including fines and business disruption.
> - Security should reduce the number and severity of public *events* that erode the customer base.

FROM ARCHITECTURE TO EFFICIENT AND SECURE OPERATIONS

Security is a key factor that is associated with all aspects of cloud operations. Long before a security engineer de-activates a former employee's various infrastructure accounts, reviews vulnerability scan results or puzzles out which Snort events warrant concern, the efficiencies around these eventual actions are already constrained. As discussed in Chapter 4 (Securing the Cloud: Architecture), the foundation of subsequent operational processes is cast when the architecture of the cloud is defined.

It is certainly true that a small prototype or department-level cloud can be designed and subsequently made operational with modest effort. With a small number of users and modest VM and storage resources, such a cloud will not present the efficiency demands on its operators that an enterprise-level or a public cloud will. But even a prototype or department-level cloud will evidence security issues in the absence of ample planning before the cloud is made operational. These security issues can easily escalate and will demand increasing attention and resources when cloud implementations become larger.

To complicate matters, VM management alone can quickly devolve into virtual server sprawl, and valuable resources and work can become lost or destroyed as a larger cloud progresses from its initial state into an operational one where resource usage flexes and control is lost over virtual and even real IT assets.

Just as architecture casts the foundation for subsequent operational processes, so does the implementation and configuration of infrastructure. A cloud is a highly complex and dynamic composition that rides on various enabling technologies and components. How these are designed, implemented, and even configured will go a long way toward enabling efficient and secure operations.

The Scope of Planning

It makes perfect sense to start the design and architecture phases of planning for a cloud by outlining the operational activities that will take place after the cloud is brought online. Planning for security operations is best done in conjunction with planning other aspects of operations. Security operations not only involve realms such as configuration management, service desk, problem management, capacity management, and service delivery, but security operations are often tightly coupled with these other aspects of operations.

The IT Infrastructure Library (ITIL[A]) is recognized for the demonstrated value it offers in terms of the detailed descriptions of the primary IT practices that an IT organization will likely face in operation. ITIL is all about capturing and organizing best practices around the full scope of IT services management, IT development, and IT operations. Hence, ITIL makes for an excellent starting point for any organization that is in the planning or early design phases of a cloud build. Of course, the focus of ITIL is on the operation and management of IT, but it has great value when one is planning and building infrastructure and defining processes that will soon form the cornerstone of daily operations.

ITIL Security Management is derived from the ISO/IEC 27002 code of practice for information security management. The goal of Security Management is to ensure appropriate information security, in other words: ensuring confidentiality, integrity, and availability of information resources. ITIL is published as a series of books, each of which covers specific practices. The overall collection is organized into eight logical sets that are grouped according to related process guidelines. In its present form, ITIL, version 2, is organized as follows:

- Service Support
- Service Delivery
- Information and Communication Technology (ICT) Infrastructure Management
- Security Management
- Business Perspective
- Application Management
- Software Asset Management
- ITIL Small-Scale Implementation

While security does have its own section, planning and architecting for security also requires understanding the other areas. Going further, sound security entails mature security practices that are integrated with other practice areas. A mature and effective operations team appreciates this on a daily basis and leverages the synergies gained by cross-domain teams. In other words, when security team members contribute their expertise to multiple teams, they gain valuable understanding of activities and issues beyond security.

Physical Access, Security, and Ongoing Costs

In order to take operational costs to their lowest possible levels, physical access to the cloud IT infrastructure must be constrained on the basis of a documented need. Since

---

[A]ITIL and IT Infrastructure Library are registered trademarks of the United Kingdom's Office of Government Commerce (OGC).

every individual with access represents additional risk to the organization, the number of individuals who should have regular access to a data center should be kept low.

Unescorted access should be limited to individuals who have undergone equivalent employment screening as regular cloud staff with physical access. But even escorted access invites unnecessary risk; for example, allowing tours of visitors in close proximity to cabling, power cords, cute little buttons, and blinking lights is inviting an accidental cable loosening brush or minor outage. What is really interesting here is that when the cloud infrastructure is designed and built out for operational efficiencies, then all physical access should be fairly limited for even operational personnel—physical access simply should not be necessary on a daily basis as lights-out operations should be the goal.

Data centers are equipped with extensive video surveillance and a foundation of environmental sensors that will detect water, smoke, humidity, and temperature. These can be further augmented with additional sensors and high-resolution cameras that can be remotely trained on critical gear to serve as a means to remotely view visual diagnostic lights or displays. Reducing the need for operations personnel to have constant physical presence will lower operations costs, high-resolution cameras are an investment that supports minimal visits to the data center, and the recordings from these can serve as a legal record if needed. The longer the retention of video data the better as at least one operations team has found it necessary to review the past month of video surveillance to determine if a backup tape was removed from an archive cage when written records were neglected by personnel.

Logical and Virtual Access

As important as physical access controls are, given that clouds are managed over the network, limiting access controls to the physical realm would be profoundly silly. No number of sophisticated multifactor physical locks or high-resolution video cameras will prevent or record operations personnel as they engage in their work managing network devices, servers, and storage devices. The use of an identity system to define and manage access by personnel to specific devices and functions is an effective way to centralize access control data. But logical controls alone are not ample to limit access to servers and other cloud infrastructure. As discussed in Chapter 4 (Securing the Cloud: Architecture), the use of network isolation between different realms within the cloud infrastructure will go a long way to limit the reach of not only a hacker but isolation will also limit the scope that authorized operations personnel have. Putting it differently: Security controls form the lowest layer of protection and network isolation provide a second protection mechanism. These reinforce each other and provide a degree of insurance against *ham handing* configuration in either realm.

Personnel Security

Not only must physical and logical access to a cloud be limited to personnel with an operational need for access, but all such individuals must also meet personnel policies. Personnel must be screened before being granted clearance for access, access lists must be maintained in a disciplined manner, periodic reviews of continuing access needs must be made, and all operations personnel with either physical or logical access should undergo at least annual certification and refresher training. Likewise, all personnel policies and procedures should be subject to continuous evaluation, especially in terms of user access rights and privileges. When personnel leave the operations team, their access must be immediately revoked, and doing that effectively entails the use of centralized identify management.

It is worthwhile adding that while personnel security is necessary it will not stop insider threats. What can be done about that? For instance, security administrators should have their work independently tested against expected outcomes. This is yet another example of the mosaic of activities that together form an ecosystem that encourages and enables security.

Training

Specific training for IT personnel is important for all staff and, especially, the cloud operations support personnel—which includes not only infrastructure staff but also the various administrators and staff associated with other aspects of operations. The cloud operations staff should have appropriate training to ensure they adhere to company policies, security, or general. With a potentially large number of virtualized servers, the potential to compromise multiple servers or perform a denial-of-service inadvertently is high. This will apply not to just when the service is fully operational, but in the initial and ongoing build up as well. The complexity and scope of a large cloud demand that personnel be more broadly and more deeply experienced than the typical enterprise systems administrator commonly is.

Categories of Cloud Security Staff

In general terms, the following types of security personnel are associated with the operation of a cloud:

- Physical security or data center facility staff
- Security analysts responsible for monitoring or associated with a physical or virtual SOC
- Scanning or penetration testing staff
- Security systems architects and engineers
- Chief Security Officer and other security management roles
- Security research analysts, security automation developers, and security content developers

---

TOOLS

The open source community has embraced cloud computing in a number of ways. First, many open source projects are hosted in various clouds. Google, Amazon, and other clouds support active development communities. Second, many open source projects are focused on enabling cloud computing. These software development efforts include:

- **Configuration Management** These tools include *Chef* and *Cfengine*.
- **Monitoring** Among several monitoring efforts are *Zenoss, collectd,* and *CloudStatus*.
- **Management** This category includes *OpenQRM, Bitnami,* and *ControlTier*.
- **Cloud Enabling Software** Several efforts in this space deliver software that enables users to build, manage, and deploy cloud environments.

    The cloud enabling software area is especially active and has some very powerful tools for fielding private, public, or hybrid cloud. These include:

    - *CloudStack* is an IaaS software platform that enables the development of private or commercial elastic cloud computing services that compete with Amazon EC2. The CloudStack platform includes a management server and hypervisor extensions to implement and manage an IaaS cloud.
    - *Eucalyptus* is an open source infrastructure to implement cloud computing on clusters and is compatible with Amazon EC2, S3, and EBS.
    - *OpenNebula* is a tool kit that allows building private or public deployments and also manage the virtual infrastructure. But OpenNebula goes well beyond those use cases by supporting many different cloud models, including hybrid cloud deployment.
    - *Enomaly Elastic Computing Platform* is used to design, deploy, and manage programmable virtual cloud infrastructure.
    - *Ubuntu Enterprise Cloud* integrates various open source projects (notably Eucalyptus) allowing very easy deployment of a private cloud.

From the Physical Environment to the Logical

The physical data center environment serves as the underlying support structure for a cloud. This is as true for a small cloud that resides in a server closet as it is for a large infrastructure cloud or for a public cloud that spans several physical data center locations. This physical support environment must be secure and safe if the cloud is to be reliable and secure. That alone represents a series of problems that must be addressed if power, Internet connectivity, other communications, and physical access are going to be reliable and safe.

The amount of advance planning that needs to be done for the data center alone is significant—in fact, it is the rare data center that gets all that right as evidenced by gaps that are exposed in contingency plans when things go wrong. This forms the physical security boundary, inside of which one manages the cloud enabling IT infrastructure.

Between the physical perimeter of the data center and this IT gear are multiple layers of physical access controls. Likewise, the typical complex computing and storage infrastructure will also evidence a number of layers of logical separation. Each of these physical and logical boundaries is an impediment to efficiency in operating the cloud, but they exist to prevent and to isolate the scope of damage that unauthorized access could otherwise lead to. These boundaries should be designed for not only protection but also with ongoing costs in mind. Inefficiencies in design and associated operational processes will undermine the cost efficiencies of managing a highly dynamic cloud. If a cloud is going to deliver on its promises of improved efficiencies, then even physical boundaries must be well designed.

Bootstrapping Secure Operations

It would be unrealistic to assume that a cloud can be operated securely without verifying the origin and security of most of the components that comprise a cloud. By example, if a piece of software to control cloud infrastructure is introduced into the infrastructure without vetting it's security, then one clearly risks compromising the infrastructure with malware. Since much software used today is open source, there is a real potential for installing software by downloading it directly from the Internet without effective control over authenticity or security. That is simply not appropriate when building a system for production. The bottom line is that security operations depend on processes and procedures that support security—even before a cloud is placed in operation.

The Refinement of Procedures and Processes over Time

In Chapter 6 in the section Risk Management: Stages and Activities, we stated that cost savings in security operations will largely stem from security planning and implementation phases. However, that chapter also indicated that procedures and operations processes are hard to design in a manner that is not only encompassing and reliable but also flexible enough to meet unpredictable challenges. Thus, one of the goals of security operations should be the refinement of procedures and processes over time.

Efficiency and Cost

In security operations, there are several kinds of activities that consume time and yet are largely avoidable. There are other security operations activities that are not avoidable but that can be streamlined. As to the first category (time consuming and avoidable), the ability of human beings to invent unnecessary work can only explain part of the problem. Identifying, assessing, tracking, remediating, and reporting on vulnerabilities are somewhat akin to wildfire fighting. Several strategies are possible: One can seek to reduce flammable underbrush (vulnerabilities) or one can employ fire spotters to identify an outbreak of fire. Clearly, it will be impossible to prevent all fires, but if you do not invest in some forms of prevention, you will spend more time identifying and reporting on a larger number of fires.

Every computing environment will periodically discover newly exposed vulnerabilities. Removing all vulnerabilities as they are discovered may seem appropriate, yet it is not universally possible or always reasonable. Some may be mitigated by other factors (or by compensating controls), and some are sometimes unavoidable when specific functionality is necessary. However, experience has shown that the equivalent of clearing out the underbrush in computing environments is not only possible but a best practice. What does this look like?

Code scanning for vulnerabilities early in the development cycle is a proven approach to reduce ongoing security costs. Likewise, developing reasonable guidelines and standards for development, for implementation, and for operations brings enduring value by preventing the accumulation of *flammable tinder* in the code base, in the infrastructure, and in operations overall. Getting back to the point above about inventing *unnecessary work*, if one does not aggressively reduce this sort of *combustible* material in a cloud implementation, one may find that management will demand report after detailed report as to the number and kind of residual vulnerabilities and the planned schedule for remediating each of them. Isn't it wiser to avoid some problems like this to begin with?

This should be especially evident with cloud computing where our collective desire to drive down operating costs should inculcate an aversion toward anything that leads to repeated and avoidable risk, work, and cost. It turns out that if you strive toward greater efficiency in cost, you will cast a cost saving eye toward the cloud computing infrastructure and operations teams. And once your gaze settles on the headcount there, you should be thinking about how to not only grow your business but also reduce your costs by making your operations more effective. Limiting ongoing costs is highly correlated with the need to avoid situations that are avoidable to begin with.

As stated above, other security operations activities may not be avoidable but many can be streamlined and made more efficient. By example, one of the periodic and necessary activities that security operations will perform is vulnerability scanning. After each scan, the results must be assessed, which involves several discrete steps including identifying false positives. This entire process can be managed as an unstructured series of activities, or the process can be made more mature and streamlined.

One way to do that is to generate vulnerability information in a machine-readable format or at the least in a representation that can be managed in a semi-automated manner. Figure 10.2 depicts such an integrated approach in managing vulnerability scan data. Note that the first step of the process is the selection of scanning parameters that are appropriate for the environment and scan target. If the scan is to be performed against a pure test environment, then the gloves can be taken off and the scanner can throw everything in its arsenal at the target—since it is not a production target, destructive testing will reveal valuable information that can be applied to the analogous production environment in order to harden and avoid a production outage. If the target has been scanned previously, it is reasonable to start with scan parameters that were previously used—unless of course new tests are available since the last scan. As Figure 10.2 shows, the next steps are to initiate the scan and collect scan results. These results will include not only vulnerability data and associated results but also a measure of how long the scan took to run—this itself is useful information to collect over many scans as the target itself

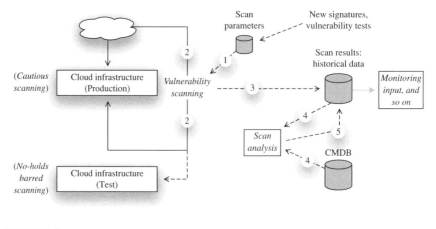

FIGURE 10.2

Managing scan vulnerability data.

changes. The scan results are then converted or captured in a database in order to perform analysis of the current results and to assess any changes from previous results. This is relatively easy to do with a database and is otherwise too time consuming and detailed to perform effectively manually. Once captured and analyzed, such vulnerability data has been scrubbed and assessed, and it can be reported on using either canned report routines or ad hoc queries. It should be noted that the analysis that can be performed can be greatly enhanced if the database routines also have access to CMDB managed information about the cloud infrastructure itself (this is further discussed in the next section). In this manner, information associated with an IP address can be used to supply the context behind a specific alert. In this manner, an alert associated with a Web server can be categorized as a false positive, whereas the same alert associated with a directory server would be verified as critical.

SECURITY OPERATIONS ACTIVITIES

There is a direct relationship between release management, configuration management, change management, and security. However, this relationship often falls prey to sloppy procedures, a lack of formal controls, or ineffective reviews of proposed changes. CM and change control demand a degree of discipline in process that includes security involvement not only for approvals but in planning. The earlier that security engineers are involved in planning, the less chance there is that such changes will bring unintended security risks.

Security engineers or architects can identify specific steps and procedures that can greatly improve not only security but also operational reliability. In many ways, security is a set of qualities that in operations contribute to availability and integrity. One of the hallmarks of effective security is an economy of functionality that is best expressed by the saying *keep it simple*. Complex steps and procedures are generally not optimized, and by their nature, they present greater opportunity for error and failure. By contrast, simpler and more atomic steps can be more robust and reliable.

Server Builds

Most environments have a number of different standards for server builds. For instance, with a Microsoft Windows Server build, you may face a number of server options that start with 32 or 64 bits, and from there you may install one or more of IIS (Internet Information Server), anonymous FTP server, Microsoft Silverlight, DHCP, and DNS. The options go on, and although you could have a server build with all the options installed, this does not result in a hardened build or optimum security. Having unlimited options also makes for greater operational work, so with a standard server build, you need to find a balance between flexibility and security. But, this should easily be able to be kept to a small number of builds.

For a private cloud, you may want to set guidelines for the use of the environment. For instance, a set of standard operating system builds should be considered, which can be developed and tested to ensure that users can easily and quickly deploy them. These may well be a mix of Linux and Microsoft Windows server, such as:

- Linux build: Red Hat with MySQL server
- Linux build: Ubuntu with Apache Web Server
- Microsoft Windows Server 2003
- Microsoft Windows Server 2008

Each of these can be prebuilt and installed with the standard applications that your enterprise requires such as antivirus, patch updates, auditing software, and so on. If you are deploying a production and development environment, these rules might be less stringent for the development environment, but any build outside the normal for your enterprise may need to be formally approved.

A brief aside about development environments: There is simply no excuse for perpetrating the disconnect between development and production environments. Cloud computing is an effective answer to this persistent problem. There is simply no reason for a development environment to be anything less than production from day one. The developers are restricted in just the ways they will be restricted in production and can manage their ways of doing things to leverage cloud advantages (like always rolling new replacement versions of software forward and never back-patching).

Each server instance should be scaled to ensure it falls within limits that you have set. Putting too many virtual instances on a single CPU server that all require a large CPU utilization will not yield satisfactory results. Asking the user for an indication of CPU and memory load and storage volumes anticipated without setting limits or charging is unlikely to be successful. If you offer a virtual instance on either a 32-bit platform with 2GB of memory or on a 64-bit platform with 6GB of memory, the user will likely choose the higher performing form unless there is a cost associated. The cost needs to be sensible otherwise users will opt for the lower performing instance, and this might end up causing local denial of service issues due to the overloaded server. The bottom line? There need to be hard restrictions on all virtual resources.

Server Updates

No matter what platform your servers run, there will be regular updates to the operating system and the applications. Operational procedures should specify how and when you perform updates on servers. Depending on the cloud architecture and the method of provisioning, you may have a lot of servers to patch. But with a virtual environment, it makes far more sense to migrate applications from an older VM to a new updated VM. The stage is then set for proper testing of the new version before deployment, availability recovery is automatically tested, and the serious problems that regularly occur (and are always underestimated) during patching are eliminated. And it's not just the virtual environments that should be managed this way. It might take a bit longer, but automated provisioning (again, started in development) will allow the same kind of management of the base OSs and/or hypervisors.

Users and operators may well consider it easier to deploy and manage applications on an individual basis, particularly those that are known to have a defined life. At the end of life, these virtual servers can just be removed and the application is terminated with no interaction with any other server. This can also make the internal cloud work in a similar manner as the external cloud by turning applications on and off as needed, which will improve the overall performance of the cloud.

As you are deploying a cloud infrastructure, the inference is that you have a relatively large number of servers to deploy. The deployment of patches will therefore require thought and a discussion. The overall security of the cloud needs to be maintained, but this does not mean that each and every patch that is released has to be deployed. Taking Microsoft as an example, they release a set of patches on the second Tuesday of each month. These will be rated by Microsoft as critical, important, and so on; however, these may be rated differently by your company due to many possible factors. Updates that are consider essential will need to be rolled out, possibly with a goal of a few days for your entire landscape of servers.

Depending on the virtualization software you are using, there are automated patch management tools that can be used that can enable the updating process. Using VMware for instance, there are patch management tools by VMware (www.vmware.com) that can be deployed to manage the patching of the host and the virtual instance. If the investment you are making in the internal cloud infrastructure is for a long period of time with sufficient numbers of servers, then some form of automation in the update process will likely be cost effective.

Business Continuity, Backup, and Recovery

In order to ensure that cloud services will be available to customers and users, business continuity refers to a broad set of activities that are performed on an ongoing basis to maintain services and availability. Business continuity is predicated on standards, policies, guidelines, and procedures that allow for continued operation regardless of the circumstances. Disaster recovery is a subset of business continuity and is focused on the IT systems and data.

From an operational standpoint, the activities that are associated with business continuity will be woven into other operational procedures and processes, including the performance of both continual backups and data mirroring to off-site recovery systems. Creating backups should be seen as a form of ongoing insurance. Although backup data may be safely stored off-site, it may be very time consuming to reconstitute a system from such storage. What is more effective from a time-to-recover perspective is the use of multiple instances that both share the processing load but that have excess capacity to allow for any one site or instance to be taken offline either for maintenance or when due to a service interruption. If such excess capacity is to serve as a failover capacity, then the data that is associated with processing at the affected site must be continuously mirrored to such additional sites or instances.

EPIC FAIL

In the early 1980s, in a classified data center located in the Pentagon, a night shift computer operator set about his duties of backing up a critical system. This was the day of washing machine–sized disk drives with motorcycle tire–sized removable disks. The way the backup process was designed was that the system to be backed up would first be taken offline. Then, a backup disk would be mounted into a second drive, and the backup program (DSC on the Digital Equipment PDP 11/70) was run. As DSC ran, the contents of the source disk would be copied to the target or backup disk. When the process was completed, the original source disk would be unmounted and put on a storage shelf (for backup). Then the system would be rebooted with the backup disk. The primary purpose of this was to verify that the backup was complete and resulted in a viable copy.

Unfortunately, on this one occasion the process failed, and the system could not be booted from the backup disk. Thinking that the backup had failed, the operator removed the non-booting backup disk from the drive, replaced it with the original source disk, and attempted to boot that. This also failed. Thinking that there might be a problem with the drive itself, the operator then took the original disk and mounted it in the other drive and attempted to boot from that device. This also failed.

The operator then went to the storage shelf and retrieved the next most recent backup disk, mounted it in one of the two drives, and attempted to boot it. This also failed. The operator went back to the storage shelf and tried the same thing with the next most recent backup.

(Continued)

(Continued)

At around this point, the shift supervisor arrived and saw about 10 disks scattered on the floor. What had happened was that the original backup had failed due to a relatively rare head crash. That generation of disk drive technology was not completely sealed from dust as are drives from the past few decades. A small hair or large piece of dust could be introduced as the disk was inserted into the drive. Since the gap between the drive heads (which float over the surface of the rapidly spinning disk) and the surface of the disk was smaller than the thickness of a human hair, a piece of hair would on occasion lead to a head crash. A head crash would physically scrape the surface of the disk platter leaving very fine magnetic dust inside the drive.

Everything the operator did was in error, by replacing a disk that was unbootable with another one he exposed the second disk to the same crashed heads. By switching a disk from a drive that had a crashed head to another drive, he introduced a damaged and gouged platter full of magnetic dust into the second drive, which now also became damaged. By retrieving the next most recent aged disk and then the one older than that into the same damaged drives, the operator was methodically destroying all recent backups for the past several days.

Managing Changes in Operational Environments

A cloud provider will periodically need to revise services offerings and underlying functionality that services are built upon. Before a new release can be deployed, it must be tested in as near an operational environment as possible. This can be a tall order, as an operational cloud can require many discrete components for cloud management. Such components include carrier grade switches, routers, directory servers, security infrastructure, provisioning, and other infrastructure. All in all, the technology footprint can be extensive and expensive. A public cloud especially will not have the luxury of a prolonged outage to upgrade the infrastructure.

Several strategies can be employed in achieving a safe and predictable system upgrade. The most straightforward approach is to have completely separate development, test, staging, and operational environments. Development environments can be quite modest in terms of supporting infrastructure but expect to require some quality time during development—if only for brief periods—with access to larger blocks of computing and storage resources. Once a release is ready for broader testing, a dedicated testing environment will be required. Depending on the nature of the release, this testing environment may require dedicated use of some of the more expensive infrastructure—such as the ingress router or a large storage instance. But generally the need for dedicated test environments should not entail sacrificing significant revenue generating percentages of the infrastructure. For a private enterprise cloud, the same kinds of issues will exist although more likely at a lower overall technology footprint.

Moving a release from testing to production will expose all manner of errors in configuration files, scripts, and procedures. Unless a release is a minor variation on a previously repeated series of enhancements, expect to run into showstoppers or debugging marathons. For this reason alone, the operations team should have at least one staging environment available where new releases and upgrades can be tested in as near to a final operational mode as possible. If the staging environment is virtually identical to the operational environment, then a new release can be staged, tested with a subset of final computing and storage resources. When it is time to go-live, the remainder of computing and storage can be switched over to staging in a hopefully seamless and nearly transparent manner.

But there is another set of reasons why operations really does need a staging and/or testing environment that can be configured identically to production: security testing and scanning. Rather than performing destructive security scanning against production, it should be performed against a sandboxed staging or testing environment that except for resources is identical to production. The same is true for other security testing, and such as may be necessary for verifying the integrity and correctness of patches and other fixes.

Release Management

Release management for a cloud is intended to ensure that proper versions of hardware and software, configuration files, licenses, and associated supporting processes are in place and correctly and reliably rolled into production. The goals of release management include effective management of all phases from planning a release to developing procedures that will be used in the rollout along with managing customer expectations during the rollout. Figure 10.3 depicts common steps within release management and indicates the underlying need for configuration management to support a new release.

Successful release management depends on discipline in process, the use of formal procedures and numerous checks and acceptance gateways. Figure 10.4 depicts the relationship between release management and operations, note that operational activities such as incident response and analysis can contribute to the need for changes to a cloud.

Releases can involve either major or minor software or hardware changes as well as emergency fixes. Emergency fixes are usually limited to addressing a small number of identified problems or security patches.

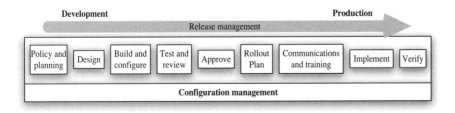

FIGURE 10.3

Typical steps in release management.

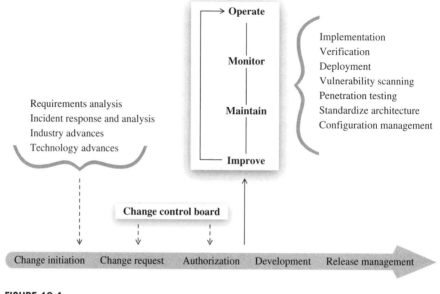

FIGURE 10.4

The relationship between operations and release management.

Information about the Infrastructure: Configuration Management

A complex cloud implementation will have several different categories of information about it. These will range from planning and design information to information about the configuration of the cloud to near-real-time data about the cloud. These different kinds of data will probably be found in completely separate realms and will likely have different representations. However, because of the highly dynamic nature of a cloud and because of the greater degree of automation in IT operation, these kinds of data about a cloud should be expected to converge or at least become more accessible to management processes as cloud computing matures. Focusing on the physical infrastructure itself (the hardware that comprises computing and storage resources along with networking), one might be tempted to use a complex computer aided design (CAD) program to represent the servers, storage, and networking—along with power cables and associated physical infrastructure. But that's just crazy—or is it? If a cloud infrastructure was designed the way complex buildings are designed with CAD systems that produce building information models, then each physical element would be reflected in the model. What would this buy you in operations, and would it be worthwhile to invest in the tools and the time to develop and maintain such models? It is hard to gauge this at this point since the upfront cost of such tools is probably too high for any, but very large cloud providers to be able to effective benefit from the investment. But this notion does point in the direction of the greater control one can achieve if one has accurate and current information about the infrastructure.

In Chapter 4, we discussed the role of a CMDB in managing knowledge about the authorized configuration of components, their attributes, and relationships. As discussed in Chapter 4, a CMDB offers tremendous advantages to the operation of a cloud. Not only can a CMDB be used to reflect the current state of the physical elements of a cloud, but it can enable tracking and even managing virtual cloud elements as well. The CMDB itself does not need to store information of virtual resources, but it does need to bridge knowledge and management of virtual resources to the physical and traditional CMDB realm. Doing so will enable automation in operations that encompasses the constant provisioning and deprovisioning VMs, virtualized networking, and security. To begin, the CMDB maintains contextual information about the physical infrastructure that security systems are reporting on and monitoring. Orchestration and VM management services maintain contextual information about the virtual infrastructure—what is left is to make all this information available to the security monitoring and assessment systems that are responsible for detecting and alerting security relevant situations as they unfold. Doing this will entail advances in the cloud management arena, but these advances and such integrated analysis and management capabilities will go far in further reducing ongoing operational costs and they will bring greater security for customers. In such a view, security monitoring will itself evolve from alerting and reporting to automated security response. In a realm where attacks are automated, and at the scale of a cloud, this is necessary.

Change Management

Everything in the data center should be covered by a change management process, which prevents any change without correct authorization and approved. This should apply to both hardware and software to ensure that there is a smooth operation of the data center. A change made in one area could inadvertently affect other areas. For instance, upgrading firmware in a router may be done without realizing that some application relies on a specific firmware version. Likewise, any updates to an operating system may be required by policy, but must still be put through change management since some applications may require specific builds.

The change management process should have access to the CMDB to both verify and assess change requests and also to update the CMDB after a change is completed. In this manner, changes that are made to the cloud are recorded and can be reviewed in the future for any number of reasons—including debugging.

Information Security Management

As discussed in Chapter 8 (in the section Information Security Management Systems), an ISMS is a necessity for a medium to large-scale cloud. Every organization that builds a cloud of this size should have a comprehensive set of policy and procedures documents. Also noted in Chapter 8, one of the most common security certifications for a company to achieve is ISO 27002, which identifies and details the best practices for companies who are implementing and maintaining their ISMS. Suffice it to say that the focus of this standard is the ongoing security of systems and that security in operations is a key aspect of that. ISO 27002 calls for certain activities to be in place prior to a system being operated, and these include the following: a risk assessment, a security policy and associated standards, asset management, personnel security, and physical and environmental security. Equally important are activities that fall into operation of a cloud, such as communications and operations management, access control, incident management, and business continuity management.

Vulnerability and Penetration Testing

Penetration and vulnerability testing of cloud infrastructure should be performed on a regular basis. In many cases, operations and security personnel may not possess the specialized skills and expertise to perform these activities in which case this may need to be outsourced to a third party. In that case, you should ensure that the third party is professional and has demonstrable skills in this area. Although the majority of the skills and techniques used to test a cloud infrastructure are the same as testing a single application, you want to be certain that testers have a firm understanding of virtualization and cloud orchestration. Penetration testing should be aimed at the whole cloud infrastructure and not just individual servers or components. Security is only as good as the weakest link, and it is pointless if you verify the security of one server and leave others unverified. In addition, network components that enable the cloud environment need to be tested to ensure that these are securely configured. Routers and switches can have exploitable vulnerabilities, and if they are not configured correctly, they can route traffic in ways that are counter to the need for cloud security.

A penetration test and vulnerability scanning may discover a multitude of vulnerabilities, not all of which must be or can be fixed. Discovered vulnerabilities need to be graded (as simply as critical/high/medium/low). As a rule of thumb, any vulnerability that is classed as a critical or high should be remediated to ensure the security of the entire cloud is maintained. On the other hand, low and medium vulnerabilities may be accepted as a reasonable risk, but this has to be determined for each cloud. Vulnerabilities that are not remediated need to have the residual risk assessed and then accepted by the business. Addressing efficiency in security operations, if you find that you have the same vulnerability across all your servers with the same build, then this should be fixed in a golden image for multiple server builds.

It does need to be pointed out that many of the vulnerabilities that are discovered by scanning or penetration testing stem from poor development and coding practices. Where commercial software is the culprit, little can be done before introducing such components into an operational environment—but when the software is developed by the cloud organization itself, better coding practices can prevent the introduction of vulnerabilities into operation. This is far more cost effective than addressing poor code after it is fully developed and even in operation. Best practices here include having developers follow secure coding guidelines and security testing their code as it is developed. What can security operations do toward that? To begin with, operations can publish guidelines for code development and enforce acceptance tests and standards to put the responsibility for vulnerability avoidance squarely on development organizations.

WARNING

Several years ago, the author was in the middle of a customer engagement that involved developing strategies for a certain Asian government's information security modernization efforts. After several days of discussions and answering customer questions on information security topics, one of the customers asked a question that conveyed their lack of background and their naivety. They began with: "I read on the Internet that ...." The point of this is the obvious one: Don't take anything you read on the Internet (or see on TV for that matter) as being correct or even realistic. The hype around cloud computing itself should offer ample evidence of that. Be skeptical, in a healthy information-respecting way. Nonetheless, the Internet is especially valuable as an information resource when information is correlated and weighed in light of the source.

Security Monitoring and Response

Overall monitoring can be split into two main areas: physical and cyber. Clearly there is a security need for monitoring of the data center. A well-run data center will be fully monitored continuously and will have defined procedures in the event of an alarm. As you grow your cloud infrastructure, so too will the need for monitoring increase as well as the complexity to undertake this task. Dependent on the size and location of the cloud facility, you may require extra staff and specialized equipment to be installed.

Physical monitoring will include:

- Video monitoring
- Door access
- Fire, water, and other environmental sensors
- Utility power
- Walk through of the facility

These activities are typically the responsibility of data center security staff. You should have well defined procedures in place to ensure that the logs from door access systems and video recordings are kept according to meet policy requirements. These procedures should be reviewed and tested when a risk assessment is undertaken, and all the perceived physical risks should then be mitigated.

Typically, video cameras are now readily available to work across a TCP/IP network, with wireless enabled cameras becoming more common. How these devices are incorporated into the network is important, both from a security point of view and from the viewpoint of the network bandwidth since video feeds are notorious for consuming large amounts of network bandwidth. If these are connected into the same network segments as data is transported over, then given a number of cameras there is a likely bandwidth contention or saturation issue. A better approach is to have a security-network for all such out of band traffic and to prioritize traffic on that network according to site needs.

Cyber monitoring can be broken into three areas:

- Housekeeping
- Threat monitoring
- Incident response

Housekeeping

Housekeeping monitoring includes monitoring of all the servers to ensure they are up-to-date in terms of patches, antivirus updates, CPU and RAM utilization, and so on. Here again a CMDB presents the opportunity to increase efficiencies in operation. Rather than scanning each system and identifying systems that require a patch, all version and associated information can be maintained in the CMDB itself making for a quick search or lookup.

Periodically, it is important to verify that the CMDB accurately reflects the physical and logical environment that it maintains information on. Doing this for the entire cloud would be a daunting task, but it should be done for the components that comprise the management infrastructure. Also, one can selectively sample and audit computing servers and VMs that are repeated hundreds or thousands of times. One way to perform a periodic audit against the logical environment is to use cataloging software. Nessus is a good example that is familiar to most security engineers. The key is to perform an authenticated scan and to collect and convert the results into format (such as a database) that can be used to perform a comparison against the CMDB.

Threat monitoring and incident response is a significant security area, and both aspects have to be well designed to be effective. Each is dependent on the other, and the whole process is flawed if they are not both present.

Threat Monitoring

The monitoring of the threats within your architecture will likely be a mix of manual and automated methods. At the base level, you need to collect the event and alert data from IDS/IPS sensors, antivirus logs, system logs from the various devices in your architecture, and others as has been described in various parts of this chapter. With a medium to large data center, the sheer amount of data would overwhelm operations personnel if they are solely using a manual method to collect and assess these. As the amount of data increase, the manual method will require a lot of extra heads or the chance of a threat passing unnoticed will increase sharply. The bottom line is that manual methods are not in the same time domain as threats and exploits operate in, so even if it could be performed, it is simply not a reasonable approach.

There are numerous automated tools that can assist in this area, and these span threat correlation engines and various security event management capabilities or systems. Chapter 6 went into great detail on this in the section Security Monitoring. Basically, these tools will be able to reduce the number of false positives that appear in the raw event stream, more likely identifying more sophisticated attacks as well as alerting to any sensors that fail. The operator is thus able to concentrate on a smaller number of threats and decide if these are real or allowed. Additionally, these tools can be tailored such that alerts are sent to the appropriate groups: virus alert to one group and failure of an IDS sensor to another group, for instance. These tools can collect data from many different sensors and then consolidate and correlate this data in one place.

The number of threat correlation engines has grown over the last few years, and there are a variety of approaches for collection, consolidation, correlation, and analysis. An assessment of these is outside the scope of this book, and, if you need one, an internal review should be held to consider your needs and compare them against the various commercial and open source tools. The security community can also be very helpful in terms of identifying tools and relating experiences —every one of these comes with some sort of cost, and perfection has yet to be achieved.

In the past, monitoring the amount of IT that comprises a cloud would entail a dedicated network operations center (NOC) and maybe a security operations center (SOC). But today, this can largely be done virtually using secured Web-based consoles that allow a security team to operate from around the world's time zones in order to have full coverage 24/7. A NOC and SOC are still reasonable, but the scale of the infrastructure or the risk needs to justify such an investment.

Incident Response

Monitoring and detecting a potential threat is only the start, and, after confirming this is a not a false positive, you need to have an incident response plan in place. This plan will have a number of different levels depending upon the severity of the incident. These will be labeled in a variety of ways: low/medium/high; major/minor; and so on and will have an appropriate response for each.

At the lowest level, incidents can be dealt with by the operations staff as part of the day-to-day activities and will typically not need to be escalated. Obviously, these need to be tracked to ensure that there is no overall pattern and to ensure that any follow-up work (such as installing critical patches) is undertaken.

The next level of incident would be when something impacts one or a small number of servers, such as a failure of the power supply into a whole rack, or network failure to one segment of your network. Although the operations staff may fix these problems, it is likely that some form of communications will need to be sent out to affected staff and tracking of the incident undertaken. Also, you need to decide if a root cause analysis (RCA) needs to be initiated to decide what went wrong and if any change to the policy and procedures, infrastructure, detection sensors, and so on needs to occur to prevent this happening in the future.

At the top level, one may have major incidents, which affect a large percentage of the user base, or such incidents may involve a security compromise or otherwise impact your reputation. Again, planning is the key to successfully responding to such incidents. Response will often involve a broader range of people than just the operations staff and require careful and skillful management of the incident. Communications will be necessary across a range of levels, from technical to management, and will need to occur on a continuing basis.

For many incidents, it may be expedient to have a dedicated team of people who are trained to undertake incident response—this will typically be a sub set of operations and management. Having a dedicated team undertake this will be especially important if the response requires that forensics be undertaken. Evidence will need to be preserved (chain of custody), and evidence can be easily destroyed or made irrelevant if the correct steps are not taken. Also, when incidents increase from those that are easy to fix to the more complicated, you may wish to have the next tier of support staff working on them to ensure they are corrected properly.

Best Practices

In the 1990s, the Information Security Forum (ISF) published the *Standard of Good Practice* (SoGP), which identified a comprehensive set of information security best practices. This set continued to be updated until 2007 (a new version is expected in late 2010). The SoGP was developed from comprehensive research and review of best practices around security and incident handling. The SoGP is often used in conjunction with other guidance or standards, such as ISO/IEC 27002 and COBIT.

In 1996, Marianne Swanson and Barbara Guttman produced the NIST Special Publication 800-14 (SP 800-14) *Generally Accepted Principles and Practices for Securing Information Technology Systems.*[1] They identified the following eight principles:

- Computer Security Supports the Mission of the Organization.
- Computer Security is an Integral Element of Sound Management.
- Computer Security Should be Cost-effective.
- Systems Owners Have Security Responsibilities outside Their Own Organizations.
- Computer Security Responsibilities and Accountability Should be Made Explicit.
- Computer Security Requires a Comprehensive and Integrated Approach.
- Computer Security Should be Periodically Reassessed.
- Computer Security is Constrained by Societal Factors.

These principles have enduring value and can be adapted for managing cloud security. As SP 800-14 stated: "These principles are intended to guide ... personnel when creating new systems, practices, or policies. They are not designed to produce specific answers."[2]

Resilience in Operations

Increasingly, security is difficult to define without including business continuity and governance. Where business continuity is oriented toward overcoming any substantial service interruption (and its consequences), IT governance is a form of command and control over IT. Governance aligns the business in a strategic manner to support enterprise IT evolution so that it will bring continuing and consistent business value. Governance is a process or series of actions and functions that are oriented toward delivering desired IT results.

Organizations face numerous barriers in making security be an effective enabling factor to achieve an organization's overall goals. To begin with, most systems are not really able to withstand even trivial failures without some degree of service interruption.

As stated in a report by CMU:

Supporting operational resiliency requires a core capability for managing operational risk—the risks that emanate from day-to-day operations. Operational risk management is paramount to assuring mission success. For some industries like banking and finance, it has become not only a necessary business function but a regulatory requirement. Activities like security, business continuity, and IT operations management are important because their fundamental purpose is to identify, analyze, and mitigate various types of operational risk. In turn, because they support operational risk, they also directly impact operational resiliency.[3]

One of the goals of resilience in IT is to reduce the effect of failures and disasters. Reducing the likelihood of disaster is a primary objective, but equally important is the ability to recover from disasters.

SUMMARY

Depending on how you adopt the cloud model (as a private, community, public, or hybrid resource) and depending on how you deliver cloud-based services (IaaS, PaaS, and SaaS), cloud computing brings different opportunities for change. As a new model for IT, cloud computing will be used to various advantages by competitors in the same industry, by vendors and providers of cloud services, and by consumers and subscribers.

How an organization benefits from cloud computing will depend on how the organization assesses its present information and communications resources and how it envisions the transition to this model of computing. Already we can see this unfolding, with success being dependent on an organization's ability to grasp the opportunities and to navigate changes to existing and emerging technologies, products and concepts—and embracing cloud as the new model for IT.

Although private clouds can achieve immense scale and serve many internal customers, most private clouds will likely be smaller. This gives public clouds several advantages in terms of return in investment for tools and security capabilities that are inherently expensive or which require an investment in expertise to properly implement and operate.

One of the IT advantages with the cloud model is that once infrastructure is in place, most of the typical IT physical hardware and networking activities are no longer performed as a matter of course. Clearly, physical sub-portions of the infrastructure can be carved out—but on an ongoing basis, this is not how a cloud is cost effectively provisioned. Cut out of the whole cloth of infrastructure, the private cloud (or clouds) and such services as SaaS, PaaS, or IaaS will be provisioned at a virtual level. From a procedural perspective, this means that the deployment and operation of a private cloud is somewhat different than normal IT operations and that you will likely need to modify existing operational procedures.

If a cloud is implemented with security along with security reinforcing operational practices and processes (from the data center up to expressed services), then there is really no reason why cloud security can't be equal to any other implementation. In fact, as we have seen at several points in the book, due to the scale of large cloud, effective security can be far less expensive as it is spread over more tenants/users. This is due to the efficiency of scale, or to put it differently it can be attributed to the relationship between massive scale and the lowered averaged entry cost of better security components (from products thru operational practices and monitoring).

By adopting cloud computing as a model for IT, organizations can continue to move away from more traditional device-centric perspectives toward information and services–based strategies. Cloud offers many benefits that go beyond the overall leaner IT infrastructure that it uses more effectively than with other models. There are clear trade-offs that involve control over data and applications, compliance with laws and regulations and even with security. The cloud model also brings greater scalability, and by its use of *fail-in-place*, cloud also brings greater reliability and redundancy. The change from a capital-heavy model of IT spending toward an operating model that is subscription-based brings new opportunities for a broader set of users and tenants to place larger bets with lower risk. Finally, the cloud model also reduces the overall energy footprint of computing, making it one of the greenest IT approaches.

The combined need for computational power, data storage, and bandwidth continues to drive demand for more highly capable systems. Data intensive applications depend on access to increasing scales of storage. Petabyte-scale storage requirements are eclipsing terabyte-scale, and soon Exabyte-scale may eclipse petabyte-scale. In addition to its other benefits, the cloud computing model makes such large-scale storage implementations more possible than are typically the case with other models.

> **NOTE**
>
> Some of the best Internet sources for information are sites where peers and professionals share and collaborate. Of these, while there are many there are several that stand out for cloud computing, these include:

- **Google Groups** Google, the 900 pound Internet gorilla has provided a great and rich set of tools for collaboration among groups of individuals with common interests. The biggest issue with Google groups is the sheer number of groups! Many of these groups have a very active membership of thought leaders in their fields.
- **Linkedin** This is the professional networking site with roughly 100 million professional members in over 200 countries. It is a very effective networking tool for finding and getting introduced to potential clients, service providers, and subject experts. Linkedin groups in the areas of security and cloud computing are very active with a broad range of ongoing discussions on numerous technical, market, and related topics. It is an excellent resource for collaboration as well as pursuing employment or filling positions in cloud computing.
- **The Cloud Security Alliance** This organization seems to be undergoing some changes in terms of becoming a self-appointed accreditation organization.

Endnotes

1. Swanson M, Guttman B. NIST SP 800-14 "Generally Accepted Principals and Practices for Securing Information Technology Systems", National Institute of Standards and Technology, Technology Administration; 1996.
2. Ibid.
3. Caralli R, Stevens J, Wallen C, Wilson W. Sustaining Operational Resiliency: A Process Improvement Approach to Security Management. CMU Networked Systems Survivability Program; 2006.

Index

Note: Page numbers in *italics* indicate figures and tables.